GEORG WILHELM FRII
Heidelberg Wr.

M000238931

The purpose of the Cambridge Hegel Translations is to offer translations of the best modern German editions of Hegel's work in a uniform format suitable for Hegel scholars, together with philosophical introductions and full editorial apparatus.

This work brings together, for the first time in English translation, Hegel's journal publications from his years in Heidelberg (1816–18), writings which have been previously either untranslated or only partially translated into English. The Heidelberg years marked Hegel's return to university teaching and represented an important transition in his life and thought. The translated texts include his important reassessment of the works of the philosopher F. H. Jacobi, whose engagement with Spinozism, especially, was of decisive significance for the philosophical development of German Idealism. They also include his most influential writing about contemporary political events, his essay on the constitutional assembly in his native Württemberg, which was written against the background of the dramatic political and social changes occurring in post-Napoleonic Germany. The translators have provided an introduction and notes that offer a scholarly commentary on the philosophical and political background of Hegel's Heidelberg writings.

BRADY BOWMAN is Assistant Professor of Philosophy at Pennsylvania State University.

ALLEN SPEIGHT is Associate Professor of Philosophy at Boston University.

CAMBRIDGE HEGEL TRANSLATIONS

General editor: Michael Baur

Heidelberg Writings: Journal Publications
Edited and translated by Brady Bowman and Allen Speight

GEORG WILHELM FRIEDRICH HEGEL

Heidelberg Writings

Journal Publications

TRANSLATED AND EDITED BY

BRADY BOWMAN

Pennsylvania State University

ALLEN SPEIGHT

Boston University

CAMBRIDGE UNIVERSITY PRESS

CAMBRIDGE
UNIVERSITY PRESS

University Printing House, Cambridge CB2 8BS, United Kingdom

Cambridge University Press is part of the University of Cambridge.

It furthers the University's mission by disseminating knowledge in the pursuit of education, learning and research at the highest international levels of excellence.

www.cambridge.org
Information on this title: www.cambridge.org/9781107499706

First published 2009
First paperback edition 2015

A catalogue record for this publication is available from the British Library

Library of Congress Cataloguing in Publication data
Hegel, Georg Wilhelm Friedrich, 1770–1831.
[Selections. English. 2009]
Heidelberg writings : journal publications / Georg Wilhelm Friedrich Hegel ; translated and edited by Brady Bowman, Allen Speight.
p. cm. – (Cambridge Hegel translations)
Includes bibliographical references and index.
ISBN 978-0-521-83300-4
1. Philosophy. 2. Jacobi, Friedrich Heinrich, 1743–1819. 3. Württemberg (Germany) – Politics and government – 19th century. 4. Hegel, Georg Wilhelm Friedrich, 1770–1831 – Correspondence. 5. Philosophers – Germany – Correspondence. I. Bowman, Brady. II. Speight, Allen. III. Title. IV. Series.
B2905.B68 2009
193 – dc22 2009021762

ISBN 978-0-521-83300-4 Hardback
ISBN 978-1-107-49970-6 Paperback

Contents

Acknowledgments

The translators wish to thank a number of individuals who have been of help in the preparation of this volume. We are grateful to the late Terry Moore of Cambridge University Press for his interest in commissioning this volume and to Hilary Gaskin and Beatrice Rehl for supporting its completion. Professor Walter Jaeschke of the Hegel-Archiv of the Ruhr University Bochum and Professor Christoph Jamme of the University of Lüneburg both gave us important early suggestions about research sources; PD Dr. Klaus Ries of the history department at the University of Jena was helpful with placing the Estates Assembly's proceedings in the context of German constitutional history in the period from the creation of the Confederation of the Rhine until the Carlsbad Decrees, and also helped elucidate textual details that otherwise would have remained obscure; Professor Gerhard Lingelbach, professor of the history of law at the University of Jena, was helpful with clarifying some older legal terminology; Falk Bornmüller compiled most of the biographical data on the members of the Estates Assembly 1815–17 and other historical persons mentioned in the text, as well as helping research terms associated with older legal and political institutions; Dr. Matthias Perkams was helpful with the translation of the medieval Latin text quoted in Hegel's *Estates* essay; and Dr. Ralf Beuthan regularly gave feedback on the interpretation of particularly idiosyncratic Hegelian formulations. Thanks also go to Toby Svoboda (Penn State), who compiled the index, and to Chris Jackson, our CUP copy-editor.

The translation was much improved by the constructive comments of Michael Baur and an anonymous reviewer for Cambridge University Press. Hallie Speight's proofreading and stylistic suggestions were invaluable in the final stages of editing.

Brady Bowman's work on the volume was carried out in the framework of the collaborative research center (*Sonderforschungsbereich*) 482 at the University of Jena, *Ereignis Weimar-Jena: Kultur um 1800.*

Introduction

This work brings together, for the first time in English translation, Hegel's journal publications from his years in Heidelberg (1816–18), writings which have been previously either untranslated or only partially translated into English. The two years Hegel taught at the University of Heidelberg mark an unusually important transition in his life and thought. Following the closing of the University of Jena in the wake of Napoleon's famous victory at the Battle of Jena, Hegel was unable to find a university teaching position. After a decade in which he worked briefly as a newspaper editor and then as a gymnasium rector, Hegel returned to a university teaching position as Professor of Philosophy at Heidelberg in 1816. During his two years at Heidelberg, before he left to take up his final academic position in Berlin, Hegel brought to fruition a number of projects that characterize the mature phase of his work: he published the first version of his mature philosophical system, the *Encyclopedia*; served as editor of a journal, the *Heidelberger Jahrbücher der Literatur* (*Heidelberg Yearbooks*), which published two important contributions of his own; and began to give the first public lectures in which his developed social and political philosophy was on display.

The move to Heidelberg marked not only an important milestone for Hegel personally, but also came – as Hegel himself articulated it in this period – during a crucial generational shift in the larger political and philosophical climate in Germany and Europe. Hegel's generation, which had witnessed the beginning of the French Revolution twenty-five years before, had seen in the intervening years the swift overthrow of old philosophical systems as well as political upheavals stemming from Napoleon's rise and fall. This post-Napoleonic period, characterized by movements toward both restoration and reform, proved to be an all-too-brief moment in the larger trajectory of pre-1848 Germany: in a series of events partly triggered by a famous politically motivated murder and largely manipulated by Metternich and forces of political reaction, a very different political climate set in.[1] Hegel's writings during the years he spent at Heidelberg reflect the tensions involved in this period of German intellectual and political history and show at its most engaged his famous attention to the universal significance of concrete events.

An important part of Hegel's intellectual engagement during those two years at Heidelberg was his role as editor of the *Heidelberg Yearbooks*. Even before coming to Heidelberg, Hegel had had a relation with the *Yearbooks*, having been privy to the plans of its organizers at a very early date and having forwarded several ideas for reviews to the editors.[2] The project of the *Yearbooks* had begun, during a reform of Heidelberg University, with the intention of giving the university a distinctive voice in comparison with the journals associated with other universities. As that project had developed, their character had indeed taken on a distinctiveness associated with Heidelberg: against the rationalistic intentions of early proposals by the poet and Homer translator Johann Heinrich Voss to bring the Jena and Halle versions of the *Allgemeine Literatur-Zeitung* to Heidelberg, the editorial board which came to run the *Yearbooks* gave them a romantic and idealist stamp.[3] The members of that board included, at one time or another, the historian of religion Georg Friedrich Creuzer (who devoted an initial issue to the importance of Neoplatonism for interpreting ancient mythology), the philologist August Boeckh, the theologian Karl Daub, the jurist Anton Friedrich Justus Thibaut, and the philosopher (and rival of Hegel's) Jakob Friedrich Fries; reviewers included Jean Paul and Friedrich

---

[1] The March 1819 murder of the reactionary German poet (and Tsarist agent) August von Kotzebue by Karl Sand, a radical student associated with the nationalist *Burschenschaften* movement, touched off a wave of political reaction leading to the famous Carlsbad Decrees, which ushered in new restrictions on academic and press freedom, among other things. For the importance of these events in the context of Hegel's emerging political and social thought, see Terry Pinkard, *Hegel: A Biography* (Cambridge: Cambridge University Press, 2000), pp. 435–450.

[2] Hegel had been told by Karl Wilhelm Gottlob von Kastner in November 1806 about the efforts to get the *Yearbooks* underway, and, early in 1807, as the faculty of the University of Jena fled to other academic (and non-academic) opportunities, Hegel's botanist friend Franz Josef Schelver had also encouraged him to apply to come to Heidelberg and participate in the founding of the *Yearbooks*. The suggestions which Hegel had forwarded to the editors for works to be reviewed (including Jacobi's and Schelling's addresses to the Bavarian Academy of Sciences and Fichte's *Address to the German Nation*) had, however, not eventuated in any reviews being actually assigned to him in the years before he arrived in Heidelberg. Two of Hegel's own writings had been reviewed in the *Yearbooks* prior to his arrival: the *Phenomenology of Spirit* by his student Karl Friedrich Bachmann and the *Science of Logic* by his rival Jakob Friedrich Fries. (See *Hegel: The Letters*, trans. Clark Butler and Christiane Seiler [Bloomington: Indiana University Press, 1984], pp. 93–94.)

[3] On romanticism and idealism at Heidelberg, cf. Otto Pöggeler, "Die Heidelberger Jahrbücher im wissenschaftlichen Streitgespräch," in *Heidelberg im säkularen Umbruch. Traditionsbewusstsein und Kulturpolitik um 1800*, ed. Friedrich Strack (Stuttgart: Klett-Cotta, 1987), pp. 154–164, and Hans-Georg Gadamer, "Hegel und die Heidelberger Romantik," in Gadamer, *Hegels Dialektik. Sechs hermeneutische Studien* (Tübingen: J. C. B. Mohr, 1980), pp. 87–97.

Schlegel (both of whom wrote famous reviews of works of Fichte for the *Yearbooks*), Isaak von Sinclair, A. W. Schlegel, and Achim von Arnim.

When Hegel arrived in Heidelberg in the fall of 1816, he took over the editing of a number of areas, including theology, that had been handled previously by Fries; he became (with Thibaut and the historian Wilken) part of the triumvirate making ultimate editorial decisions.[4] His own published contributions to the *Yearbooks* both concerned important generational shifts – the first a re-assessment of a "noble elder" who was central to the philosophical climate of the generation in which Hegel had come of age, and the second a significant political turn in the development of post-Napoleonic Germany. As it turned out, both also entailed significant milestones in Hegel's own personal relationships – the first a consummation of a reconciliation between Hegel and that "elder" (who had been sharply criticized in Hegel's earlier work) and the second a complete break with an old friend.[5]

The first of Hegel's two writings to appear in the *Yearbooks*, his review of the collected works of the philosopher F. H. Jacobi, has never been translated into English.[6] The importance of Jacobi for the development of German Idealism can hardly be overstated: for Schelling, Hegel, and Hölderlin – the generation that came philosophically of age in the 1790s – the interpretation of the Kantian critical philosophy was inflected in an important way by their encounter with Jacobi, and particularly by Jacobi's engagement with Spinozism.[7] Although contemporary interest from both German- and English-speaking scholarship in the relation

---

[4] See Pöggeler, "Die Heidelberger Jahrbücher im wissenschaftlichen Streitgespräch," p. 166.

[5] Hegel's reconciliation with Jacobi is discussed in the section below. The break connected with the Württemberg *Estates* essay concerned the theologian Heinrich Eberhard Gottlob Paulus, whose essay about the same topic had been submitted to the *Yearbooks* and rejected by Hegel and the other editors as "too long"; Hegel's own publication of what turned out to be an even longer review concerning the same issue did not of course help matters. See Pöggeler, "Die Heidelberger Jahrbücher im wissenschaftlichen Streitgespräch," pp. 166 ff.

[6] There is a translation of the review into French: Andre Droz, *Rezension des oeuvres de F. H. Jacobi* (Paris: Vrin, 1976).

[7] Like Schelling and Hölderlin, Hegel read Jacobi's book *On Spinoza's Doctrines in Letters to Herr Moses Mendelssohn*, as well as other writings of Jacobi's, while still a student in the seminary at Tübingen. On the importance of this work and the pantheism controversy for German Idealism see, among other recent accounts, Frederick Beiser, *The Fate of Reason: German Philosophy from Kant to Fichte* (Cambridge, MA: Harvard University Press, 1987), pp. 44–49; Dieter Henrich, *Between Kant and Hegel: Lectures on German Idealism*, ed. David Pacini (Harvard: Harvard University Press, 2003), pp. 82–112; Paul W. Franks, *All or Nothing: Systematicity, Transcendental Arguments, and Skepticism in German Idealism* (Harvard: Harvard University Press, 2005), pp. 9–12; and Terry Pinkard, *German Philosophy 1760–1860: The Legacy of Idealism* (Cambridge: Cambridge University Press, 2002), pp. 90–96.

between Hegel and Jacobi has been strong, Hegel's important review has remained untranslated.[8]

The second writing has never been fully translated into English but is without rival as the most influential piece of political journalism Hegel ever wrote.[9] In fact, of the five striking writings on specific contemporary political issues and events that span his career – from his first publication in 1798 to his last in 1831 – *The Württemberg Estates* is the only piece that was fully published under Hegel's name in his lifetime.[10] Hegel was a Württemberg native and had been drawn, since an earlier unpublished essay in 1798, to write about the political events of his homeland. The convening of the Württemberg Estates in 1815 for the purpose of ratifying a new constitution aroused Hegel's political interest not merely as a chapter in the particular history of Württemberg but rather more broadly (as it turned out) as an important moment in the development of European and German constitutionalism during the post-Napoleonic era. Hegel's take on the political and constitutional issues surrounding *The Estates* has been widely debated, but it has been a genuinely underestimated document for the construal of his political and social philosophy, upon which the present translation and critical commentary hopes to shed some light.

THE JACOBI REVIEW

Hegel's early published engagement with Jacobi's works had been distinctively critical. In his Jena essay on *Faith and Knowledge* (1802), Hegel directs a searching and frequently harsh critique at the assumptions of subjectivity and immediacy which he took to underlie Jacobi's philosophical position.

---

[8] George di Giovanni recently published, for example, an almost 700-page volume translating many of Jacobi's works for the first time into English; his introduction to that volume ends in fact with a brief discussion of Hegel's review: *The Main Philosophical Writings and the Novel "Allwill,"* trans. George di Giovanni (Montreal: McGill-Queen's University Press, 1994), pp. 165–167.

[9] The existing translation of the *Estates* essay by T. M. Knox is only a partial translation of approximately 53 of the 123 pages of text in Lasson's German edition (*Hegel's Political Writings*, trans. T. M. Knox with an introductory essay by Z. A. Pelczynski [Oxford: Clarendon Press, 1964]).

[10] Of the five political writings Hegel devoted to specific contemporary issues – the *Confidential Letters on the Previous Constitutional Relation of Wadtland to the City of Berne* (1798), the essay *On the Recent Domestic Affairs of Württemberg* (1798), the *German Constitution* (1799–1802), *The Württemberg Estates* (1817), and *The English Reform Bill* (1831) – the first was an anonymously published translation of an essay written by another author, the second and third were never published, and the fifth was partially suppressed by the Prussian king before Hegel's death. Translations of three of the other four essays can be found in *G. W. F. Hegel: Political Writings*, ed. H. B. Nisbet and Laurence Dickey (Cambridge: Cambridge University Press, 1999) and in Knox and Pelczynski, *Hegel's Political Writings*.

Although Hegel's published work in the intervening years makes scant or oblique reference to Jacobi,[11] there was behind the scenes a substantial effort, particularly under the auspices of Immanuel Niethammer, a common friend of both men, to effect a personal reconciliation of some sort.[12]

The roots of that reconciliation, as Jaeschke has observed, may have had initially more to do with political, professional, and personal factors than with philosophical ones.[13] Jacobi and Niethammer had become comrades-in-arms in their efforts to reform higher education in Bavaria, Jacobi serving as president of the Bavarian Academy of Sciences and Niethammer as Bavaria's central commissioner of education. The attacks on Jacobi – who, like both Niethammer and Hegel, was non-Bavarian and Protestant – became an issue about which Hegel could express some alliance with Jacobi, in spite of his harsh early critique of Jacobi's work.[14] Hegel's frequent correspondence with Niethammer during this period – about, among other things, the possibilities of a position in Bavarian higher education for the underemployed Bamberg newspaper editor[15] – shows an increasing sense of support for Jacobi's position. (By the end of 1807 Hegel claims, in response to an attack on Jacobi's address to the Bavarian Academy, that he "belonged to Jacobi's party in advance.")[16] In 1812, when the two men actually met

---

[11] Jacobi seems clearly to be on Hegel's mind in important sections of the *Phenomenology of Spirit* (1807) on sense certainty and conscience, but he is not explicitly mentioned there; the first references in Hegel's *Science of Logic* come in the 1816 *Begriffslogik*; the discussion of Jacobi in the third remark to "Becoming" is part of Hegel's reworking of the text in Berlin (Walter Jaeschke, *Hegel Handbuch. Leben-Werk-Wirkung* [Stuttgart/Weimar: J. B. Metzler, 2003], p. 254).

[12] Pinkard, *Hegel: A Biography*, pp. 251–255, 384–388; Jaeschke, *Hegel Handbuch*, pp. 32–34, 254–257. The poet Jean Paul Richter, a close friend of Jacobi's, also plays an important role here: Hegel had made a favorable impression on him when the two met in Bamberg in July of 1807.

[13] Jaeschke, *Hegel Handbuch*, p. 32.

[14] Hegel certainly recognized the delicacy of his situation: in a letter to Niethammer on May 30, 1807, about apparent prospects for a job that would need Jacobi's approval, he says: "You are, to be sure, kind enough to keep up courage for me, but at the same time the condition at once seems to be added *sine qua non* that I should become reconciled with Jacobi, that from my side I must do something or other which – however delicate the turnabout might be – could only, I fear, be a 'Father, forgive me!' [pater peccavi!] You know that you can command me unconditionally; but I am convinced you will spare me of this. You yourself say that Jacobi's relationship to me is more [a matter of] pain than opinion. If it were only a matter of opinion, some alteration would be possible. But the pain would be hard to alter – without transferring it to me instead, without receiving coals of fire upon my head, which I would even help to heap on myself" (*Hegel: The Letters*, p. 129).

[15] Hegel remained in the newspaper position until late 1808, when Niethammer secured for him an appointment as rector of the Nuremberg gymnasium.

[16] From Hegel's letter to Niethammer of December 23, 1807, which discusses Karl Rottmanner's *Critique of F. H. Jacobi's Essay on Learned Societies* (*Hegel: The Letters*, p. 153). In a letter to Karl Joseph Windischmann (December 31, 1807), Schelling by contrast applauded Rottmanner's attack, a fact which may be interpreted as a further symptom of the increasing philosophical and political distance between Schelling and Hegel.

during a visit by Jacobi to Nuremberg, there was a great deal of apparent good will on both sides.[17] Hegel repaid the visit with a trip to see Jacobi in Munich in 1815, the two men exchanged recent books,[18] and Jacobi was even supposed to become godparent to an expected child of Hegel and his wife.[19]

Hegel's arrival in Heidelberg in 1816 thus appears to mark an occasion on which he could make public the turn in his relation to Jacobi. The personal change, as Pinkard has noted, coincided with a shift in Hegel's own status within the philosophical profession: with the publication of both volumes of the *Science of Logic* behind him, as well as the imminent completion of the Heidelberg version of his philosophical system as a whole, the *Encyclopedia*, Hegel could view Jacobi's works from a perspective that was no longer that of a critical rival but rather that of an established philosopher reviewing the work of a precursor.[20] What emerges is not only an extended review of a volume of Jacobi's collected works, but something of a reassessment on Hegel's part – one which involves, in tone, content, and presentation, a significantly different attitude toward Jacobi.

The volume of Jacobi's collected works which Hegel reviews is the third in that series – the last, as it turned out, that would be edited by the aging Jacobi himself. The four Jacobian texts included in the volume concern Jacobi's critique of Kant (the essay *On Critical Philosophy's Attempt to Bring Reason to Understanding and to Transform Philosophy as Such*), his contribution to the so-called "atheism dispute" over Fichte's departure from Jena (the famous public *Letter to Fichte*), and his contribution as well to the so-called "dispute on divine things" that featured a disagreement between Jacobi and Schelling (the two essays *On Divine Things and Their Revelation* and *On a Prophecy by Lichtenberg*).

Hegel's review does not simply take these writings up in order of publication, but instead places them as a group in the context of an Hegelian construal of the importance of Jacobi's work as a whole for the history of philosophy. As Hegel sees it, this construal requires the consideration of a text not included in the volume itself, but which had been of unusually decisive importance to Hegel's own generation: the *Doctrine of Spinoza in*

---

[17] Jean Paul observed about the reconciliation that it was impossible not to love Jacobi "and indeed his philosophical enemy Hegel loves him now." Hegel wrote Niethammer in July of 1812 with thanks for his help in the reconciliation, noting Jacobi's "kind disposition toward me" (Jaeschke, *Hegel Handbuch*, p. 33).

[18] Hegel sent Jacobi the second volume of his *Science of Logic*, and Jacobi sent Hegel the second volume of his collected works (the volume preceding the one which Hegel reviews in the *Heidelberg Yearbooks*).

[19] Hegel's wife Marie miscarried, however, at the end of 1815.

[20] Pinkard, *Hegel: A Biography*, pp. 384, 388.

Letters to Moses Mendelssohn. With this essay as its central point of departure, Hegel's review is thus thematically organized into roughly four parts that reflect Jacobi's philosophical engagement, respectively, with Spinoza, Kant, Fichte, and Schelling, while a coda takes up what Hegel finds distinctive about Jacobi's philosophical style.

(i) *Spinoza:* "Every consistent system of philosophy must in the end lead to Spinozism" had been the well-known claim of Jacobi's *Doctrine of Spinoza in Letters to Moses Mendelssohn,* published originally in 1785 and in a second edition in 1789. Jacobi had intended his work as a warning against the deterministic, mechanistic, and consequently nihilistic trajectory of all modern, i.e., Spinozist, philosophy, but it had had, on many in Hegel's generation, an opposite effect – rather of leading them to a more serious study of the philosopher whose view of substance had been famously captured by the phrase Jacobi attributed to Lessing: *hen kai pan* ("one and all"), words that Hölderlin inscribed as a sort of watchword in Hegel's *Stammbuch* during their days in the Tübingen seminary.[21]

Hegel's review does not focus on the historical details of the so-called "pantheist" controversy that followed upon the publication of Jacobi's book, but rather on the importance he sees Jacobi's appeal to Spinoza as having within the broader perspective of the history of modern philosophy. According to Hegel, both the French and German Enlightenments had moved from a critical encounter with givenness in the natural and social worlds to the positing of abstract determinations (such as "force" or "totality") in which, however, thought was equally unable to "possess itself." Against the sterility of the metaphysics which resulted, it was the achievement of Spinoza, according to Jacobi, to show that the "only relation in which . . . [such] determinations of knowledge attain their truth" was the "unwavering and infinite contemplation and knowledge of the one substantial being," or Spinoza's substance.

For a correct construal of this "Spinozism in possession of which we find Jacobi,"[22] everything depends, says Hegel, on understanding the notion of

---

[21] On the paradoxical effect of Jacobi's Spinoza book on Hegel's generation, see, for example, Frederick Beiser, *German Idealism: The Struggle against Subjectivism, 1781–1801* (Cambridge, MA: Harvard University Press, 2002), pp. 362–364 and Henrich, *Between Kant and Hegel,* pp. 82–95. On the significance of Hölderlin's inscription for the two friends, see H. S. Harris, *Hegel's Development: Toward the Sunlight 1770–1801* (Oxford: Clarendon Press, 1972), pp. 97–99.

[22] Hegel's claim here about "the Spinozism in possession of which we find Jacobi" is interesting, given the harsh Jacobian criticism of Spinoza that Hegel had acknowledged already in *Faith and Knowledge.* As Rolf-Peter Horstmann has suggested, this appeal bears remarkable similarity to that of the 1795 Schelling, who stressed the common interest of Jacobi and Spinoza in seeking to integrate the role of the unconditional in their respective philosophical approaches. Rolf-Peter Horstmann, *Die Grenzen der Vernunft. Eine Untersuchung zu Zielen und Motiven des Deutschen Idealismus* (Frankfurt: Anton Hain, 1991), p. 277, n. 32.

negativity at work. Spinoza's substance implies the determinateness of finite things – as in the phrase which Hegel follows Jacobi in ascribing to Spinoza, *omnis determinatio est negatio*. But negation in this sense, as Hegel credits Jacobi with seeing, "fails to be seen as internal to substance" because there is no comprehension within that substance of the very work of negation. Jacobi's demand that God be not merely substance but "spirit," which is both "free and a person [*persönlich*]," thus presages, on Hegel's view, his own distinction between substance and spirit: "the difference between determining the Absolute as substance and determining it as Spirit boils down to the question whether thought [*das Denken*], having annihilated its finitudes and mediations, negated its negations and thus comprehended the One Absolute, is conscious of what it has actually achieved in its cognition of absolute substance, or whether it lacks such consciousness."

Although Hegel goes on to criticize Jacobi's notion of spirit for a further problem of immediacy – i.e., for staying put in the immediacy of intuition – he nonetheless makes the implicit concept of Spirit he finds in Jacobi into the organizing concept of the review and thus the key point of his assessment of Jacobi's importance for the history of philosophy. For it is "chiefly against the conception of Spirit as Jacobi finds it in his vision of reason that he measures the philosophical systems which are his subjects in the writings contained in the present volume" – i.e., those of Kant, Fichte, and Schelling.

(ii) *Kant:* Hegel credits Jacobi and Kant in the review with a shared achievement for the state of contemporary philosophy as a whole: they "put an end to the metaphysics of the old school" of Leibniz and Wolff and thus "established the necessity of a complete revision of logic." When Hegel turns to an account of the criticism which Jacobi ultimately directed at the Kantian categories of space, time, identity, and difference, he praises Jacobi for undertaking it, at least in part, "in accord with true method, that is, dialectically." But while Jacobi shows the contingent character of Kantian categories, he nonetheless "fails to give Kant the infinite credit due him for having seen that the freedom of the Spirit is the fundamental principle" of both theoretical and practical philosophy.

(iii) *Fichte:* As Jaeschke has observed, Hegel's discussion in the review of Jacobi's famous *Letter to Fichte* focuses not so much on the issues of the atheism dispute surrounding the publication of that letter as on Jacobi's critique of the one-sidedness of the Fichtean approach, particularly, to morality.[23] Hegel compares Jacobi's criticism of Fichte's rationalist moral

---

[23] Jaeschke, *Hegel Handbuch*, p. 256.

principle to Aristotle's criticism of the Socratic attempt to "make the virtues into knowledge": "in the realm of the practical, universals articulate only what *ought to be*, and Aristotle (like Jacobi) finds this insufficient to account for the manner of the *existence* of the universal and the possibility of such existence." Yet, Hegel claims, Aristotle's appeal to "drives and character" – and moreover to the situating of an individual's ethical life within the context of the life of the *polis* – is to be distinguished as more richly concrete than Jacobi's appeal to the "mere *heart*." While Hegel thus praises (as he had earlier in *Faith and Knowledge*) the "fine passage" in which Jacobi insists upon the importance of individual moral decision when it must oppose the weight of conventional norms, he nonetheless ends the section on Jacobi's view of Fichte with a criticism of the temptation to romanticism.

(iv) *Schelling:* The final section on the controversy over "divine things" with Schelling gives the shortest discussion of any of the texts covered in the review. While there may have been some intentional reasons for Hegel's brevity here in discussing the dispute between Schelling and Jacobi,[24] Hegel claims that it is "without doubt still sufficiently present in public memory that it would be superfluous to spend much time on it here." Following two short paragraphs that concern the relation of the human spirit to God and the difficulties of the Schellingian project in the philosophy of nature, Hegel segues to a discussion of the distinctiveness of Jacobi's philosophical style – the particular *ésprit* (*das Geistreiche*, a term close to untranslatable in English) that makes use of a wealth of images and "simple juxtapositions." However much such *ésprit* may probe contradictions inherent in the claims of the understanding, it is, on Hegel's view, still "a kind of surrogate for methodically developed thought."

What, in the end, did Hegel's review of Jacobi achieve? First of all, the developing reconciliation between the two men was clearly sealed – and Jacobi, who had earlier evinced an extraordinary charitability toward Fichte's and Schelling's quite different philosophical construals of his own work, reacted with similar openness to Hegel's account here.[25] While

---

[24] Jaeschke (ibid., p. 257) suggests that the brief treatment may have arisen from Hegel's awkward position – between a developing friendship with Jacobi on the one hand and a philosophical stance on the issues in the dispute that actually may have come closer to Schelling's position, despite the distance that had developed between the two former Jena colleagues in the years since the publication of the *Phenomenology of Spirit*.

[25] Jacobi acknowledged that Hegel's work had "on the whole pleased me very much" (F. H. Jacobi to Jean Paul [Munich, 11.5.1817], Günther Nicolin, ed., *Hegel in Berichten seiner Zeitgenossen* [Hamburg: Meiner, 1970], p. 142). Regarding Hegel's criticism, Jacobi said in a letter to his friend Johann Neeb, "He may well be right" (F. H. Jacobi to Johann Neeb [Munich, 30.5.1817], ibid.,

Hegel's Jacobi review certainly heralds a shift in tone in his treatment of Jacobi, there are also more importantly elements of a new philosophical contextualization of Jacobi's work that will be present in Hegel's later treatments of Jacobi in the *Encyclopedia Logic*, the *Science of Logic*, and the *History of Philosophy*.[26]

THE REVIEW OF THE WÜRTTEMBERG ESTATES *PROCEEDINGS*

Hegel was born – as Terry Pinkard puts it in his recent biography – not in Germany, but in Württemberg. The experience of "Germanness" for Hegel's generation was one which continually oscillated between the local appeal of the specific area in which one grew up (the large number of principalities, duchies, and free cities which composed the German-speaking realm) and the aspirations – fired not only by the principles of the French Revolution but by the collapse of the Holy Roman "Empire" of the German Nation – to a more universal political life. While Hegel's life introduced him to a wide variety of German-speaking cities (from Swiss Berne to Bavarian Nuremberg to Prussian Berlin), it also provided in its experiences a distinct focus for his interest in the development of universal and rational political institutions. Hegel's interest at once in the specificity and the broader meaning of political institutions gave him an unusually careful eye – certainly in comparison with the rest of his German Idealist contemporaries – for the fine nuance of significant administrative detail. (One can indeed occasionally see in Hegel perhaps some inheritance from his father, who had been a secretary to the revenue office at the court of the duke of Württemberg – for example, in the aspiration of the young philosopher, abroad in Switzerland for the first time, to "work through the financial constitution of Berne to the smallest detail, even to highway funding [*Chausseegeld*].")[27]

---

p. 143). Reacting in 1797 to Fichte's and Schelling's citations of him, Jacobi had said in a letter to Baggesen that it was possible that "these men have understood me better than I have myself." The relevant portions of these letters, along with part of an important contemporary letter of Hegel's concerning the Jacobi review, are translated below in the Appendix (pp. 137–139).

[26] The 1827 and 1830 editions of the *Encyclopedia Logic* follow Hegel's review in placing Jacobi's philosophical position not, as in the earlier *Faith and Knowledge* essay, with Hume and Locke, but rather with Descartes, who did not come up for discussion in *Faith and Knowledge* at all. The Berlin *Lectures on the History of Philosophy* begin, as does the review, by locating Jacobi in the context of a reaction to French Enlightenment philosophy and contemporary German metaphysics. The 1832 *Science of Logic*, as Jaeschke points out (*Hegel Handbuch*, p. 254), also follows the lines of Jacobi's Kant criticism as discussed in the review (*Science of Logic*, trans. A. V. Miller [Atlantic Highlands, NJ: Humanities Press International, 1989], pp. 95–98).

[27] Karl Rosenkranz, *Georg Wilhelm Friedrich Hegels Leben* (Berlin: Duncker and Humblot, 1844), p. 61.

While such smaller details are part of what Hegel must contend with in the *Estates* essay, there are clearly larger issues on his mind. For the essay is one of the important documents in the explicit development of Hegel's mature social and political philosophy – a development which can in many respects be dated to Hegel's time at Heidelberg, where he lectured on the philosophy of right for the first time, but a development which itself takes place against the background of an unusually pregnant moment in European political and constitutional history. In the wake of Napoleon's defeat and the Congress of Vienna, a number of new political rearrangements emerged in Europe.[28] In Germany, the old empire had been replaced with thirty-nine "sovereign principalities and free cities of Germany" within a loose confederation, including the Kingdom of Württemberg, which, because of its strategic position in the Napoleonic wars, had not only risen in stature from its former status as a duchy, but had more than doubled in size.[29]

Above all, however, this post-Napoleonic era was a time ripe for new attempts at constitution-making: Louis XVIII had just given the French a new *Charte Constitutionelle* in 1814, and the Acts of Confederation emerging from the Congress of Vienna would specify that the new realms incorporated under those acts each provide for their citizens "estates constitutions" (*landständische Verfassungen*).[30] With an eye on both of these developments, Württemberg's King Friedrich I presented his country's Estates Assembly a new constitution in March 1815. This overture was initially rejected by the Estates, which argued for a return to its "old" rights under the constitution which Friedrich had declared null in 1805 on the eve of the collapse of the remaining "institutions" of the Holy Roman Empire.

This *contretemps* between king and Estates over the outlines of a new constitution – the central dramatic event analyzed in the *Estates* essay – presents a number of questions for the political theorist and the historian of ideas. Both the notions of an "Estates" and of a constitution appear, in fact, to be part of a larger set of terms in the political vocabulary of post-Napoleonic Europe which are shifting and under conflictual pressure.

---

[28] On these developments more generally, see James Sheehan, *German History: 1770–1866* (Oxford: Oxford University Press, 1989) and Thomas Nipperdey, *Germany from Napoleon to Bismarck: 1800–1866* (Dublin: Gill and Macmillan, 1966).

[29] See footnote 4 on p. 33.

[30] Article 13 of the Acts of the German Confederation stipulated that every member state have a constitution providing for an assembly of the Estates (*landständische Verfassung*). On the contemporary interpretation of this important phrase – and the distinction made between it and the notion of an explicitly *representative* (*repräsentative*) constitution – see Rolf K. Hočevar, *Stände und Repräsentation beim jungen Hegel. Ein Beitrag zu seiner Staats- und Gesellschaftslehre sowie zur Theorie der Repräsentation* (Munich: C. H. Beck, 1968).

King Friedrich's constitution was the first to be proposed within the new German states that were represented at the Congress of Vienna; his constitution involved rationalistic and representative elements that had not previously been seen in the existing political frameworks in German-speaking lands.[31] Even prior to the 1815 Estates Assembly, however, Württemberg had had a constitutional history which in many ways set it apart from the political structure of other German realms – a fact acknowledged in the famous remark of the English statesman Charles James Fox that "there were only two constitutions in Europe, the British constitution, and that of Württemberg."[32] Perhaps the most distinctive element of the Württembergian constitution in this regard was the status of the *Landtag* (Estates Assembly or Parliament), which not only had acquired significant political powers in relation to the ruling duke but was also almost entirely dominated by an urban class of burghers. The role of the Württemberg Parliament was rooted in the Treaty of Tübingen, signed on July 8, 1514, which had granted the Estates basic civil rights and liberties, a say in decisions concerning war and peace as well as in major legislation, and – crucially – the administration of public finances. In return, the Estates had agreed to take on the responsibility of repaying the duke's foreign debts and to submit to taxation as necessary to supply the needs of the state. Effectively, this treaty was Württemberg's constitution, and talk of the "old law" or the "old constitution" invariably refers to the Treaty of Tübingen which had made Württemberg's Estates the most powerful in Germany.

While the term "estates" suggests a body broadly representative of the interests within the feudal state[33] – i.e., those of nobility, peasants, church, and bourgeoisie (the burgher class) – the Württemberg Estates

---

[31] See Hartwig Brandt, *Parlamentarismus in Württemberg 1819–1870. Anatomie eines deutschen Landtags* (Düsseldorf: Droste, 1987), p. 25. The "firstness" of Württemberg's constitutional proposal is not without some historical irony, as Rolf Grawert points out, given the length of time it ultimately took Württemberg, in comparison with other realms of the German Confederation, to approve it (Grawert, "Der württembergische Verfassungsstreit 1815–1819," in *"O Fürstin, der Heimath! Glükliches Stutgard." Politik, Kultur und Gesellschaft im deutschen Südwesten um 1800,* ed. Otto Pöggeler and Christoph Jamme [Stuttgart: Klett-Cotta, 1988], p. 126).

[32] Fox's remark is cited in a review of the *Proceedings* of the Württemberg Assembly for the *Edinburgh Review* by a contemporary of Hegel's: "Verhandlungen in der Versammlung der Landstände des Königreichs Würtemberg," in *Edinburgh Review* 29,58 (February 1818): 340. For a broader comparison of the emergence of parliamentary government in German political history, see F. L. Carsten, *Princes and Parliaments in Germany: From the Fifteenth to the Eighteenth Century* (Oxford: Clarendon Press, 1959).

[33] Pelczynski comments that both the notion of "estates" (*die Stände*) as the corporate entities within a state and that of the "Estates" as the parliamentary forum of the various parts of a state are words at some distance from active political vocabulary in English, whereas *Stand* and *Stände* have had a somewhat longer life in German (*Hegel's Political Writings* [Oxford: Clarendon Press, 1964], p. 82).

Assembly was almost entirely made up of burghers. From the Treaty of Tübingen on, the nobility had refused to participate in the Assembly on the grounds that they had an "immediate" legal status (*Reichsunmmitelbarkeit*) within the larger German Empire and stood under no intermediate authority;[34] the peasants, despite early attempts to press for representation, had been effectively excluded,[35] and the prelates had become, through intermarriage and co-optation, effectively side-lined as a separate "estate."[36]

The representativeness and effectiveness of the Estates Assembly in the years between the Treaty of Tübingen and 1815 had been blunted on two sides. On the one hand, a so-called "committee" that putatively was to meet only between adjournments of the Assembly came instead to be a political entity in its own right and was almost entirely dominated by a ruling class of burgher families (the Württemberg replacement for politically active nobles):[37] during the eighteenth century, the Assembly as a whole met only four times, as the committee controlled important political and financial issues within the duchy.[38] On the other hand, there was an ongoing battle between Assembly and dukes, and the latter occasionally got the decisive grip on power: Friedrich shut down the Assembly in 1805, and it did not meet again until he convened it for the constitutional process in 1815.[39]

Within this power structure, there were clearly competing views of what a constitution was and what the political machinery in constitution-making exactly involved.[40] On the one hand, the king's motives in proposing the constitution were clearly mixed. Friedrich had been the last to join the German Confederation but was the first to draft a constitution. While

---

[34] The nobles had declared in 1519 that they were "*kein Staind in der Wirtemberg Landschaft*" but instead "*frey Edelleut*" (free nobles). Cited in James Allen Vann, *The Making of a State: Württemberg 1593–1793* (Ithaca: Cornell University Press, 1984), p. 48.

[35] The 1514 "Poor Conrad" uprising, for example, had failed to produce a peasant representation in the Assembly. Despite the lack of political representation, the peasants still had some significant rights in Württemberg in contrast with other German states: Carsten cites, for example, the right of peasants to leave the state freely, and the general disintegration of the manorial system and duties associated with serfdom (Carsten, *Princes and Parliaments in Germany*, pp. 2–3).

[36] On the history of the Württemberg estates, see Brandt, *Parlamentarismus in Württemberg 1819–1870*; Carsten, *Princes and Parliaments in Germany*; Vann, *The Making of a State*; Walter Grube, *Der Stuttgarter Landtag 1457–1957* (Stuttgart: E. Klett, 1957).

[37] There were actually two committees, the inner and outer committees, with eight and sixteen members respectively.

[38] It was only the duke's need for emergency funds during the Napoleonic wars that forced the re-convening of the Estates in 1796, since the committee itself could not approve the emergency outlays required.

[39] On Friedrich's closing of the Assembly, Napoleon was said to have exclaimed: "I have made your master a sovereign, not a despot!" (see Hegel's letter to Niethammer citing this remark in August of 1807: *Hegel: The Letters*, p. 141).

[40] See Grawert, "Der württembergische Verfassungsstreit 1815–1819," pp. 126 ff.

Introduction

he had autocratically closed the Estates in 1805, he now had a political interest in subduing the newly "mediatized" nobles in his land; and, given the concern with constitution-making emerging from the Congress of Vienna, taking the initiative might ensure the final product would be more to his liking than something that might be imposed from outside. On the other hand, the burghers of the Estates were trying to reclaim the "good, old right" that had been suspended, yet – as Hegel never tires of pointing out – they started to give the appearance of oligarchs simply trying to hold on to their privileges. Besides king and Estates, there were other movements afoot as well. The Estates received numerous petitions from towns and citizens (*Volksadressen*) demanding that the king grant the people a constitution rooted in the Estates, and there was significant interest outside Württemberg from German intellectuals (including Görres, Stein, Fries, and Kotzebue) who favored the Estates' cause. Finally, there emerged as well a "moderate" group between the two positions (taken especially by the publisher Johann Friedrich Cotta and Tübingen University Curator August von Wangenheim).

The constitutional debate that emerged – if it can be properly so called – lasted four years and fell into three distinct phases.[41] Friedrich I initiated the first phase with his 1815 presentation of a draft of the constitution to the newly convened Estates Assembly; Hartwig Brandt characterizes this phase as a long-drawn-out stalemate that persisted until Friedrich's death in October of 1816. A second phase beginning with his more liberal successor, Wilhelm I, fell in the year 1817: Wilhelm proposed in March of 1817 another draft version of the constitution that had been much influenced by the proposals of Tübingen chancellor Wangenheim, whom Wilhelm had now made minister of state.[42] After an ultimatum from Wilhelm to vote

---

[41] For an analysis of these three phases, see especially Brandt, *Parlamentarismus in Württemberg 1819–1870* and Joachim Gerner, *Vorgeschichte und Entstehung der württembergischen Verfassung im Spiegel der Quellen (1815–1819)* (Stuttgart: W. Kohlhammer, 1989).

[42] Wangenheim's anonymously published *The Idea of a State Constitution in its Application to Württemberg's Old Estates Constitution and a Proposal for its Renewal (Die Idee der Staatsverfassung in ihrer Anwendung auf Württembergs alte Landesverfassung und den Entwurf zu deren Erneuerung)* had suggested, among other things, a bicameral estates, as opposed to the unicameral situation envisioned by Friedrich. Wangenheim and his constitutional proposal play an important role in the assessment of Hegel's stance during the second phase of the process, since it was alleged by Rudolf Haym that Hegel had written his review of the *Proceedings* to gain influence with Wangenheim for an appointment to his old position at Tübingen. Haym, however, later recanted this story. On Wangenheim's proposal, see Dieter Wyduckel, "Die Idee des Dritten Deutschlands im Vormärz. Ein Beitrag zur trialistischen Verfassungskonzeption des Freiherrn von Wangenheim," in "*O Fürstin, der Heimath! Glükliches Stutgard*," pp. 159–183. For an analysis of the Haym charge, see especially Franz Rosenzweig (*Hegel und der Staat* [Munich and Berlin: Oldenbourg, 1920], vol. II, pp. 30–62), who finds also important textual grounds – including the rather circumscribed mention of bicamerality that appears in the *Proceedings* essay below – for casting doubt on Haym's claim.

on the new proposal, the Estates voted it down on June 2, 1817 by a margin of 67–42. The third and final phase, following Wangenheim's departure, was dominated by the conservative minister Theodor Eugen Maucler and culminated in the ratification of the constitution on September 23, 1819, in the wake of the adoption of the Carlsbad Decrees.

Hegel's essay on the Württemberg Estates was written and published during the second phase of this dispute,[43] but limits itself almost exclusively to discussing the published *Proceedings* concerned with the events of 1815–16. In his review of those *Proceedings*, Hegel sees that what is at issue is the inheritance of a generation of political experience in the wake of the French Revolution: these twenty-five years, Hegel says, are "perhaps the richest that world history has had," years which "teach us the most, because our world and our ideas belong to them."[44]

The central philosophical concern for political philosophy and constitutional law emerging from this period is, for Hegel, the notion of the *rational* justification of institutions and governmental structures. The desire of the Estates to return to their old rights is, however, rooted in a "positive" conception of right (following his earlier writings, Hegel means here by "positive" a notion of right as what happens to be posited by authorities in a given historical or political situation). But if the members of the old Estates see things in a "positive" light that takes no account of the rational import of the French Revolution, theorists who would wish to construe political matters in the overly "abstract" French terms of "pure number and quanta of wealth" employ "atomistic principles" which are, in science as in politics, "death for every rational concept, articulation and liveliness."[45]

The notion of an "articulated" or "organic" rather than atomistic relationship at the heart of the citizen's relation to the state implies as well that the terms of a contractual relation between ruler and people are equally off the mark. In an argument which links closely to the stance Hegel will take on Hobbes, Rousseau, and the contract tradition in the *Philosophy of Right*, Hegel holds that what is at issue in acts of constitution-making is a notion of the relation of citizen to state which cannot be understood in terms of a contract between a ruler and the people. This relationship demands instead philosophical consideration of a notion of the

---

[43] The essay was originally published in two installments in the *Heidelberg Yearbooks*: the issue of November 1817 and the continuation in the December 1817 issue (which did not actually appear until January 1818).

[44] G. W. F. Hegel, *Gesammelte Werke (GW)*, vol. XV, *Schriften und Entwürfe I (1817–1825)*, ed. Friedrich Hogemann and Christoph Jamme (Hamburg: Meiner, 1990), pp. 61–62.

[45] Ibid., p. 45. As examples of such "atomistic principles," Hegel mentions age and property qualifications for voting.

political – defined, as Hegel presents it here, as a set of obligations which extend beyond those of merely private interests.

Hegel begins his account with a description of the opening of the Estates Assembly by the king, followed by a characterization of the rigid political stance taken by members of the Assembly advocating the "good, old right," the stultifying style of *verbatim* speech-reading, and lack of actual political dialogue among members. Hegel also devotes a significant section of the review to a consideration of the various abuses of existing administrative arrangements in Württemberg (including the notorious network of "notaries" whose interests are defended by many of the Estates members).

The review does not offer a chronological analysis or account of the proceedings, even of the limited phase of them that Hegel discusses (as Rosenzweig remarks, Hegel seems to focus unduly on the first few days of the Assembly). And, although the essay was once called "one of the best pamphlets that came from a German pen,"[46] it is rather the polemical sharpness and apparent one-sidedness that most readers have in fact noticed. Rudolf Haym called it "Asiatically eloquent," a "servile and syco-phantic defense of the government line."[47] Fries, one of Hegel's bitterest rivals, describes the essay as one phase of an accommodationism that characterized Hegel's relations with whatever regime was in power at the moment.[48] Even Hegel's close friend Niethammer told him that he had "cleverly supported a dubious cause."[49]

Hegel's not entirely unfair attack on the Estates ignores some legitimate complaints on their part which Hegel himself in earlier contexts had endorsed – for example, the Estates' criticism of Friedrich's autocratic dissolution of its meetings.[50] But Hegel's philosophical aim is, he says, not to give a concrete description of this particular Estates but rather – in a wider public compass – to show the concept or *Begriff* of an Estates Assembly. That concept, Hegel holds, concerns precisely the educative function that he wishes to elucidate for the public by means of the essay: an education

[46] M. Lenz, *Geschichte der königlichen Friedrich-Wilhelms-Universität zu Berlin* (Halle: Waisenhaus, 1910–18), p. 203, cited in Pelczynski.

[47] Rudolf Haym, *Hegel und seine Zeit. Vorlesungen über Entstehung und Entwicklung, Wesen und Werth der Hegel'schen Philosophie* (Hildesheim: Olms, 1962 [Berlin: Rudolf Gaertner, 1857]), p. 352.

[48] See the letter from Fries to L. Rödiger on January 6, 1821: "Hegel's metaphysical mushroom did not spring up in the gardens of science, anyway, but on the dung-heap of servility. Until 1813 his metaphysics was French, then it became royal Württembergian, and now it is kissing von Kamptz' whip . . ." (Nicolin, ed., *Hegel in Berichten seiner Zeitgenossen*, p. 221). [Our translation.]

[49] Hegel, *Briefe von und an Hegel*, ed. Johannes Hoffmeister (Hamburg: Meiner, 1969), vol. II, p. 172.

[50] See his approving remark on Napoleon's complaint about Friedrich's dissolution of the Assembly.

both of the government concerning the people's needs and an education of the people themselves about what their genuine political needs and will are.

Seen from this perspective, the review essay gives an interesting window onto the development of Hegel's political thought, in that the articulation of his stance on the shaping of the Württemberg constitution appears to contribute to the increasingly concrete character of his "official" philosophical teaching concerning political institutions. As the editors of the Hegel Archive edition of the Heidelberg writings note, the essay was written in the fall of 1817, exactly between the publication of the first edition of the *Encyclopedia* (summer semester 1817), with its relatively sparse section on political institutions in the "Objective Spirit" section, and the richer account of political institutions in the lectures on the philosophy of right which Hegel began giving in the winter semester 1817–18.[51]

One of the most prominent philosophical concerns at issue between the sparse *Encyclopedia* account of political philosophy and Hegel's *Philosophy of Right* is the emergence of Hegel's articulation of the difference between civil society and the state. Rolf-Peter Horstmann has suggested that it may have been exactly the (negative) public reaction to Hegel's review essay that prompted him to formulate more clearly his position regarding the relation between civil society and the state.[52] There are in fact a number of concerns that Hegel appears to be developing simultaneously between the review essay and the new lectures on the philosophy of right: (a) the explanation of the Assembly as a "mediating" body (*Vermittlung*) between ruler and people;[53] (b) the role of the Assembly for the political education (*Erziehung*) of the people;[54] (c) the difficulty of "permanence" in a constitution and the importance of the monarch establishing the constitution from "outside," as it were (as the ancient figures Solon, Moses, and Lycurgus presented fundamental laws to people from whom they had a certain

---

51 For a comparison of the institutional analysis of the "Proceedings" essay with the philosophical stance Hegel takes in the Heidelberg lectures on the philosophy of right, see Christoph Jamme, "Die Erziehung der Stände durch sich selbst: Hegels Konzeption der neuständischbürgerlichen Repräsentation in Heidelberg 1817/18," in *Hegels Rechtsphilosophie im Zusammenhang der europäischen Verfassungsgeschichte*, ed. Hans-Christian Lucas and Otto Pöggeler (Stuttgart-Bad Cannstatt: Frommann-Holzboog, 1986), pp. 149–174.

52 Rolf-Peter Horstmann, "The Role of Civil Society in Hegel's Political Philosophy," in *Hegel on Ethics and Politics*, ed. Robert Pippin and Otfried Höffe (Cambridge: Cambridge University Press, 2004), pp. 208–238.

53 GW vol. XV, *Schriften und Entwürfe I (1817–1825)*, p. 80; compare *Vorlesungen über Naturrecht und Staatswissenschaft. Heidelberg 1817/18 mit Nachträgen aus der Vorlesung 1818/19. Nachgeschrieben von P. Wannenmann*, ed. C. Becker *et al.* (Hamburg: Meiner, 1983), §§147–148.

54 GW vol. XV, pp. 114, 121; cf. *Vorlesungen*, §154.

distance);[55] and (d) the role of opposition in Parliament (especially in relation to the English system).[56]

The *Estates* essay thus opens an intriguing window on to Hegel's emerging concrete political philosophy in the years prior to the publication of the *Philosophy of Right*. As is well known, Hegel's articulation of his political philosophy at Berlin came to be complicated by the repressive measures of the period of the Carlsbad Decrees shortly after he moved to Berlin. A letter from Hegel in Berlin back to his Heidelberg colleague Creuzer captures well how the political tone of things had changed from the somewhat more optimistic vein of the *Estates* essay's praise of what the twenty-five years since the French Revolution had wrought:

I am about to be fifty years old, and I have spent thirty of these fifty years in these ever-unrestful times of hope and fear. I had hoped that for once we might be done with it. Now I must confess that things with us remain as ever; indeed, in one's darker hours it even seems that they are going to get worse.[57]

It is difficult not to look back from this somewhat grayer perspective when assessing the political contribution of the *Estates* essay. While the essay's re-publication at government expense[58] gave it a far wider influence than anything else Hegel ever wrote about contemporary events, it also lent particular currency to the charges of Hegelian accommodationism (even though Hegel's brief on behalf of the king's constitution clearly had not been uncritical).[59] Rosenzweig's account of the new political situation in Württemberg after 1819, however, notices that both parties which emerged at that time – both the "liberal party" of officials and the educated classes, as well as the more leftist, so-called *Bürgerfreunde* party – recognized a truth that was central to Hegel's analysis of the constitutional situation: that the days of the positive claims of the "old right" were over.[60]

---

[55] Ibid., p. 77; cf. *Vorlesungen*, §134A.   [56] Ibid., p. 67; cf. *Vorlesungen*, §156.

[57] Letter of October 30, 1819 (*Hegel: The Letters*, p. 451).

[58] The essay was republished in the *Württembergischer Volksfreund* (see GW vol. XV.291–2).

[59] Jamme's essay stresses three aspects of Hegel's criticism of the king's proposal that each link to larger elements of the emerging *Philosophy of Right*: the insistence that state officials not be left out of the Assembly, the criticism of the "atomism" of voting rights connected merely to age or property qualifications, and the criticism of the tax-approval right demanded by the Estates (see Jamme, "Die Erziehung der Stände durch sich selbst").

[60] Rosenzweig, *Hegel und der Staat*, vol. II, pp. 57–62.

Translators' note

We have used the corrected text of the Jacobi review and the *Estates* essay in volume XV of the critical edition of Hegel's collected works produced by the Hegel-Kommission of the Rheinisch-Westfälischen Akademie der Wissenschaften and the Hegel-Archiv at the Ruhr-Universität Bochum (*Schriften und Entwürfe I: 1817–1825*, ed. Friedrich Hogemann and Christoph Jamme).[1] The marginal numbering in our translation refers to the pagination of this edition. The (few) lettered footnotes in the translations are Hegel's own, while numbered footnotes are ours. In the *Estates* essay, Hegel cites page numbers of the official *Proceedings* of the Estates meetings in parentheses in the body of the main text; we have chosen to put these references in the numbered footnoting sequence.

In the numbered footnotes, we refer in the majority of cases to standard English translations of Hegel's and Jacobi's works, occasionally modifying them. As there is currently no complete translation of Jacobi's major works, however, we frequently make reference to the standard German edition by Klaus Hammacher, Walter Jaeschke *et al.* In the case of Hegel's works in German, preferential treatment is given to the critical edition. In the few instances in which Hegelian texts have yet to appear in this edition, we refer to the widely used edition revised by Eva Moldenhauer and Klaus Markus Michel (Frankfurt am Main: Suhrkamp, 1970/1986). While neither of the two Heidelberg texts presents the sort of technical challenges familiar to the translators of, say, the *Science of Logic* or the *Phenomenology of Spirit*, Hegel's more "public" journal style still requires some editorial decisions for translators. The first of the issues concerns the rather long, unbroken expository style Hegel seems to prefer here: neither text features

---

[1] (Hamburg: Meiner, 1990), pp. 7–125. We are grateful to Felix Meiner Verlag for permission to consult their critical edition in the preparation of our translation. There were a number of mostly slight corrections to the text of this edition, which are printed in volume XVI, *Schriften und Entwürfe II: 1826–1831*, ed. Friedrich Hogemann with the assistance of Christoph Jamme (Hamburg: Meiner, 2001), p. 441.

basic divisions or subject headings of any sort, and Hegel tends toward what are, for contemporary English (or for that matter, German) readers, rather long sentences and paragraphs. Hegel does break up sentences at places with semi-colons, and his long paragraphs are likewise punctuated by occasional end-of-sentence dashes within those paragraphs to suggest points of transition (the longer paragraphs thus often have two, three, or more indicated sub-divisions).

In our translation, we have attempted to indicate the most basic subject-matter shifts in Hegel's texts as a whole with the insertion of bracketed headings and sub-headings. We have tried where possible to preserve Hegel's sentence and paragraph structure, but since the mid-sentence semi-colons and the mid-paragraph dashes often correspond, respectively, in today's usage to periods and paragraph breaks, we have often divided the larger sentences and paragraphs at just those points. These correlations are, of course, rough and ready and hence do not allow for mechanical substitution. In no case, however, have we inserted a paragraph break where there is no dash or paragraph break in the original.

We do not keep to Hegel's practice of italicizing text both for emphasis and to indicate indirect speech. Clear cases of indirect speech are indicated by quotation marks, and, in keeping with contemporary stylistic sensibility, we have not always reproduced Hegel's italicized emphases.

The other main set of translational difficulties connected with these texts concerns Hegel's use of terms. Though both texts are remarkable for presenting a far less technical mode of philosophical argument than many other Hegelian works, the reader will nevertheless encounter frequent instances of Hegel's "speculative" terminology. In rendering technical terms into English, we have adopted the principles formulated by Terry Pinkard in the preface to his forthcoming translation of *The Phenomenology of Spirit*, and for a reasoned account of these principles the reader is directed to that volume.

Several remarks may nonetheless be in order here. Perhaps the most distinctive conception in Hegel's philosophy is what he calls "*Geist.*" Like the French *ésprit*, German *Geist* has a number of distinct meanings not directly associated with the English word "mind," so that the latter is often (and especially in Hegelian contexts) a poor equivalent of the German term. Frequently, "spirit" would serve as a better translation, as when Hegel speaks of the "great spirit [*großer Geist*] of the Cartesian *cogito ergo sum*" in his review of Jacobi. There *Geist* is used in a sense similar to the French *ésprit de corps* or our "spirit of the age." *Geist* in the further sense of intelligence or wit (*ingenium*) is a virtue that Hegel repeatedly and emphatically attributes to Jacobi; he even goes into some detail in appraising the uses and general value of what he refers to as "*das Geistreiche der Philosophie*," a kind of philosophical *ésprit* he sees as the distinguishing feature of Jacobi's philosophical style. That Hegel's nominalization of the adjective *geistreich*, which in most contexts would appropriately be rendered as "witty," "inventive," or "intelligent," resists translation is not only due to its resonance with Hegel's more technical use of the term *Geist*. For one thing, the term "wit" has almost entirely lost its association with the Latin *ingenium* as the faculty of discovering (*inventio*) subtle similarities and connections between disparate things and creating incisive, suggestive, or especially vivid expressions of thought, while the etymologically more closely related "ingenuity" has taken on a too narrowly instrumental sense, and "genius" is both too vague and too emphatically positive to allow of the kind of critical analysis to which Hegel subjects what is *geistreich* in philosophy. Like the German *Witz*, "wit" nowadays refers almost exclusively to the brilliant but superficial quality typical of so-called witticisms.[2] Thus, depending on the context, we have translated *Geist* variously as either "mind" or "spirit," *geistlos* as "spiritless," and *das Geistreiche* as *ésprit*. In contexts which made a different translation desirable, the German word *Geist* or its cognate is supplied in a footnote.

The verb "sublate" (and its cognates, e.g., "sublation") is a term of art introduced by James Hutchison Stirling in his 1865 work *The Secret of Hegel*[3] in order to have an equivalent for Hegel's term *aufheben*. The term appears to have been in common use in English-language textbooks of logic in the nineteenth century[4] and is formed from *sublatum*, the past participle of the Latin verb *tollere*. Apart from its semantic aptness, Stirling's choice of *sublatum* as the root from which to form the English term of art may have been motivated by Hegel's own observation in a scholium to the section of

---

[2] Cf. Kant's remarks on the terms *Witz, Geist, ésprit*, and *genius* in his *Anthropology from a Pragmatic Point of View*, trans. and ed. Robert B. Louden (Cambridge: Cambridge University Press, 2006), §§44 and 54–59.

[3] *The Secret of Hegel: Being the Hegelian System in Origin, Principle, Form and Matter* (Edinburgh: Oliver and Boyd, 2nd ed., 1898. Reprint: Dubuque, Iowa: William C. Brown, 1972), pp. 242 ff.

[4] Cf. Sir William Hamilton, *Lectures on Metaphysics and Logic*, ed. H. L. Mansel and J. Veitch (Boston: Gould and Lincoln, 1860), vol. i, Lecture XVII, p. 234: "If the essential character of the Disjunctive Syllogism consists in this – that the affirmation or negation, or, what is a better expression, the position or sublation, of one or other of two contradictory attributes follows from the subsumption of the opposite; – there is necessarily implied in the disjunctive process, that, when of two opposite predicates one is posited or affirmed, the other is sublated or denied; and that, when the one is sublated or denied, the other is posited or affirmed."

the *Logic* entitled "*Aufheben des Werdens*" that the ambiguity of *aufheben* bears strong affinity to that of the Latin *tollere*, although he remarks that "the double meaning of the Latin *tollere* (which the Ciceronian wit – *tollendum esse Octavium* – has made notorious) is more circumscribed [sc. than that of the German expression], its affirmative character amounting only to a lifting-up."[5] Hence although "sublation" will sound a good deal stranger to English ears than Hegel's term *Aufhebung* does to German ones, both its long standing as a favored English equivalent and its etymology, which links it to a term Hegel himself viewed as close in meaning to *Aufhebung*, led us to retain it in this translation. It should be noted that although Hegel consciously plays on the "double meaning" of the term, he does not always use *aufheben* in its full technical sense and that it is sometimes debatable whether he means to include both its usual senses or whether he intends it to be taken in the sense of negation (abolishment, annulment, or revocation) only. In cases in which Hegel arguably uses the term only in this one sense, it has been translated accordingly and the German term has been supplied in a note.

Hegel explicitly distinguishes his use of the term *Begriff* ("concept") from its more ordinary use.[6] We have departed from the older custom of translating *Begriff* as "notion" (which stressed its relation to the scholastic term *notio*), adopting "concept" as the translation for Hegel's technical term. Due to the specific technical meaning Hegel gives to this term, however, it would seem misleading and inappropriate to render Hegel's frequent use of *begrifflos* as "non-conceptual." In analogy to the translation "spiritless" for *geistlos*, we render *begrifflos* as "concept-less."

The specific political and legal vocabulary employed in the *Estates* essay presents difficulties of a different kind. Hegel's review of the *Proceedings* draws on a wide variety of often archaic terms for governmental functions and legal and economic relationships which have few or no equivalents in contemporary parliamentary or administrative practice. The familiarly named *Schreiberei-Institut* is not (as one might otherwise guess) an authors' guild but an oppressive layer of local officialdom; we have translated *Schreiber* consistently as "notary," indicating a particular class (or actually caste) of officials whose approval was needed for the most diverse

---

[5] Translated in *The Secret of Hegel*, p. 244. Thus Stirling himself was clearly familiar with the passage, and since he also seems to consider "resolution" a possible equivalent for *Aufhebung*, he certainly did settle on "sublation" in the light of other alternatives.

[6] For a concise exposition of Hegel's speculative notion of the concept and its difference from what are ordinarily referred to as concepts, see the initial section of the "Subjective Logic" in Hegel's *Science of Logic*.

transactions. In some cases we resorted to (usually periphrastic) descriptive equivalents, translating, for example, the difficult term *Virilstimmführer* as "non-elected member." Throughout the text of the *Estates* essay, footnotes provide glosses on historical terminology and supply background information on the relevant institutions where necessary. For an overview of terms and their translations, the reader may refer to the Glossary (pp. 143–162).

Heidelberg Writings:
Journal Publications

Friedrich Heinrich Jacobi's Works, Volume III

Friedrich Heinrich Jacobi's Works, Volume 3, Leipzig: Gerhard Fleischer, 1816. 568pp. + xxvi

The reviewer is pleased that a new volume of Jacobi's collected works has 7 appeared so soon after the last, and wishes both that noble elder and his readers all the best for the uninterrupted continuation of their publication. This third volume contains four writings which, in the words of the preface, "to a certain extent originated simultaneously and are but divergent parts of a single whole that recapitulates itself differently in each of them." They are: (1) Jacobi's *Letter to Fichte*, first published in 1799; (2) an essay which first appeared in Reinhold's *Contributions* (no. 31, 1801), with the title *On Critical Philosophy's Attempt to Bring Reason to Understanding and to Transform Philosophy as Such*;[1] (3) *On a Prophecy by Lichtenberg*,[2] first printed in 1801; and (4) the text *On Divine Things and their Revelation*,[3] with a foreword written for this new edition. An interesting appendix of twenty-three letters to Johann Müller, Georg Forster, Herder, Kant (among them one from Kant to Jacobi), Privy Councillor Schlosser, J. G. Jacobi, and several unnamed recipients concludes the volume.[4]

---

[1] *Über das Unternehmen des Kriticismus, die Vernunft zu Verstande zu bringen und der Philosophie überhaupt eine neue Ansicht zu geben.* Jacobi's lengthy essay appeared in the periodical *Beyträge zur Leichteren Übersicht des Zustandes der Philosophie beym Anfange des 19. Jahrhunderts* [*Contributions to a Simpler Overview of the Situation of Philosophy at the Beginning of the 19th Century*], edited by the philosopher Karl Leonhard Reinhold (1757–1823). Jacobi's title contains a play on the words *Vernunft* (reason) and *Verstand* (understanding). "To bring someone to understanding" (*zum Verstand bringen*) means to bring him to his senses.

[2] *Über eine Weissagung Lichtenbergs.*   [3] *Von den göttlichen Dingen und ihrer Offenbarung.*

[4] Johann Friedrich Müller (1749–1825) was a painter and poet. Jacobi and Goethe had made his acquaintance together in 1775. Georg Forster (1754–94) was a natural historian, ethnologist, and essayist who accompanied James Cook on his circumnavigation of the globe between 1772 and 1775. He was a founding member of the short-lived Mainz Republic (1792), and his revolutionary sympathies took him to Paris in 1793, where he died of pneumonia in 1794. Johann Georg Schlosser (1739–99) was a prominent intellectual, long-standing member of Jacobi's circle, and Goethe's brother-in-law. He was well known both for his numerous translations of classical Greek works of

[SPINOZA]

One might have wished that in the order of publication of these collected works Jacobi's earlier *Letters on the Doctrine of Spinoza*[5] had preceded the treatises contained in the present volume, for these *Letters* respond to an historical interest that is older and prior to the forms of philosophy dealt with by these treatises, namely the metaphysics of Leibniz and Wolff, which at the time of the *Letters* was at its last breath. That metaphysics was a common point of departure for both Jacobi's philosophy and the philosophy of Kant which Jacobi was later to oppose. The *Letters* also offer a more extensive and reasoned presentation of Jacobi's views on the vacuity of claims to scientific knowledge of the divine. These views are also at the fore of the present writings, not only as limited to the philosophical systems dealt with there, but in their full generality. Yet despite the spiritedness[6] and warmth that attend them, they still leave much to be desired by those who, when it comes to truth, are in the habit of demanding reasons. The prior publication of the *Letters* might have been viewed as a sign of more respect for this habit than was the publication of the dialogue *David Hume on Faith*[7] in the second volume in the series. – How Jacobi confronts the philosophies dealt with in the present volume, an attitude which this review must convey, will gain in clarity and perspicuity if we first remember how Jacobi immersed his mind in the study of Spinozism and how he had thereby established the position at which, already fully matured, he encountered Kant's philosophy upon its original publication. In order to clarify that, however, we must first recall a few things about the state of philosophy in those days.

The great spirit of the Cartesian *cogito ergo sum* had consisted in knowing that thought[8] is the ground of being and in comprehending the various

---

literature and philosophy and for his outspoken criticism of the Enlightenment. His work *Platos Briefe* [*Plato's Letters*] (1793) provoked Kant's critical response in the essay *On a Newly Arisen Superior Tone in Philosophy* (1796). Johann Georg Jacobi (1740–1814) was Friedrich Heinrich's older brother, a prominent poet in the anacreontic style popular in eighteenth-century Germany, and professor of beaux-arts in Freiburg.

[5] Jacobi's *Über die Lehre des Spinoza in Briefen an den Herrn Moses Mendelssohn* (Breslau: Gottl. Löwe, 1785), with an important second edition in 1789. An English version of the 1785 edition with excerpts from the 1789 edition can be found in *Friedrich Heinrich Jacobi: The Main Philosophical Writings and the Novel "Allwill,"* trans. George di Giovanni (Montreal: McGill-Queen's University Press, 1994). In the following, this text is cited as *Jacobi: Main Philosophical Writings.*

[6] *Geist.*

[7] *David Hume über den Glauben, oder Idealismus und Realismus. Ein Gespräch* (Breslau: Gottl. Löwe, 1787).

[8] The English word "thought" is used to translate two different words in German. On the one hand, it renders the gerund *das Denken* ("thinking"). In the present context, on the other hand, the same

forms of being only in and through that ground. But French philosophy had given up that spirit and embarked instead on the opposite pathway of Lockeanism, seeking to derive thought from the immediate givens of the *world of appearance*. To the extent that the need still remained for a universal ground in this world of appearance, its fundamental essence was declared to be a conceptless universality, namely an indeterminate *nature* or rather a nature onto which a few barren determinations of reflection such as totality, forces, composition, and similar forms of externality and mechanism were superficially tacked. German culture had essentially taken the same direction. In every quarter, the Enlightenment had eroded the traditions of venerable doctrine and mores, the passively *received* and immediately *given* content of a world charged through with the divine; it abandoned and rejected these so-called *posits* on the grounds that self-consciousness was not to be found in them or (what comes to the same) because self-consciousness could not find them within itself.[9] What remained was the *caput mortuum*[10] of an abstract, empty entity that *cannot be comprehended*, i.e., an entity in which thinking[11] is not present to itself. That which is being in and for itself had thus been reduced to nothingness, for what self-consciousness found in itself were *finite purposes* and the things related to such purposes by *utility*.[12] There were some for whom their religious feeling was sufficient to counteract this contagion; they attributed the theoretical results to mistakes in cognition[13] and sought to support and save the truth, as it were, by correcting and improving the cognition of it.[14] Jacobi, on the contrary, did not counter with just the certitude of his soul. Rather than

9

term renders the German word *Gedanke*. Hegel uses the term *Gedanke* both in the usual sense and in a special sense closely related to his technical use of the term *Begriff* ("concept").

[9] Hegel's term *das Positive* most frequently refers to what has been *merely* posited, i.e., posited from a source external to the consciousness of those who accept it as binding and valid. Hegel offers a critical analysis of the Enlightenment's struggle against the merely positive in the *Phenomenology of Spirit* (trans. Terry Pinkard [Cambridge: Cambridge University Press, forthcoming], §§537–583).

[10] *Todtenkopf* ("skull") is the literal German translation of the alchemical term of art *caput mortuum*, which designated the chemical residue that remained after a distillation or sublimation in the process of which everything of value had been removed from the substance that was left over. Hegel himself generally uses the Latin term; in fact, this use of a German equivalent is the only instance in all his published writings. Cf. §44 of the *Encyclopedia*, where in a similar vein he characterizes Kant's thing-in-itself as a *caput mortuum*.

[11] *Das Denken*.

[12] Hegel presents his views on the historical conflict between the Enlightenment and the religious tradition and the ascendance of the category of utility in more detail in the *Phenomenology of Spirit*, §§562–563 and 575.

[13] Here and throughout the text, the English expression "cognition" serves to render the German terms *Erkennen* and *Erkenntnis*.

[14] Hegel may be referring to a stream of thought represented by Christian August Crusius (1715–75, professor of philosophy and theology in Leipzig) in the middle of the eighteenth century. In his *Entwurf der notwendigen Vernunftwahrheiten* (1745: *An Outline of Necessary Truths of Reason*) and

lingering with the barren remains in which metaphysics was eking out its wan existence and nourishing its stale hopes, his deeply thorough mind conceived philosophy in its relation to the sources of knowledge and delved down to their undiluted purity. Philosophical endeavors may slave away at the analysis, distinction, and recombination of metaphysical topics, inventing new logical possibilities and refuting others. Yet if their foundation does not lie in the infinite intuition[15] and cognition of the one substantial being that is Spinozism and in whose possession we find Jacobi – if that Spinozism is not the standard by which they measure every further determination – then the only relation linking the determinations of cognition to truth will be missing. Spinoza expresses that relation when he says that all things must be contemplated *sub specie aeternitatis*. Because the purity of this intuition was present in Jacobi, he made his appearance in the time of the metaphysics of the older school[16] with such exceptional superiority, while others still took the interest of knowledge to lie in a few barren, conceptless determinations of understanding such as existence, possibility, concept, and so on. It makes no difference that God was supposed to be the object and goal of such determinations, for it is those determinations themselves which form the *content* of cognition when we seek to understand God by their means. *Outside and apart from* such finite content, the idea of God itself remains nothing more than a mere representation[17] or sentiment, the infinite character of which remains external to the cognition. The finitude

---

Weg zur Gewißheit und Zuverlässigkeit der menschlichen Erkenntnis (1747: *The Path to Certainty and Reliability of Human Knowledge*), Crusius took issue with the logic, metaphysics, and philosophical theology of Leibniz and Wolff. Hegel could also be thinking here of the Jewish rationalist thinker Moses Mendelssohn (1729–86), who was intimately involved in the original controversy on Lessing's alleged Spinozism. It is noteworthy that Mendelssohn criticized Jacobi for his fideist conception of intuition (cf. Friedrich Heinrich Jacobi, *Werke*, vol. I,1, ed. Klaus Hammacher and Irmgard-Maria Piske [Hamburg: Meiner, 1998], p. 115). Hegel briefly discusses Crusius and Mendelssohn in his *Lectures on the History of Philosophy* (*Werke*, ed. Eva Moldenhauer and Karl Markus Michel [Frankfurt: Suhrkamp, 1970], vol. XX, pp. 263 ff.).

[15] "Intuition" renders *Anschauung*. In the few passages which seem to call for a rendering of *Anschauung* different from "intuition," the German word will be indicated in a footnote. In the passage at hand, Hegel may be referring to Spinoza's *scientia intuitiva* and the contemplation of things *sub specie aeternitatis* (cf. Baruch de Spinoza, *Ethica*, part 2, prop. 40–47, esp. 44, corollary 2).

[16] When Hegel speaks of the "metaphysics of the older school" (*vormalige Metaphysik*) he is invariably referring to the methods, concerns, and doctrines of the Leibniz–Wolff school of philosophy that dominated German thought well into the latter years of the eighteenth century. Cf. *Encyclopedia*, §27.

[17] Kant gave the German word *Vorstellung* a technical meaning equivalent to the Latin term *repraesentatio* (cf. *Critique of Pure Reason*, ibid., pp. 398 f. = B 376). Although in Hegel's philosophical psychology the term takes on a highly specific meaning somewhat different from its meaning in Kant (cf. *Encyclopedia*, §§451–454), he most frequently uses it with pejorative connotations in contradistinction to the properly speculative conception of a category or determination of thought, speaking of "mere representations" (*bloße Vorstellungen*).

of such content, however, and thus also of the subjective grappling it occasions, is consumed in the one absolute. Spirit only achieves the absolute and becomes consciousness of reason,[18] however, by recognizing its limitations as *illusory*, as mere forms of *appearance*, and thus consigning them to the abyss. – Jacobi had achieved this highest intuition not only in the form of feeling and mere representation, the form at which mere religiosity halts; he achieved it on the higher path of *thought* and recognized with Spinoza that this vision[19] is the ultimate and true result of all thinking, and that every consistent system of philosophy must in the end lead to Spinozism.[20]

A substantial difference enters in at this point, however, in that the one absolute substance must be considered merely an *initial* form of the necessary result and that it is necessary to go beyond this form. The unshakeable feeling was manifest in Jacobi that in this initial immediacy the truth could not suffice for spirit, which is not something immediate, and hence that the truth had not yet been grasped as *absolute spirit*. The object as taken by *sensuous* consciousness is the believed being[21] of finite things. As consciousness progresses toward Reason, however, it comes to reject the truth of immediate *sensuous belief*. Being, raised to infinity, is the *pure abstraction of thinking*, and this thinking of pure being is not sensuous intuition but rather *intellectual intuition* or the intuition of reason.[22] Since, however, in its immediacy infinite being is only something abstract, unmoving, and non-spiritual, we find that what is *free*, i.e., self-determining, is missing in that abyss into which all determinateness has been cast and destroyed.

10

---

[18] Hegel distinguishes between subjective and objective reason (cf. *Encyclopedia*, §§441, 467 and the introduction to the *Science of Logic*, *GW*, vol. XXI, p. 30). In the present passage, the phrase "consciousness of reason" is therefore importantly ambiguous and can be read as referring both to (subjective) consciousness of (objective) reason and to objective reason's own realized consciousness as speculative philosophy.

[19] *Anschauung*.

[20] "Lessing: . . . There is no other philosophy than the philosophy of Spinoza. I: That might be true. For the determinist, if he wants to be consistent, must become a fatalist: the rest then follows by itself" ("Concerning the Doctrine of Spinoza in Letters to Herr Moses Mendelssohn," in *Jacobi: Main Philosophical Writings*, p. 187).

[21] *Geglaubtes Seyn*.

[22] *Vernunftanschauung*. Jacobi had introduced this term to characterize his own rational intuitionism in the preface to the dialogue *David Hume on Belief* in the second volume of his collected writings, a preface he describes as an introduction to his complete writings (Friedrich Heinrich Jacobi, *Werke*, ed. Friedrich Roth and Friedrich Köppen [Fleischer: Leipzig, 1815], vol. II, pp. 3–123). There (p. 59) Jacobi writes, "This above all must be borne in mind: Just as there is sensible intuition, intuition by means of the senses, there is also such a thing as rational intuition by means of reason. Both stand over against each other as proper sources of knowledge and neither one can be derived from the other . . . For the same reason, no demonstration can be valid against rational intuition or the intuition of reason, a faculty which enables us to know supersensible objects [*jenseitige Gegenstände*], i.e., a faculty which renders certain their existence and truth." [Our translation.] In the rest of the text, we translate *Vernunftanschauung* as "rational intuition."

Immediately and for itself, freedom is *personality* as the infinite point of *determination in and for itself.* The one unalloyed substance, however, or pure intuition (which is the same as *abstract thinking*) represents only *one* side of freedom, namely the side on which it has only just arrived at the simple element of universality and left the two finitudes of being and consciousness behind it, without, however, positing self-determination and personality within that element. For it is to no avail that in absolute substance *Thought*, the ground of freedom and personality, is just as much an attribute as *Being* or extension; since substance is the undifferentiated and undifferentiable unity of both, their *fundamental determination* remains *immediacy* or *being.* Such being, however, contains no transition from itself to an understanding or to anything singular. An even more obvious requirement would be to demonstrate some transition from the absolute unity to the divine attributes, for it has merely been *assumed* that there are such attributes, just as the existence of a finite *understanding* or *imagination* and of particular, finite things was assumed.[23] Their being is constantly being revoked as something untrue and immersed in the infinity of substance, yet despite this recognition of their negativity they retain the status of a *given point of departure.* Conversely, absolute substance is not understood as the point of departure for distinctions, particularization, individuation, or whatever form distinctions may take, be it as attributes and modes, as being and thought, understanding, imagination or what have you. And hence everything is merely submerged and perishes in a substance which remains motionless within itself and out of which nothing ever resurfaces.

Upon reflection, however, it is not hard to discover the internal principle of separation in substance itself, for we need only reflect upon that which is so to speak *in fact* contained within substance. For since substance has been defined as the truth of the particular things that are sublated and extinguished in it, *absolute negativity* has effectively already been posited as its determination, and absolute negativity is itself the source of freedom.[24] – Everything depends here on a correct understanding of the status and significance of negativity. If it is taken only to be the determinateness of

---

[23] Cf. *Ethics*, part 1, def. 4 & 6 and prop. 10, schol., part 2, prop. 1, 2, and 7, schol.; cf. also Letter 64 to G. H. Schuller from July 29, 1675. Spinoza's assumption of a finite understanding is evident in the wording of part 1, def. 4: "By *attribute*, I mean that which the intellect perceives as constituting the essence of substance" (*Benedict de Spinoza: On the Improvement of the Understanding, The Ethics, Correspondence*, trans. R. H. M. Elwes [New York: Dover, 1955], p. 45).

[24] Cf. Hegel's exposition of the concept of spirit (*Begriff des Geistes*) in the *Encyclopedia*, §382, where the connection between freedom and absolute negativity is spelled out in greater detail.

finite things (*omnis determinatio est negatio*),[25] then we are already thinking of it outside of absolute substance and have allowed finite things to fall outside of it; our imagination *maintains* them *outside of* absolute substance. Conceived of this way, however, negation fails to be seen as *internal to the* *infinite* or *internal to substance*, which is supposed rather to be the sublated being of finite things. – Yet the manner in which negation is internal to substance has in fact *thus already been said*, and systematic progress in philosophical reflection really consists in nothing other than knowing what one has already said oneself. Substance, namely, is supposed to be the sublation of the finite, and that is just to say that it is the *negation of negation*, since it is precisely negation which we took to be definitive of the finite. And as the negation of negation, substance is absolute *affirmation*, and just as immediately it is *freedom* and *self-determination*. – Thus the difference between determining the absolute as substance and determining it as spirit boils down to the question whether thinking, having annihilated its finitudes and mediations, negated its negations, and thus comprehended the one absolute, is conscious of what it has actually achieved in its cognition of absolute substance, or whether it lacks such consciousness.

    In his innermost, Jacobi had made just this transition from absolute substance to absolute spirit and had proclaimed with an irresistible *feeling of certainty*, "*God is spirit, the absolute is free and has the nature of a person.*" – In terms of philosophical insight, it was of the utmost significance that Jacobi brought out the moment of immediacy in our knowledge of God so distinctly and emphatically. God is not a dead god, but a *living* one; indeed, he is more than merely a living God, he is *spirit* and *eternal love*, and this only because his being is not abstract being, but an internal movement of self-differentiation, and because he is cognition of himself in the person differentiated from himself. His essence is the immediate, i.e., determinately existing unity,[26] only insofar as the eternal mediation eternally returns to unity, and this returning is itself that unity, the unity of life, feeling of self, personhood, and self-knowledge. – Thus Jacobi claimed that reason, as that which is *supernatural* and *divine* in man and which is aware of God, is *intuition*, and hence that, since as life and spirit reason is

---

[25] Although Hegel attributes this principle to Spinoza, it does not occur literally in the cited form in his writings. (Cf. Spinoza's letter to Jarig Jellis of June 2, 1674, in *Benedict de Spinoza*, p. 370.) Hegel presumably models his formulation on Jacobi's use of the principle in the *Briefe über die Lehre des Spinoza* (1789 edition), p. 182: "XII. *Determinatio est negatio, seu determinatio ad rem juxta suum esse non pertinet*. Therefore particular things, to the extent that they exist only in a certain determined manner, are *non-entia*; and that undetermined, infinite being [*Wesen*] is the only true *ens reale, hoc est, est omne esse, & praeter quod nullum datur esse*." [Our translation.]

[26] *Seiende Einheit*.

essentially mediation, it could only be immediate knowledge by sublating that mediation. Only an inert, sensuous thing has its immediacy otherwise than by mediating itself with itself.

However, in Jacobi's thought the transition from mediation to immediacy has more the character of an external rejection and dismissal of mediation. To this extent, it is reflective consciousness itself which, isolated from the intuition of reason, isolates the mediating movement of cognition from that intuition. Indeed, he goes so far as to declare the movement of cognition to be an obstacle to such intuition and ruinous of it. Here we must distinguish between two acts. First there is finite cognition itself, which is concerned exclusively with objects and forms which do not exist in and for themselves, but are conditioned and grounded by something other than themselves. The very character of such cognition thus consists in mediation. The second type of cognition is the reflection just referred to, which recognizes both the first, subjective mode of cognition itself and its objects as not absolute. Thus on the one hand this second mode of cognition is itself mediated, for it essentially refers to the first mode of cognition, having it as its presupposition and object. On the other hand, though, it is the sublation of that first mode of cognition. Therefore, as was stated above, it is a mediation which is itself the sublation of mediation, or in other words it is a sublation of mediation only to the extent that it is itself mediation. As the sublation of mediation, cognition is *immediate* cognition. If cognition does not understand its immediacy in this way, it fails to grasp that this is the only sense in which it is the immediacy *of reason*, and not that of a rock. For natural consciousness, knowledge of God may well appear as merely immediate knowledge, and natural consciousness may see no difference between the immediacy with which it is aware of spirit and the immediacy of its perception of a rock. But the business of philosophical knowledge is to recognize in what the activity of natural consciousness truly consists, to recognize that its immediacy is a living, spiritual immediacy that only arises within a self-sublating process of mediation. This insight is precisely what natural consciousness lacks, just as, being an animate, organic entity, it digests without possessing the least knowledge of physiology.

Apparently it was cognition of God in the form once known as the proofs of God's existence which led Jacobi to believe that the idea behind them was that consciousness could not count as knowledge of God without first having *formally* worked through the chain of inferences, concepts, and implications contained in those proofs – which is like telling a man that he could not digest, walk, see, or hear without first having studied anatomy and physiology.[27] A closely related misunderstanding is that the mediating process of cognition makes *knowledge of God* and *God's being* itself into something dependent, something whose ground lies in something other than itself.[28] This apparent disproportion vanishes, however, as soon as we examine the matter itself. For since *God* is the result, the mediation in question immediately reveals itself to be a mediation which sublates itself in that result. What is *last* is seen to be that which is *first*; the *end* is the *purpose*; and when we discover it to be that purpose, indeed the absolute purpose, we recognize the product as the immediate first mover.[29] This progression toward a result is thus at the same time a returning into itself, a repelling that is in itself its own self-repelling.[30] It is what was described above as the true nature of spirit, i.e., of the active final purpose that creates itself. If spirit were immediate being without effective activity, it would not be spirit, indeed it would not even be life.[31] And if it were not purpose and purposive activity, then spirit would not discover in its product that its activity consists wholly in its own merging with itself, a mediation that mediates its own determination in immediacy.

13

[27] Jacobi denies the possibility of proving God's existence and insists that the very attempt leads to fatalism and moreover involves the absurdity of making God, the unconditioned, into a conditional entity (cf. *Briefe über die Lehre des Spinoza*, p. 122 and the seventh supplement [*Beilage VII*], pp. 423–434; *Jacobi: Main Philosophical Writings*, pp. 375–378). Hegel's disagreement with Jacobi over this question ran deep. In the summer of 1829 and again in the fall of 1831, Hegel was busy preparing a manuscript on the proofs of the existence of God. As Jaeschke notes, the reflections in Hegel's manuscript revolve around a detailed critique of Jacobi's position on the idea of a rational demonstration of God's existence, while Kant – prominently associated with the philosophical demise of such attempts – is not even mentioned by name (cf. Walter Jaeschke, *Hegel-Handbuch. Leben-Werk-Wirkung* [Stuttgart/Weimar: J. B. Metzler, 2003], p. 499). Hegel's analogical reference to physiology and digestion is paralleled in the preface to the first edition of the *Science of Logic* (*GW*, vol. XI, p. 6) and in §19 of the *Encyclopedia*.

[28] Cf. Jacobi, *Werke*, vol. I,1, p. 288.

[29] This is a compact re-statement of the idea Hegel articulated in the *Phenomenology of Spirit* that "the true is the whole" (*Phenomenology of Spirit*, §20).

[30] Hegel's highly emphatic metaphor of a *Gegenstoß gegen sich* is nearly impossible to translate, nor can any literal interpretation be given for it without entering into the complexities of Hegel's concept of absolute negativity, the paradoxical nature of which the metaphor forcefully conveys. The metaphor is prominent in central passages of Hegel's *Science of Logic*; cf. esp. "Das Wesen als Reflexion in sich," the initial chapter of the *Doctrine of Essence* (*GW*, vol. XI, pp. 252, 291; cf. also p. 328).

[31] The *Science of Logic* culminates in Hegel's exposition of what he refers to as the idea (*die Idee*), which Hegel associates with the Aristotelian conception of the divine as *noēsis noēseōs* (cf. *Encyclopedia*, §577). The idea itself develops through three stages, the first of which Hegel refers to as *life*. (The other two are knowledge and the absolute idea, respectively.) Life Hegel characterizes as "the concept inasfar as it at once distinguishes itself simply in itself from its objectivity and pervades that objectivity and, being an end in itself, finds and posits in that objectivity its own means, all the while remaining immanent within that means as the self-identical purpose realized in it" (*GW*, vol. XII, p. 177). [Our translation.] The gist of this description is that living beings use their own bodies as a means to continuing their physical existence, so that in the case of life means and ends coincide. As Hegel will go on to suggest in the main text, the ultimate significance of scientific and philosophical inquiry is a conscious form of this same structure.

Now since Jacobi dismisses the *mediation* inherent in cognition and fails to see how it restitutes itself as the essential moment *within* the nature of spirit itself, his *consciousness of absolute spirit* remains fixated in the form of *immediate*, merely *substantial knowledge*. The sole content of Spinoza's simple, fundamental intuition is substantiality. Now if the intuition of the absolute knows itself to be intellectual, i.e., cognitive intuition, and if furthermore its object is no longer substance in its motionless rigidity, but spirit, then it would also be necessary that knowledge dispense with the leftover form of substantiality, namely the form of immediacy. For it is precisely life and cognitive movement within itself[32] by which alone absolute spirit differs from absolute substance, and knowledge of spirit is itself something spiritual, something intellectual.

The conception of spirit Jacobi finds in his intuition of reason is the standard against which he measures the philosophical systems which form the subject matter of the present volume of essays. Jacobi urges not only the content, but also the substantial form[33] of his rational intuition against those philosophies. Kantian and Fichtean philosophy and the philosophy of nature[34] are the systems he examines, and the basic character of his treatment should be clear from the foregoing.

The texts themselves are well known to the reading public, but the passion of the times in which they were first published has passed away. Thus we can be brief in our consideration of their main points, confining ourselves to the essentials, and we need not worry about stirring up controversy. Neither the publication of this collection nor its close study will seem superfluous simply because some of the philosophies it deals with now belong to the past, and I regret to hear Jacobi himself speak in that tone (p. 340),[35] saying that it is well known how quickly philosophical systems have changed in Germany in the past twenty-five years. For this is usually the talk of people who seek to justify their contempt of philosophy and even think themselves quite clever in pointing out that since such systems contradict each other so blatantly and change so frequently it is plain good sense to ignore them, especially since the whole point is supposed to be to find everlasting truth, which is hardly to be discovered in so transient a thing

---

[32] *Wissende Bewegung in sich.*

[33] "Substantial form" is a term of art referring to the form something has to the extent that it is understood to be substantial, i.e., neither dependent on nor mediated by anything outside itself for its determinate existence. Thus substantiality is another way of saying immediacy, and the "substantial form" of Jacobi's intuition is the form of immediacy.

[34] The term "philosophy of nature" refers unambiguously to Schelling's philosophy.

[35] See Friedrich Heinrich Jacobi, *Werke*, vol. III, ed. Walter Jaeschke (Hamburg: Felix Meiner Verlag, 2000), p. 73.

as a philosophical system.[36] – What has indeed proven to be transitory are **14** the various endeavors that leave the *philosophy* out of philosophizing.[37] Yet even such transitoriness can seem eternal, the flux itself seem perennial. – Jacobi's claim that science is incapable of comprehending the divine is not entirely innocent of having provided ignorance and lack of spirit with a convenient pillow upon which to rest their conscience and even of having given them occasion for arrogance. Similarly, Kantian philosophy first reduced the object to a problematic something and then, in Jacobi's own witty phrase (p. 74),[38] recompensed it with an *otium cum dignitate*[39] in its status as a thing-in-itself.

[KANT]

Kantian philosophy is the main subject of the second treatise, whose title was given above. The other treatises, especially the third, also return to it frequently. Since it comes first, I would like to deal with it and Jacobi's polemic against it first and briefly explain why the Kantian doctrines were bound to appear very inadequate when compared with Jacobi's great conviction that the absolute must be conceived as spirit. For the *highest* thing in Kant's philosophy that can be found by theoretical means, i.e., by cognition of that which *is*, is in general mere *appearance*. Upon analysis, the essential constituents of appearance resolve into three determinations. First, there is the thing-in-itself which is exhaustively determined as being the conceptless thing-in-itself just mentioned; secondly, the I of self-consciousness insofar as it originates connections, remaining, however, all the while conditioned by a given manifold and producing only finite connections among finite things; and finally, as the other extreme term corresponding to the thing-in-itself, the I as pure unity. Insofar as the I consists in that finite activity, Kant refers to it as the "understanding," whereas "reason" is his term for the I qua pure unity.[40] Thus we find the cognition of *that which is* represented as

---

[36] Prominent examples are the self-styled skeptic Gottlob Ernst Schulze (*Kritik der theoretischen Philosophie*, 2 vols. [Hamburg, 1800], esp. vol. 1, pp. 5 ff.) and his disciple J. F. E. Kirsten, Hegel's colleague in Jena, who propagated Schulze's skepticism in lectures (*Grundzüge des neuesten Skepticismus* [Jena, 1802], preface).

[37] Hegel might be thinking here of Karl Leonhard Reinhold: cf. *Differenzschrift*, *GW* vol. IV, p. 81; *Bouterwek review*, *GW* vol. IV, p. 104; *Science of Logic*, *GW* vol. XI, p. 34.

[38] See Friedrich Heinrich Jacobi, *Werke*, vol. II,1, ed. Walter Jaeschke and Irmgard-Maria Piske with the assistance of Catia Goretzki (Hamburg: Felix Meiner Verlag, 2004), p. 267.

[39] Literally, "leisure with dignity." Cf. Cicero, *De oratore*, I, 1, 1.

[40] Hegel elaborates on this (basically Fichtean) identification of Kantian *reason* with the *pure I* in *Encyclopedia*, §45.

a *syllogism*,[41] the two *extreme terms* of which, namely the thing-in-itself and the pure unity of self-consciousness, are abstract universals. When fixated as such, these extreme terms thoroughly lack the nature of spirit. Similarly, while the syllogism's *middle term* is indeed concrete, it nevertheless consists merely in the external coming together and bringing together of ingredients which remain essentially external to one another. This makes it impossible to discover spirit either insofar as it is certain that it is itself identical with the true or insofar as it is certain of something other than itself as the true.[42] When it comes to knowledge of that which *ought to be*, i.e., *practical* knowledge, the same formal unity of self-consciousness that made up the one extreme term of the previous syllogism serves again as the principle which is supposed to constitute duty and the Good. Opposed to this principle is the manifold of Nature, which forms the other extreme, and the *concrete*, universal unity of these extremes remains forever beyond human ken. Inner certainty of self and externally given reality are maintained as existing in radical separation and independence; consequently, the unity of that which *is* and that which *ought to be*, of existence[43] and the concept, can emerge only as a perennial postulate, not as true being. For the same reason, Kant's practical philosophy does not have spirit as its final result, and hence (as we explained above) spirit does not serve as the primary basis and truth of his practical philosophy.

Now, Jacobi did not merely assume his standard as valid and then apply it to Kant's philosophy, but treated it rather in accord with true method, namely dialectically. It was Kant's own determination of the form in which the problem of philosophy was supposed to be formulated and solved that supplied the ammunition. Kant posed the question, "How are synthetic a priori judgments *possible?*",[44] instead of making the *necessity* of such judgments the object of philosophy. Kant shared this formulation of the problem with the metaphysicians of his time, who thought that they had to begin by demonstrating a concept's possibility (including for example that

---

[41] The English word "syllogism" translates the German *Schluß*. The German expression connotes ideas of conjoining and merging more immediately than the Greek term *syllogismos*, connotations frequently played on by Hegel (cf. *Encyclopedia*, §24). Hegel develops his theory of the syllogism in self-conscious distance from traditional formal logic, giving it a metaphysical import that is only "imitated" by the formal syllogism (cf. *Science of Logic*, *GW* vol. XII, pp. 90–126, and *Encyclopedia*, §§181–193).

[42] Hegel's remark is a condensed formulation of a criticism of Kant he formulates in "The Idea of Cognition" (section 3, chapter 2 of the *Doctrine of the Concept* in the *Science of Logic*).

[43] In Hegelian terminology, "existence" (*Dasein*) is a technical term within the "doctrine of being" distinct from the terms *Existenz* and *Wirklichkeit* (actuality), which are treated of in the *Doctrine of Essence* (*GW*, vol. XI).

[44] See *Critique of Pure Reason*, ibid., p. 146 = B 19.

of the concept of God).[45] Now when taken thus in isolation from actuality and necessity, possibility is a mere abstraction, and as such it is grounded in abstract *identity*, the *formal* unity of the understanding. Jacobi takes up this form, and thus holds *space* fixed as one thing, *time* as one thing, *consciousness* as one thing; he holds the pure synthesis of the latter, the synthesis in itself, independent of thesis and antithesis, i.e., as a thoroughly abstract copula is, is, is, without beginning or end; he holds them fixed in the dry understanding where they occur, and he then rightly questions how the *possibility* of tying a knot might be found there. Indeed, if white is only white, and black only black, then it is impossible that gray or any other color should come into or continue in existence. – Jacobi rightly goes on to portray such abstractions as empty *entia rationis*, as ghosts and sorcerer's smoke.

Now Jacobi does not go beyond regarding the vacuity of abstract space, abstract time, abstract identity, and abstract diversity[46] as his own reflection and as external to those abstractions themselves. This is quite consistent, insofar as the dialectic is here directed only against Kant's presentation and aims merely to demonstrate its *abstract* nothingness; the *objective* dialectic of such abstractions, however, would have consisted in their immanent vacuity and would have led to the *necessity of the concrete*, the necessity of the here merely so-called synthetic a priori. Jacobi would then have **16** demonstrated the untruth of those *entia rationis*, and his proof of the impossibility of the concrete, conducted on the assumption of their validity, would have turned into a proof of the opposite, the necessity of the concrete. – Now the concrete in its various forms as imagination, judging, and the apperception of self-consciousness is also treated of in its *relation to those abstractions*. Since those abstractions have been fixated as independent entities, the result is that both those abstractions and the forms of the concrete are maintained in their abstract difference and form a fixed substrate for each other instead of sublating themselves dialectically. Thus

[45] Cf. Leibniz, *Über die universale Synthese und Analyse oder Über die Kunst des Auffindens und Beurteilens* (Lat. *De synthesi et analysi universali seu arte inveniendi et judicandi*, in *Philosophische Schriften*, vol. IV, ed. Herbert Herring (= *Schriften zur Logik und zur philosophischen Grundlegung von Mathematik und Naturwissenschaft*) (Frankfurt am Main: Insel Verlag, 1992), pp. 134–151. In his *Letters on the Doctrine of Spinoza* (*Jacobi: Main Philosophical Writings*, pp. 375 ff.), Jacobi formulates similar criticisms of the demand that the possibility of every concept be demonstrated. On the importance of Jacobi's Spinoza-interpretation for German Idealist conceptions of modality and the idea of intellectual intuition, see Dieter Henrich, *Der Grund im Bewußtsein. Untersuchungen zu Hölderlins Denken in Jena* (Stuttgart: Klett-Cotta, 1992), pp. 48 ff.

[46] "Diversity" here renders *Verschiedenheit*. In the *Doctrine of Essence* (*GW* vol. XI, pp. 265–272), Hegel distinguishes between two forms of difference, *Unterschied* (difference) and *Verschiedenheit* (diversity).

reason comes to *rest* upon the understanding, the understanding upon the imagination, imagination upon sensibility, and sensibility itself in turn upon imagination. – It is, however, arguable that Kant's own conception of the relation in which those powers stand to each other is more exactly expressed in terms of conditioning and being conditioned by each other.

More importantly, however, we must not overlook that in his treatment of the Kantian critique of reason Jacobi fails to call attention to the infinite credit due to this critique for recognizing that the freedom of spirit is also the fundamental principle in the theoretical side of reason. This principle – albeit in an abstract form – is implicit in the idea of an original synthetic apperception of self-consciousness,[47] the essence of which is to strive for *self-determination* in cognition. Though this theoretical freedom is abstract, yet it is no more abstract than *moral* freedom, of which Jacobi (p. 324)[48] says that it is the faculty of man, "which makes his life his own and makes man conscious of a power for good[49] that surmounts all resistance, but which is partly conditioned by the presence of such resistance and partly fails to realize itself fully, remaining only an approximation and striving." Jacobi does touch upon theoretical freedom when he says (p. 80)[50] that an original synthesis would be an originary act of determination, but this concept is not to be gotten rid of by noting that an originary act of determination would be tantamount to creation *ex nihilo*. This implication or rather this expression, "creation *ex nihilo*," is ill-suited for discrediting the notion of freedom in the realm of the theoretical, for the same argument would do away with moral freedom as well.

For the rest, though, the narrative manner of Kant (whose own main concern was only to establish the basis of universality and necessity in cognition) gives just cause to assume that the materials of his story of thought, feeling, time and space, imagination, understanding, and finally reason are quite as contingent in respect to each other as their coincidence in a mere story would make them appear. Thus, since they are fixated as abstract substrates, we are entitled to point out the contradiction involved in *bringing them together* and *positing them as a unity*. Jacobi's critique brings out both the lack of insight into spirit inherent in Kant's apprehension of the faculties and the general deficiency of an account which neither demonstrates the *necessity* of those mental activities[51] in their determinateness nor accounts for their *concreteness*.[52] These criticisms grow yet more important

---

[47] Cf. *Critique of Pure Reason*, ibid., p. 246 = B 131.   [48] See Jacobi, *Werke*, vol. III, p. 65.
[49] *Kraft zum Guten*.   [50] See Jacobi, *Werke*, vol. II,1, pp. 271 f.   [51] *Tätigkeiten des Geistes*.
[52] This is a recurring point in Hegel's Kant critique. Cf. *Lectures on the History of Philosophy*, in *Werke*, vol. XX, p. 351, and in a similar vein §42 of the *Encyclopedia* and Hegel's note to that section.

in view of the fact that even Jacobi's friends claim that it would actually *improve* the Critical Philosophy if the study of the cognitive mind[53] were made the subject of an *anthropology* – a mere narration of *facts* that are supposed to be found in consciousness, so that knowledge would consist in nothing more than an analysis of those facts.[54] Thus, as though it were the only legitimate course, they deliberately give up on comprehending the activities of the mind in their *necessity*, since in Kant it is rather the *lack of necessity*, the *contingency* and *externality* that characterize the determinations of the mind and their relation to each other. Yet it is precisely this lack which gave Jacobi the basis for his dialectic against the synthesis of faculties and against the false, finite relations which arise when we assume that the activities of the mind are external to each other.

At this point we should briefly mention how Jacobi sees the deficiency of the Kantian theory of practical reason. The ideas of God, freedom, and immortality are indemonstrable for theoretical reason, which is to say that its proper objects are unknowable. Theoretical reason aims at that which *is*, and knowledge of that which is requires the faculty of understanding, which in turn requires experience or rather the perception of temporal and spatial things and materials taken from sensation in order to apply its categories to them. Such cognitions get no further than *appearances*. God, freedom, and immortality, however, do not fall within such experience and within the world of appearance. Practical reason then postulates these ideas, which are theoretically indemonstrable. Their *subjectivity* need not be postulated, for as ideas they are subjective; their objectivity, rather, is the aspect which belongs to theoretical reason. To rebuke practical reason for this one-sidedness is of the utmost importance, especially since it has become a widespread prejudice that everything of truth is to be found in

---

[53] "Study of the cognitive mind" serves here to translate Hegel's phrase "*Erkenntniß des erkennenden Geistes.*"

[54] Cf. Gottlob Ernst Schulze (*Kritik der theoretischen Philosophie*, esp. vol. 1, pp. 51 ff.); Wilhelm Traugott Krug, *Entwurf eines neuen Organons der Philosophie oder Versuch über die Prinzipien der philosophischen Erkenntnis* (Meissen und Lübben, 1801 [reprinted in the series Aetas Kantiana, Brussels, 1969], esp. §5, pp. 25–50); Friedrich Bouterwek, *Idee einer Apodiktik. Ein Beytrag zur menschlichen Selbstverständigung und zur Entscheidung des Streits über Metaphysik, kritische Philosophie und Skepticismus* (Halle, 1799). All of these philosophers stressed their affinities with Jacobi's thought. Köppen, the editor of volumes IV–VI of Jacobi's works, was also a close personal friend. Jacob Friedrich Fries (1773–1843) deserves special mention. He consistently sided with Jacobi against Fichte, Schelling, and Hegel throughout his career (cf. for example his polemical pamphlet from 1812 entitled *On German Philosophy, Culture and Art: A Vote for Friedrich Heinrich Jacobi against F. W. J. Schelling*). Fries was also the most systematic and productive proponent of treating epistemology as a branch of anthropology and empirical psychology. See his *Neue Kritik der Vernunft* (1807), which he later worked out in greater systematic detail in his *Neue oder anthropologische Kritik der Vernunft* (1828).

the practical sphere, in the heart's striving alone, while thought, knowledge, theoretical reason are held to be dispensable, indeed detrimental and even dangerous. The awareness that God *is*, that freedom *is*, that immortality *is*, is something quite different from the postulate that these ideas merely ought to be. The theoretical side of reason forms the complement to that "ought," and the foundation of the practical is only complete when the conviction is present that the rational *is* as it ought to be. The mere "ought" by itself, the subjective concept without objectivity, is devoid of spirit, just as mere *being without the concept*, without its own "ought" to which it must conform, is an empty illusion.

18

[FICHTE]

We now turn to the *Letter to Fichte*. The inadequacies of Fichte's philosophy that Jacobi demonstrates in this essay, the first in the volume, are essentially the same as those he criticized in Kant's philosophy. As is well known, Fichte's system raised Kant's to a higher level of abstraction and developed it with greater logical consistency. It is an attempt to give a systematic account of the necessary relations among the categories, the determinations of thought both in the theoretical and in the practical sphere.[55] Whereas in Kant, the cognition of the so-called faculties of the soul results in the object dwindling as it were over the course of the *Critique* to an unknown and unknowable thing-in-itself, falling outside the bounds of the understanding and hence of reason, too, in Fichte the pure unity of the I with itself presents itself immediately and from the very outset, as does the equally abstract thing-in-itself, the non-I, in its opposition to the I.[56] The further development of the forms taken on by the determination of the one by the other is consistently carried out on the basis of their opposition, such that every new form presents a richer synthesis of the opposition but nevertheless fails to overcome it. The resulting resolutions thus continue in their status as *relations* and *finite forms*, whose ultimate resolution is deferred to the practical realm – where, however, it also fails to be achieved, ending in a one-sided "ought" and a striving that remains vitiated by a beyond.[57] As a *moment*, Fichte's principle is of infinite importance both in terms of its content and in terms of its form, which raised Kant's principle to so high

---

[55] Cf. *Encyclopedia*, §42.

[56] Cf. the first three basic principles in Fichte, *Foundations of the Entire Science of Knowledge* (*The Science of Knowledge, with the First and Second Introductions*, trans. and ed. Peter Heath and John Lachs [Cambridge: Cambridge University Press, 1982], sect. 1–3).

[57] Cf. Fichte, *Foundations of the Entire Science of Knowledge*, ibid., sect. 5.

a level of abstraction. Even so, his principle fails to capture concrete spirit precisely because Fichte understands it as an absolute principle in spite of its one-sidedness and refuses to reduce it to a mere moment.

As opposed to the way in which he treated the philosophy of Kant, Jacobi did not treat Fichte's philosophy dialectically, even though its scientific form would have made it more susceptible to such a treatment. For when Fichte begins with I = I as the *first* absolute principle of his philosophy, he follows up immediately with the *second*, namely that the I is absolutely opposed by a non-I, and states that in terms of its form as an *opposite* principle it too is *unconditioned*. These two unconditionals are self-identical abstractions of the same kind as abstract space and abstract time or the abstract "is" in Kant. Against Fichte's third principle, which contains the *synthesis* of those abstractions, one could urge the same *impossibility* that was urged against the Kantian synthesis. Jacobi is here content to oppose his unwavering intuition of the absolute as concrete, i.e., the spiritual, to the abstraction of an ego which does not cease to be an abstraction even after its synthesis. This is the basis on which he rejects Fichtean subjectivity as one-sided. On p. 40[58] Jacobi refers to the "moral principle of reason" (which is actually the principle of reason in a form degraded to the level of the understanding, i.e., to the abstract agreement of the human being with himself) and rightly characterizes it as dreary, desolate, and void, contrasting it with the faculty of non-empty ideas, concrete reason, which he refers to by a popular term, calling it the "heart."

This is basically the same thing Aristotle criticized about the moral principle (Ηθικ. μεγ. A).[59] For he says that the first teacher of morals, Socrates, made the virtues into *knowledge*, ἐπιστῆμας. Goodness and beauty are the practical idea only insofar as they are universals. But that is impossible, he added, for all knowledge is bound up with a reason (λόγος), and reasons belong to the cognitive side of the mind; and so it befalls Socrates that he negates[60] the a-logical side of the soul, which consists in the passion and the character (πάθος καὶ ἦθος).[61] – In the realm of the practical, universals articulate only what *ought to be*, and Aristotle (like Jacobi) finds this insufficient to account for the manner of the *existence* of the universal and the possibility of such existence. Aristotle's *passion* and *character* mean something far more definite than the mere *heart*, however. It has always been deemed the work of the wisest men not only to be familiar with the universal as such, i.e., the abstract laws, but also to have insight into the

---

[58] See Jacobi, *Werke*, vol. II,1, p. 212.   [59] *Magna Moralia*, 1182a 15–23.
[60] *Aufheben*.   [61] *Magna Moralia*, 1182a 22.

unconscious side, that is, the passions, habits, and customs, and to discover ways to regulate this side. It is by way of such regulation that the abstract side comes to have a natural *reality* among a particular people, for it is in the form of custom that the law has its existing validity[62] for the individual. In this way the law is *given* both as the individual's own drive and in respect to as yet undetermined, undirected passions. The morality of a more highly cultivated character requires an even more universal cognition: not merely awareness of what *ought to be* in the form of a particular people, but knowledge of it in the form of *being*, in the form of what appears as *nature, world*, and *history*. Similarly, Kant's formulation of the practical principle was shown above to be one-sided to the extent that it abstracts from the *theoretical* moment and thus remains subjective.

It may seem as though Aristotle's censure is directed at precisely the opposite and that he intends to criticize Socrates for making virtue into a kind of knowledge, i.e., for making the moral principle into something *theoretical*. In the first place, however, Aristotle does not criticize attempts to grasp and formulate what is universal in morals, i.e., the good. On the contrary, later in the work he finds the contemplation of the good to be necessary, though he distinguishes such contemplation from the investigation of virtue. Jacobi differs from this point of view in that he rejects this form of the good and any theory of duties, referring us instead to the heart. – Now, the immanent purpose of self-consciousness is the good, and the being of the good is a being in and for itself. To this extent it is something theoretical. But it becomes one-sided when it is fixated in the form of universality in isolation from the concrete idea. The content of the good, on the other hand, is that which *ought to be*, and thus it is posited as subjective purpose. The other side of this is *reality*, the properly *theoretical* moment, and we find it as something non-rational, as external, corporeal nature and equally as inner nature, feelings, passions, habits, customs. Knowledge of this nature preserves its form of non-rationality to the extent that it lacks the concept of how this nature *ought to be* and does not recognize absolute purpose within nature, i.e., does not recognize nature as the mere realization and manifestation of that purpose. In the same way, the good remains without spirit and fails to rise above the standpoint of existence[63] (namely mere striving) as long as it is not complemented by a view of reality.

[62] *Seiende Gültigkeit.*

[63] "Existence" here renders the term *Dasein*. In the first volume of the *Science of Logic*, Hegel situates Fichtean "striving" within his treatment of *Dasein* and sees it as a form of "bad infinity." See *GW*, vol. XXI, pp. 117–123 and 220–229.

There is, however, a further sense in which Jacobi contrasts the *heart* with the good-in-itself and the true-in-itself. He says (p. 37)[64] that he is not acquainted with it and has but a vague intimation of what it could be. He expresses his indignation when someone tries to force upon him *a will that wills nothing*, this empty husk of self-sufficiency[65] and freedom in a sphere of absolute indeterminacy, and to convince him that that is the good-in-itself. In the fine passage following the one just cited, Jacobi finds even more solemn words:

Yea, I am the atheist and the Godless one, who, against the *will that wills nothing*, will tell lies, just as Desdemona did when she lay dying; the one that will lie and defraud, just as Pylades did when he disguised himself for Orestes; will murder, as Timoleon did; or break law and oath, like Epaminondas, or John de Witt; commit suicide like Otho, perpetrate sacrilege like David – yea, I would pluck ears of wheat *on the Sabbath* just because I *have hunger, and the law is made for man, not the man for the law* . . . I know, with the most sacred certainty that I have in me, that the *privilegium aggratiandi* for such crimes against the pure letter of the absolutely universal law of reason is man's true *right of majesty*, the seal of his worth, of his divine nature.[66]

The absoluteness of which self-consciousness is aware within in itself cannot be expressed more warmly or nobly than in those words. Yet why do the majesty, dignity, and divinity of self-consciousness appear here as opposed to reason? Is it not otherwise Jacobi's frequently stated and express opinion that *reason* is the supernatural, the divine in man, and that it is God's revelation? – Here, however, what is divine is opposed merely to the *law* of reason, the *letter* of the law, and, in the examples cited, to the laws with *determinate* content which raise that determinate content to the status of something absolute – determinate laws which *absolutely* prohibit

---

[64] See Jacobi, *Werke*, vol. II,1, p. 210.   [65] *Selbständigkeit.*
[66] Hegel quotes here directly a (slightly abbreviated) version of Jacobi's famous claim in his *Letter to Fichte* (*Werke*, vol. III, p. 37). We have used here (in correspondingly abbreviated and slightly modified form) the translation of this passage by di Giovanni in *Friedrich Heinrich Jacobi: The Main Philosophical Writings and the Novel "Allwill,"* p. 516. The allusions are to Shakespeare, *Othello*, act 5, scene 2, where Desdemona lies with her dying breath to divert suspicion from her murderer, Othello; Aeschylus, *Libation Bearers*, in which Pylades disguises himself to aid Orestes in his matricidal revenge (but see also Goethe's *Iphigenie*, act 2, lines 765–768). Timoleon's fratricide of his tyrannical brother is recounted in Plutarch's *Lives* (trans. Dryden [New York: Modern Library], pp. 293–320), as is Epaminondas' public censure for having retained command of an army beyond his term (cf. Jacobi, *Woldemar*, in *Werke*, vol. V, ed. J. F. Köppen and C. J. F. Roth [Leipzig: Gerhard Fleischer, 1820], pp. 84–86) and Otho's suicide (*Lives*, p. 1296); Johan de Witt was a Dutch political leader who faced down opposition from the Orangeist party. Samuel I, 21:7, recounts how David eats the consecrated bread in the temple, an episode referred to in the Gospels of Matthew (12:3 f.), Mark (2:25 f.), and Luke (6:3 f.), all of which recount how Christ's disciples plucked corn on the Sabbath. Jacobi's words "The law is made for man, not man for the law" echo Christ's words in Mark 2:27.

21 lying, deceit, murder, perjury, and transgression, suicide, sacrilege, and the breaking of the Sabbath. *I shall* do such, says Jacobi, justified by the majesty inherent in humankind. – Does he not here give expression to an absolute will that wills nothing, i.e., *no determinate law, no determinate universal* – self-sufficiency and freedom in a sphere of *absolute indeterminacy?* The actions of Desdemona, Pylades, Timoleon etc. are externally concrete realities, but their interior is the will, the internally concrete which only achieves this sovereignty and majesty by virtue of the infinite power[67] of abstracting from all that is determinate. That will becomes self-sufficiency and freedom only to the extent that it recognizes itself as the absolutely indeterminate, the universal, the good-in-itself, and thus constitutes itself as absolute indeterminacy, though at the same time and for that very reason it is determined only by itself and is concrete action. – Furthermore, as important as it is for the will to be recognized as such omnipotent, purely universal negativity in relation to the determinate, it is equally important to recognize and acknowledge the will in its particularization, i.e., rights, duties, and laws. They make up the content of the ethical or moral sphere. Though Jacobi merely *appeals* to the indeterminate side of the majesty of personhood and speaks of it merely on the basis of the certainty he finds within himself, to a certain extent that appeal has the same basis and results in a dialectic which brings to consciousness the limitations of *determinate* rights, duties, and moral or religious commandments. At the same time, however, it is equally important not to leave the recognition of these limitations to the heart alone. As we remarked before, Jacobi's appeal is not directed against the good-in-itself, i.e., not against the will as it is after having sublated all particularity in the pure self-consciousness of its essentiality. And if Jacobi's appeal is directed against determinate insights into the finitude of determinate laws, rights, and duties, then we hardly need spell out where that would lead, just as we need not justify any determinate insight of the kind, since it is an insight into something that is itself determinate, e.g., a right, a duty, or a law.

Neither, however, can the appeal be directed against these determinations themselves. For even if the dialectic manifests their *limitations* and hence their conditioned nature and finitude, thus recognizing their subordination to something higher, we must nevertheless acknowledge the sphere within which they possess positive validity. Philosophy must both demonstrate the necessity and validity of ethical determinations and uncover the higher ground upon which they are founded and which for that very reason has power and majesty over them. – Indeed, one might even desire to make

[67] *Kraft.*

the consciousness of such majesty the locus of science or the inner sanctum **22**
of religion and thus exclude it from popular treatments in which appeals
to emotion and the inner certainty of individual subjects are permitted –
especially when one considers how easily *romanticism* makes inroads into
ethical life, how much more inclined people are to be *generous* than to be
lawful, to act *nobly* rather than *morally*, and that in permitting themselves to
act against the *letter* of the law they more often than not absolve themselves
from the *law* itself rather than just from its letter. Besides, the actions that
appeal to divine majesty in absolving themselves from the law and which
Jacobi cites as positive examples are themselves *conditioned* – conditioned
by a particular character and temperament and above all by situation and
circumstances. – And what circumstances those are! Embroilment in crass
misfortunes, rare and extraordinary distress into which individuals find
themselves plunged. Freedom would be in a sorry state if it could only
prove its majesty and achieve reality in extraordinary cases of dreadful
conflict and in extraordinary individuals. The ancients, by contrast, saw
the highest form of ethical life in the life of a well-ordered state. – Of such
a life it could well be said that there man was indeed made for the sake
of the law and not the law for the sake of man. The well-known adage to
the opposite effect, quoted above, contains a lofty truth when it refers to
positive, i.e., merely statutory, law. But taking the moral law universally,
it is truer to say that man was made for its sake, for if one goes so far
as to separate man and law and oppose them to each other, then there is
nothing left over for man except his bare particularity, sensuous purposes of
desire, and these cannot be considered to be more than *means* in relation to
the law.

[SCHELLING'S PHILOSOPHY OF NATURE. REMARKS ON JACOBI'S
PHILOSOPHICAL STYLE]

We turn now to the treatise *On Divine Things*. Its original publication is
without doubt still sufficiently present in public memory that it would be
superfluous to spend much time on it here.[68] – The first part is concerned
to show that positivity in religion becomes one-sided when it remains a

---

[68] *On Divine Things* appeared in 1811, occasioned in large part by the explicit contradiction of Jacobi's
Spinoza interpretation in Schelling's *Philosophical Investigations into the Essence of Human Freedom
and Matters Connected Therewith* (1809). The ensuing controversy and the exchanges that led up to
it are documented in Walter Jaeschke, ed., *Der Streit um die göttlichen Dinge (1799–1812)* (Hamburg:
Meiner, 1999). For Jacobi's contributions, see Jacobi, *Werke*, vol. III. Jaeschke also supplies useful
background information on personal constellations between Hegel, Schelling, and Jacobi that might
account for why this section of the review is so brief and relatively circumspect in its formulations
(see his *Hegel-Handbuch*, pp. 256 f.).

mere external attitude, thus representing the relation of the human being in a way that fails to capture it as a relation of spirit. In a fine passage, Jacobi insists on the necessity of the *subjective* moment, underscoring (as he expresses it on p. 292)[69] that sight does not arise from the things seen, nor hearing[70] from that which is heard, nor the *self* from the *other*, just as on the other hand sight, taken by itself, sees *nothing*, hearing hears *nothing*, and the self, finally, does not become aware of itself by itself, but that we must learn of our existence from an other – and that in humans the spirit alone is evidence of God.

The other part of the treatise concerns the philosophy of nature. The basic idea of this philosophy is distinct from the abstractions and one-sidedness that form the basis of the systems considered so far, for it consists in the concrete, in spirit itself. Thus in this case it is no longer a question of contrasting such abstractions with the intuition of spirit or of demonstrating a contradiction – a task easily achieved, since contradiction lies in the nature of the concrete. It would be a vain and fruitless labor to try to untangle the misapprehensions that occurred in the controversy. I will limit myself to two remarks. First, it is obvious from the philosophy of nature's own repeated attempts to find a proper scientific form that even its proponents are still not satisfied. None of the series of systematic expositions completely exhausts its content, for each one of them has broken off unfinished at some more or less advanced point. Both these circumstances expose to the polemicist weak points for an advantageous attack. As long as the scientific form has not gained a determinate and secure method, the relation of *nature* to *spirit* will retain an aspect of immediacy exposing it to well-founded dialectical attack. Furthermore, only a completed execution will be able to transfigure that relation into its truth, stripping away all the imperfect relations in which it appears before its completion.

Secondly, however, Jacobi's dialectic depends less on the *content* of his position than on the persistent *form* in which he asserts that position. It is this form that I will seek to describe in more detail. Its distinctive character lies in its opposition to conceptual development, proof, and methodical thought. Presented in a manner bare of these forms of cognition by which we show an idea to be necessary, Jacobi's ideas have the value of *mere assurances* only: *emotion, intimation, immediacy of consciousness, intellectual*

---

[69] See Jacobi, *Werke*, vol. III, p. 49.
[70] Jacobi employs here not the more usual word *hören* (to hear), but the term *vernehmen*, which forms the root of *Vernunft* (reason).

intuition, belief,[71] the irresistible *certainty* of his ideas are offered as the basis of their *truth*. What rescues this offering of assurances and the mere appeal to such foundations from inanity is Jacobi's noble spirit, the deep soul and the broad cultivation of this admirable and loving individual. In these surroundings, his ideas emerge with feeling, often with deep clarity of late, and always with *ésprit*.[72]

Esprit is a kind of surrogate for methodically cultivated thought and for the reason progressing in it. Far superior to the understanding, the soul of Jacobi's *ésprit* is the idea, for it grasps the antithesis in which the idea lies. But since *ésprit* brings to consciousness neither the abstract thought of the idea nor the dialectical transition in concepts, it has as its material only concrete representations and thoughts of the form of understanding, and is a struggle to make that which is higher reflect in that material. This seeming appearance of the higher in the element of understanding and in representations as has been forcibly effected by the mind in such a material is melded with the gentle charm that makes twilight so seductive to us. Thus in all the writings collected here we encounter a wealth of ingenious expressions and images in which Jacobi's profundity emerges in its clarity and naiveté – often quite simple juxtapositions that intimate a richness of meaning, individual passages that in themselves are universally significant aphorisms. The merit of such sudden inspirations and suggestive conceits is not only undeniable; we may safely abandon ourselves to their enjoyment, since their sense and imagery are there to stimulate thought and what is spiritual. Nor must we let Jacobi's occasional exaggerations of his insights and their consequences spoil our enjoyment of them, for he is only striving for clarity and it is his right to carry himself to such extremes; for the form and manner of his utterances are only a means, and their seeming violence is itself just one of those means.

Jacobi's style is only distracting when it comes to speculative matters and then especially when Jacobi uses it to polemical ends. For though the speculative is the inner, hidden, motivating force behind philosophical *ésprit*, the speculative as such reveals itself fully only in the form of the concept. If the glow of the idea is what makes the twilight of *ésprit*

24

---

[71] German *Glauben* has two meanings, "belief" and "(religious) faith," and Jacobi plays on both. He also uses the term in a more technical sense, namely that of an *immediate certainty* that is in principle not susceptible of proof. All these meanings are in play at the *locus classicus* for Jacobi's understanding of the term in *Werke*, vol. I,1, p. 115. Cf. *David Hume über den Glauben*, passim.

[72] In the following, *ésprit* and phrases containing it always translate either the adjective *geistreich* or its substantive form, *das Geistreiche*. Where, for stylistic or more narrowly linguistic reasons, a more viable term or phrase has been substituted for *ésprit*, the German is included in a note. On the connotations of the term *geistreich*, see the note on translation prefacing this volume.

so sweet, it forfeits this merit when the light of reason itself shines forth,[73] leaving only darkness to distinguish twilight from it. Though elsewhere we readily permit Jacobi his disjointedness, leaps, bold expressions, intellectual acuity, and his exaggerations and persistence, his use of sensuous images, and appeals to emotion and common sense, here they are inappropriate. – It is plain from their outward form that the treatises contained in this volume, too, were prompted less by methodical and doctrinal concerns than by chance occasions; in the individual forewords, Jacobi explains how they came to have that form, telling what prompted him in each case to write them, how his work on them was often interrupted, and how his original intention changed over the course of time and the progress of the work. Thus, he himself confirms their character as contingent outpourings or rather as an intermediate genre more akin to the epistle than to the treatise.

The peculiar thing about Jacobi, though, is that the contingency of the form and the predominance of *ésprit* are not merely the natural and unselfconscious character of his spirit, but that he makes the positive and polemical claim that speculative knowledge, conceptual cognition[74] is impossible – nay, worse than impossible, for we find him saying for example that a *God* that could be *known demonstratively would not be God*, that man is as *unfathomable* to himself as God's essence is, since otherwise man would have to possess a superdivine faculty and would have been able to *invent* God, and so on. It is hardly deniable that Jacobi's and Kant's common achievement was to have put an end to the metaphysics of the older school and thus to have established the necessity of a complete revision of logic. Jacobi thus initiated a new era in German philosophy and (since outside of Germany philosophy has degenerated to the point of extinction) in the history of philosophy as a whole. However, his contribution to knowledge goes no further than that, for whereas Kant cemented his *negative* result in opposition to the finite forms of knowledge, Jacobi cemented it against *knowledge in and for itself*. He abstained from taking the further step of replacing the understanding by reason and *spirit* as the *soul of cognition*, and having cognition born again in reason and spirit and baptized in the spirit after having before been baptized in the water of the understanding.[75] – Jacobi's assurances on the matter can only be countered

[73] Here there is a difficult-to-translate play on the German terms *scheinen* and *leuchten*. When Hegel says that the idea "*scheint*" in philosophical *ésprit*, he is playing on the double meaning of *Schein* as illumination and illusion or (mere) appearance. *Leuchten* is synonymous with the first meaning of *scheinen* but carries none of its potentially negative secondary meanings.
[74] *begreifendes Erkennen.*   [75] Cf. Matthew 3:11.

by opposite assurances, his authorities by other authorities such as the authority of *Christianity*, for which *knowing God* is the highest goal, or Delphic Apollo's injunction to self-knowledge, i.e., knowledge of the absolute nature of self-consciousness.

The crucial point in the matter was indicated above, but to argue against *ésprit* polemically and dialectically would be clumsy and inappropriate. In one respect, *ésprit* is already on its side given to misunderstanding. Since the character of contingency is inseparable from the form of *ésprit*, it is free to seize upon any given aspect of a philosophical system and urge some point of view or other against it. For example, Jacobi's dialectical criticism is admittedly justified when directed against the barren abstractions that compete with the idea of the original-synthetic within Kant's system, for that idea is the element in Kant's philosophy that is of a properly spiritual nature, despite being bound up with those abstractions in a thoroughly non-spiritual fashion. However, Jacobi might as easily have mobilized this very idea of the original-synthetic against those abstractions. Had he done so, he could have demonstrated the untruth of abstraction by insisting on the synthetic, or even better, he could have derived the truth of the latter from the untruth of the former, instead of showing how ill-founded the **26** synthetic is by harping on the abstractions.

Since, however, *ésprit* knows its apprehension and possession of the true only as an immediate consciousness, and therefore dogmatically excludes the concept, it inevitably fails to recognize itself and its own intuition either in form or content when they are enclosed in expressions and shapes different from its own, even when they contain the very same content and material results and differ only by having thinking and the concept as their soul. For example, it is not hard to discover something higher than mere rigid being and non-spiritual necessity even in Spinoza's first definitions, in the very notion of a *causa sui* and in its definition as that whose *nature* can only be *conceived as existing*, or in the definition of substance as that which *exists in itself* and can be *conceived through itself*, i.e., whose concept does not require the concept of any other thing.[76] For these definitions contain the pure concept of freedom, of thinking as it is in its being-for-itself, of spirit, just as much as the concept of the subject-object contains them. Of course, one must not think of the *causa sui* as having originated in mechanical fashion, as Jacobi understands it on p. 416[77] of the *Spinoza Letters*, where he says that, in order to save the principle "Everything has a cause," Spinoza superficially sheered off external causes and effects from

---

[76] Spinoza, *Ethics*, part 1, definitions 1 and 3.   [77] See Jacobi, *Werke*, vol. I,1, p. 256.

God and made God himself into his own cause and his own effect merely in order to be able to subsume him under that principle. In that case, the concept of a *causa sui* would in effect be nothing but a superficial dressing and not a thought in and for itself.

Speaking of the notion of *cause*, we may mention in passing that, considering Jacobi's aversion to concepts and conceptual determinations, it might seem inconsistent of him to attach so much importance to the claim that God must not be thought of as the *ground* of the world, but rather as its *cause*. In popular contexts or as a temporary stop-gap in philosophical ones, it may be deemed legitimate to call on such relations as determinations of God's nature or of his relation to the world; perhaps the one concept may even have a slight advantage over the other in certain respects. Both, however, are mere *determinations of the understanding, finite* relations (cf. p. 413)[78] and thus incapable of expressing the concept of spirit. In this respect, *causa sui* is the concept that is richer in spirit,[79] since it expresses both the causal relation and the self-repelling within it, as well as the sublation of its finitude. The point is not that it does not exist at all, but that it is at the same time this movement of sublating itself. Similarly, when God is thought of as a self-determining ground, it is essential that he be thought of as eternally sublating that relation.

Determinations such as these and especially the more obscure determinations expressed in mere prepositions like *outside* myself, *over* or *above* myself, etc., are ill-suited to preventing misunderstandings; their effect has rather been to occasion and multiply them. For the otherwise predominant idea of spirit is repugnant to the mere understanding expressed in those determinations (and which, moreover, the prepositions express very imperfectly). However, when the emphasis is placed on them, as though they truly expressed the intended opposition, that is enough to justify criticism, the more so as other passages necessarily contradict the one side of the opposition. Often the very side that is supposed to be affirmed is itself bound up with and suggests the side that corrects and sublates it. Thus Jacobi claims throughout that it is the *supernatural within* man which reveals God (p. 424),[80] the supreme being within him, and that this bears witness to a supreme being *without* him; it is the spirit *within* him which alone bears witness to God (p. 325).[81] This majesty *within* man is also referred to as man's *divine* nature, as cited above. – Now this is as much as to say that God is *not outside* me, for what could that divinity

27

---

[78] See Jacobi, *Werke*, vol. III, p. 110.   [79] *Geistreicher*.
[80] See Jacobi, *Werke*, vol. III, p. 117.   [81] Ibid., p. 65.

within me be if it were God-forsaken? It would not even amount to "*das Gott*,"[82] as Jacobi suggestively[83] refers to the unconscious god of nature, nor could it be something evil, since it supposed to be God's holy witness. Nor again will the main thesis of the *Letter to Fichte* appear consistent with the idea of spirit as an inward evidence of God's existence, for there (p. 49)[84] Jacobi expresses himself thus: "Either God exists, and is *outside of me*, a *living being with an enduring existence*,[85] or *I am God*. There is no third alternative." This strict dichotomy clearly contradicts everything else Jacobi says, above all what he says about Christianity in a beautiful image that expresses the manifest tendency of the treatise *Of Divine Things*, namely "to demonstrate in every possible way that the religiously minded *pure* idealist and the religiously minded *pure* materialist are but the two cups of the oyster-shell that hold the pearl of Christianity." Jacobi's Either-Or and his *tertium non datur* assume the validity of the *principium exclusi tertii*. Yet this is a *principle of one-sided understanding* belonging to traditional logic, which in this highest principle, as well as in all other regards, constituted the epistemological law of the old metaphysics – a law of thought whose explicit rejection is one of Jacobi's main ideas and, as we've said, one of his main contributions.

Jacobi's spirit and basic intuition are so remote from such determinations of the barren understanding that his use of them to determine the nature of God would inevitably provoke misunderstandings if we were to take them more seriously than is consonant with the depth of Jacobi's mind[86] and the many other ingenious expressions we have of it. – In the general preface to the volume and in the foreword to the treatise *Of Divine Things*, Jacobi goes into some of the misunderstandings that have befallen him, for instance concerning his Christianity. Throughout these philosophical proceedings we encounter many remarks on personality. In his *Letter to Fichte*, for example, Jacobi says (p. 46)[87] that he does not hold him to be an atheist or a godless man *personally*, although he nevertheless sees no way around qualifying his teaching as atheistic, just like that of Spinoza. He testifies to the latter's character in a similar vein and cites the fine passage where he calls out to him thus: "May you be blessed, O great, nay holy Benedictus! No matter how you philosophized on the nature of the supreme

28

---

[82] Untranslatable play on words. The grammatical gender of the German substantive *Gott* is masculine; hence the grammatically correct definite article (in the nominative case) is "*der*." By employing the neuter definite article "*das*," Jacobi suggests that the Spinozist "god of nature" (*deus sive natura* – cf. Spinoza, *Ethics*, part 4, preface) is an inanimate god, which he implicitly contrasts with the "living God" of Christianity and of his own philosophical theology.

[83] *Geistreich*.   [84] See Jacobi, *Werke*, vol. II,1, p. 220.

[85] *für sich bestehendes Wesen*.   [86] *Sinn*.   [87] See Jacobi, *Werke*, vol. II,1, p. 216.

being and erred in words, his truth was in your soul and his love was your life."[88] This deeply felt and sincere homage is paid to a noble, much maligned shade. Public statements on the personal convictions and religion of a contemporary individual, on the other hand, are a different matter, and it is strange that Jacobi should issue them. Given Jacobi's manner of expressing his opinions about the highest ideas, it is not surprising that he should slip from discussion of ideas to the person whose ideas they are. And thus I too, without further vain attempt to prevent misunderstanding, will conclude this review with the expression of a feeling that most readers of Jacobi's writings will share, the feeling of having, through the study of these writings, conversed with a loving and noble spirit and to have been stimulated variously, deeply, instructively, and suggestively.

[Footnote in the original:][89] Here of course is the place to mention the welcome addition of twenty-three letters that present Jacobi at his most distinctive as a loving, thoughtful, and serene personality. They will hardly require further recommendation to our readers. I shall merely quote a few things as a sample of what Jacobi has to say about an especially notable friend of his, *Hamann*, of whom we catch an interesting glimpse in Jacobi's letters and whose writings we may perhaps hope to see collected by Jacobi.

The enjoyment which I take in him is indescribable, just as the peculiar individual impression that extraordinary people make on us always consists precisely in what is indescribable or inexpressible about them. The degree to which he unites almost all the extremes is amazing. That is why, even as a youth, he had rejected the principle of contradiction (and thus all the more so the *principium exclusi tertii* mentioned above [Hegel's interpolation]) as well as that of sufficient reason, and never subscribed to any principle but that of the *coincidentia oppositorum*. I have yet to discover the *coincidentia* (Jacobi understands it here not as an empty abyss, as formlessness, chaos, radical indeterminacy, and nothingness, but rather as the highest form of the life of the spirit [Hegel's interpolation]), the formula that would resolve some of his contradictions, but each day sheds new light on the matter, and in the meantime I continuously graze on the freedom of his spirit which produces the most delicious harmony between us. He is as inclined as I am to give free rein to his fancy and to pursue the inspiration of the moment. Buchholz said of him jokingly that he was a perfect indifferentist, and I have retained the epithet. He takes the same keen pleasure in diverse and heterogeneous things, whatever displays some special beauty, truth, or integrity, whatever has

29

---

[88] Friedrich Heinrich Jacobi, *Sendschreiben an Fichte*, in: Walter Jaeschke, ed., *Transzendental philosophie und Spekulation. Der Streit um die Gestalt einer ersten Philosophie (1799–1807)*, vol. II (Hamburg: Meiner, 1993), p. 19.

[89] Hegel's quotation significantly abbreviates this passage taken from a letter to Jacobi's older brother, Johann Georg, written on September 5, 1787, from which an excerpt is included in the volume Hegel reviewed (pp. 503–507).

some life of its own or betrays an inner richness and virtuosity: *omnia divina, et humana omnia*. He finds Lavater's thirst for miracles distasteful, and it makes him suspicious of the man's devoutness, though he loves and honors him with all his heart.

Then may we not feel certain that Jacobi, portraying Hamann's spirit as he does and finding himself in harmony with it, must also find himself in harmony with a form of thought that consists only in a consciousness of *coincidence* and a knowledge of the ideas of personhood, freedom, and God, and not in the category of inconceivable mysteries and miracles?

Proceedings of the Estates Assembly of the Kingdom of Württemberg, 1815–1816 (33 sections)

[INTRODUCTION]

30   The task that was begun two and a half years ago – of introducing a representative constitution and thereby bringing to completion a German monarchy that has arisen in our time[1] – awakened from its beginning such a universal interest in the German public that nothing could be more agreeable to it than the publication of the *Proceedings of the Württemberg Estates Assembly*. In place of the hopes which accompanied the beginning and the progress of this effort, there must appear at the end a result and the judgment of it. The thirty-three volumes with which this review is concerned of course do not yet contain the completion of the main goal, but they do form an historical whole. For, on the one hand, they present the progress up to the death of the king who founded the monarchy and who began the second step – the inner, free structuring[2] of that monarchy – and the characteristic development of this event in its principal features falls within his reign. On the other hand, the work of the Estates appears to have been brought to completion, since a representative committee is finished with its draft of a constitution, which likewise has appeared in print.

    Of course, these *Proceedings* present only one side of the efforts of that endeavor: the public efforts, insofar as they enter into the Estates Assembly. The inner history of the efforts of the cabinet and of the ministry, as well as what happened outside of the Assembly among the people, the possible external goals and activities of members of the Estates – all that is

---

[1] Württemberg became a monarchy "in our time" because Duke Friedrich II had taken the title "king" and become King Friedrich I only at the beginning of 1806, in the wake of Napoleon's annexation of the left bank of the Rhine and reorganization of the Holy Roman Empire (see footnote 6 below). Hegel views the attempts made by Friedrich and his successor, Wilhelm I, to introduce a representative constitution as part of the political maturation or "completion" (*vollenden*) of the new Kingdom of Württemberg.

[2] *Constituirung.*

customarily attributed to the secret connection of events and actions – is here hidden. The interest of the public, however, has mostly centered on the public part of the proceedings, which in any case are the main sources of worthy material for history. Until recently, a psychological perspective on history was popular which stressed the importance of so-called secret motives and the intentions of specific individuals, as well as of anecdotes ₃₁ and subjective influences. This perspective has, however, fallen out of repute, and history strives to regain the dignity of presenting the nature and the course of the substantial issue at hand and of allowing the characters of historical agents to be recognized from their deeds. The conviction has become more widespread that it is not contingent factors that reveal the real issue or the characters of historical agents in all their solidity.

The historical events which we see before us have the peculiar charm that they do not contain such a considerable part of the past as a history of distant times would; the great purposes and interests as well as the smaller characteristics and externalities still retain their presence. The concepts which we bring to bear on the object of interest in this event could not be demanded from any distant age, even that of cultivated Greece and Rome; they are characteristic of our time. Hence also these ideas about the constitution of a state and in particular about granting the people political influence and a public life are to be regarded not merely as the thoughts of one writer compared with those of another, for what we see is a German government and a German people engaged in spiritual labor over these matters and whose thoughts are occupied with the rebirth of an actuality.[3]

The age had presented Württemberg with a new task and the demand for its resolution: the task of building the parts of Württemberg into a state.[4] After the absurd institution known as the German Empire (and rightly called the "constitution of anarchy" by an historian gifted at least with *ésprit*)[5] finally had reached its deserved – and also externally its appropriate

---

3 *Wirklichkeit.*
4 The most important political task facing Württemberg in this regard was the union of "New" Württemberg – i.e., the territory acquired in the aftermath of the Napoleonic wars – with the former duchy. After Württemberg's surrender in the War of the Second Coalition (1802–03), Napoleon, intent on establishing strong allied states in southern Germany, had more than doubled its pre-1797 territory in recompense for its losses in Alsace after the War of the First Coalition (1793–97), thus increasing its population from about 600,000 to about 1,500,000. Until Württemberg became a sovereign kingdom and member state of the Confederation of the Rhine in 1805–06, Friedrich had ruled over the new territories as a state separate from Old Württemberg and with a different (more autocratically fashioned) political organization.
5 This comment of Voltaire's was apparently a favorite political quotation of Hegel's: see its use in his unpublished work *The German Constitution* (Hegel, *Frühe Schriften*, in *Gesammelte Werke*, ed. Eva Moldenhauer and Klaus Markus Michel, vol. I: 452, 461; translated in T. M. Knox and

and humiliating – end, the former territory of Württemberg received not only an enlargement more than double its prior extent, but this new whole, composed of former fiefs of the German Empire (the part which comprised the dukedom having also been a Bohemian sub-fief), threw off this subjection and, with the monarchical dignity of a prince, stepped forward to claim its sovereignty and the status of a state, the status of one of those actual German realms which are taking the place of the absurdity that bore only the empty name of an empire.[6]

Such epochs are extremely rare – as rare as those individuals to whom fate has allotted it to found states. The historical traces of these few epochs are lost in dark antiquity and in a condition of wild or at least underdeveloped customs,[7] where a state has come into existence externally but the inner arrangement lies in the simple habits of the people and in the character of the leader. The historical emergence of articulated constitutions has spread out over a long series of centuries; the few chief features which were at the basis of this emergence were developed and added on to at each particular point by the need of the moment, necessity and the power of circumstances. The issue around which the more specific endeavors of this development turn is rather simple. On the one hand, there were the efforts of the regime to overcome the power and presumptions of the intermediate class of aristocrats,[8] and to give the state its rights against that aristocracy; on the other hand, there were the exertions of the third estate, which is often also called the people, to force this middle-power and occasionally also the government to grant it civil rights.[9] Thus, upon survey,

---

Z. A. Pelczynski, *Hegel's Political Writings* [Oxford: Clarendon Press, 1964], p. 143) and in the Heidelberg *Lectures on Natural Right and Political Science*, which he gave during the same academic year in which the *Estates* essay was published (cf. *Lectures on Natural Right and Political Science*, transcribed by Peter Wannenmann and edited by the staff of the Hegel Archives with an introduction by Otto Pöggeler, trans. J. Michael Stewart and Peter C. Hodgson [Berkeley: University of California Press, 1995], p. 135). Hegel's qualification of Voltaire as being gifted "at least with *ésprit*" may be compared with his remarks in the Jacobi review concerning *ésprit* (*das Geistreiche*) as an imperfect surrogate for reason and the concept.

[6] Not only did the new Napoleonic order along the Rhine allow Württemberg to expand its territories, but the former duchy – which had been one of the principalities ("fiefs," as Hegel puts it in feudal terms here) composing the Holy Roman Empire of the German Nation – now became itself a kingdom, and Duke Friedrich II of Württemberg took the title King Friedrich I. Hegel here employs an important distinction between *Reich* and *Staat*, using the term *Reich* to refer both (in the singular) to the now defunct "empire" and (in the plural) to the "realms" of the emergent German Confederation that have now attained a political sovereignty – i.e., the status of *statehood*, which, on Hegel's view, both the empire and its subordinate parts previously lacked.

[7] *Sitten.*

[8] The aristocrats form an "intermediate" class (*Mittelglied*; Hegel also uses the term *Mittelstand*) between the king and the people.

[9] *Bürgerrechte.*

a constitution appears to have arisen as an aggregation. The development has not progressed uniformly; several parts have remained undeveloped and others expanded to troublesome excesses. Such a constitution is like an old house whose simple original plan has been altered by a long series of owners, according to expansions of the family and the needs of the moment, into a collection of extensions and corners which have their individual comforts but together make up a misshapen and ill-conceived whole. The intellectual culture[10] of the age has produced the idea of a state and its essential unity, while twenty-five years of a mostly terrifying actuality have afforded the rich and valuable experience of the diverse attempts at grasping that idea. The third factor, the external conditions, was granted to Württemberg's ruler by the favor of circumstances, along with the exceptional advantage that here the aristocratic middle estate did not pose the usual hindrance of a privileged landed nobility, for this element was only just on the verge of entering into the state. The king thus appeared to be in the singular historical position of being able to give a constitution that was all of a piece.

The one side of achieved sovereignty – the existence and recognition of the new Württembergian state from the outside – had been attained. The first period of its development took place in circumstances under which it was necessary to dictate measures for external creation and preservation, so that within the state means were concentrated in a powerful ministerial regime and made ready for use by a strong hand. Now the time had come in which not merely the *power* of the state but also its *will* could be brought to life. The luck and exertions of the European governments and their peoples brought it about that the sovereignty of the German realms[11] could be freed from their persistent limitations, and thus enabled them to extend to their peoples at least the promise of free constitutions. But higher than the necessity implicit in the merely external[12] bond of a promise is the necessity inherent in concepts that have come to be general conviction – i.e., that it is essential to a monarchy to have a representative constitution, a body of laws, and popular participation in legislation. Friedrich II now took this second step of instituting the monarchical state on its internal side.

The promise could have been fulfilled in a way which would have been regarded as the wisest – even the most just – yet would also have been the most perfidious counsel ministers could ever give. If the princes of the new realms had wanted to deceive their peoples thoroughly and to acquire, so to

33

---

[10] *Geistesbildung.*   [11] *Reiche.*   [12] *in dem positiven Band.*

say, honor before God and men, they would have given their peoples back the so-called old constitutions. Indeed, it would have brought them honor before God and the world because, to judge by recent historical events and the many public voices, one might have thought that the people would have flooded the churches and sung loud *Te Deums*. For Machiavelli's shade the princes would have won the fame of the refined politics of Augustus and Tiberius, who likewise allowed the earlier republican forms to persist, even though the republic existed no longer and could no longer be called back – a deception to which their Romans succumbed and which made the institutions of a rational, monarchical condition (whose concept the Romans failed to discover) impossible. This policy could have seemed an obvious course to our princes when they considered the dangers and terrors of the experience of the last twenty-five years, which are bound up with the creation of new constitutions and of an actuality that proceeds from thought, and compared them with the safe tranquillity and nullity into which the institutions of previous Estates constitutions have sunk. Indeed, it might have seemed even more attractive had they connected the nullity that was already there with the further reflection that outside a German imperial fief and in the new context those institutions would lose the little meaning and consistency they might have had (just like the Roman institutions that Augustus and Tiberius had allowed to persist).

King Friedrich rose above the temptation of this deception. On March 15, 1815, he called together the heads of the princely and ducal families of his realm and a selected group of the rest of the nobility, as well as a number
34 of deputies chosen by the citizens. The history of these *Proceedings* opened with the invariably grand scene of the king on his throne first addressing the full Assembly of the Estates of his own realm. In his speech, he first spoke of what had already happened, namely that the previously diverse elements of the country and his subjects had been united into an inseparable whole, that differences of religious confession and of class had disappeared in the relation of citizenship, and that public tax burdens for all had been brought to the same level and thus everyone made into citizens of one state. Then he gave testimony to the loyalty and obedience of his people, the courage and honor the army had brought the name of Württemberg, the support of the civil servants in all his efforts, and the willing submission of all classes in the difficult burdens of the time and efforts of all sorts through which security and preservation had been achieved.

Then he declared that he was laying the keystone of the edifice of the state by giving the people a constitution. Afterwards he reminded the present representatives that they were called upon to unite the nation with the head of state in order to exercise the most important rights of the government's power. He exhorted them: "Let us, united for the furtherance of the concerns of the nation, to which the constitution calls this Assembly, secure the holy bond between me and my subjects with mutual trust."

He then had the minister of the interior announce the Constitutional Charter. After it was read he pledged to uphold it and presented it with his own hand to the President of the Assembly.

There is perhaps no greater secular drama[13] on earth than when a monarch adds a further foundation to the power of state – which at first lies exclusively in his hands – by bringing his people into it as an essentially influential part of the whole. Since the great work of a state constitution, as in fact most other governmental action, usually takes place only in a series of divided acts and contingent events without oversight or publicity, and the public appearance of princeliness and majesty has gradually become restricted to birthday celebrations and marriage observances, it is tempting to dwell for a moment on such a beneficent, sublime, and powerful scene[14] as that in which the appearance of majesty so corresponds to the inner substance of its action. But one might also be inclined to think that one should apologize for dwelling on such a moment. For the occasions on which the king's official presence has been customary, and the emptiness and ineffectuality of the previous national assembly,[15] the German Imperial Diet,[16] and in general the nullity and unreality of public life, have brought about a prevailing mood of irksomeness toward such ceremonies and of moralistic and hypochondriacal self-conceit toward the public and the appearance of his majesty. This has happened to such an extent that the mention of his majesty's appearance – and, for instance, the view that such an appearance is capable of arousing feelings of magnanimity – runs the risk of being taken as anything but serious, and hardly as good will, but rather of being judged as courtly stupidity, slavish blindness, and tendentiousness. Our political deadness is unreceptive to becoming happy at such scenes, and seriousness demands turning away from them as mere externalities and to the substance of the matter and to one's own thoughts about it. Here then, to cite it briefly, is the substance of the matter, the content of the Constitutional Charter which the king gave.

It consists of sixty-six paragraphs, divided into two parts, in which the first part (sect. 1–46) bears the title "The Constitution of the Estates" and the second part (sect. 47–66) the title "General Provisions in Relation to the Constitution of the Kingdom and the Rights and Duties of His Majesty's

---

[13] *weltliches Schauspiel.*   [14] *Anschauung.*   [15] *Staatsversammlung.*   [16] *Reichstag.*

Subjects." The first part appears thus to be the more detailed, the second part the less developed.

By the first part the king grants an Estates representation with the following chief provisions: the Assembly is to consist both of non-elected members[17] and elected members, together in a single chamber. Eligibility for the latter is not limited to any estate; crown officials, junior officers and soldiers, clergy, doctors, and surgeons are excluded. The only further condition is an age of thirty years and membership in one of the Christian confessions. The possession of a certain amount of property is not included under the conditions. To be a voter, a net income of 200 guilders from real estate is required. The Estates assemble only at the summons of the king and at least once every three years. After this period, half of the elected representatives step down, but are re-electable, and are replaced by new elections. The Assembly is not to last more than six weeks and is to be dismissed, adjourned, or completely dissolved by the king. The elected deputies, as well as the chancellor of the university, the general superintendent of the protestant church[18] and the catholic dean, receive their travel expenses and daily allowance (5 florins, 30 crowns per day).

36   Ministers can attend the Assembly at any time. In the years when the Estates Assembly is not summoned, a committee of twelve members chosen from the Assembly for three years meets to complete pressing business; raising taxes or changing the laws is not, however, in its competence.

For the introduction of new taxes, direct as well as indirect levies, and for raising them, the consent of the Estates is necessary. Existing taxes remain the basis of the government of the current king. The reckoning of income and the expenditure of taxes are presented to the Estates every year. The determination of a civil list[19] for the king is left for further proceedings.

The Estates have a similar part in legislation; without their approval, no new general law concerning personal freedom and property or the

---

[17] The first set of members, the so-called *Virilstimmführer*, included certain nobles and officials in the kingdom (e.g., the university chancellor and the heads of church bodies) who were not *elected* in a representative manner but rather granted individual votes in the Assembly by the king strictly on the basis of their being peers or having an official status. In the Holy Roman Empire, a *Virilstimmführer* had been a member of the Imperial Diet (*Reichstag*) in Regensburg who was entitled to cast an individual vote (*votum virile*) rather than sharing in a collective vote from the bench representing a particular estate. (Knox translates this term as "*ex officio*" members, but it included here not only specific governmental figures in their official capacity but also princes, counts, and nobles of various houses whom the king wished to have present in the Assembly.)

[18] The German term *evangelisch* is roughly equivalent to the English word *protestant*; in fact the coextensive term *protestantisch* became increasingly common in Germany in the course of the nineteenth century.

[19] *Civilliste* – an English loan-word, referring to an annual sum paid out of the public treasury to a monarch for the royal household's use.

constitution can be promulgated. The king retains the initiative in this matter, but the Estates can present suggestions for laws as requests to the king; in the case of a negative answer, they can repeat them three times in future assemblies, and at the final answer, which must be justified, they can make new appeals in response to the justification.

It is further allowed that the Estates can present general requests, appeals, and complaints to the king, and the king promises to give a decision to every petition of the Estates. He also promises to take up complaints brought to the Estates by individual subjects, if proof can be shown that the governmental authorities have refused to take them up.

Finally the Estates can demand investigations against state officials,[20] and upon the king's mandatory approval judgment is to be passed – in the case of high treason and of extortion[21] by an Estates court and in other cases in the usual legal mode of proceeding.

[COMPOSITION OF THE ESTATES]

The infinite importance and liberality of the rights here allowed to the Estates, as well as the simplicity and openness of their stipulation – considered purely and disinterestedly according to their content and with regard to nothing else – certainly honors the prince who gave them and the age in which constitutional law[22] has purified itself of privileges and matured into principles. Such an accomplishment gains even more in comparison with the formlessness, pettiness, and lack of clarity of local and foreign constitutions – especially that of Old Württemberg – where the rights of the people have been veiled and vitiated by privileges and particularities, qualified and equivocated on to the point of becoming empty shams. Are the provisions cited not such constitutional foundations, which must be recognized and taken up with nothing other than highest approval? Whatever might be missing from them certainly cannot be anything that 37 would be incompatible with such constitutional foundations, but only such additions and more developed provisions as would accord with those universal truths of constitutional law.[23] For the most part, the only thing that has been retained from the *positive* constitutional law is the privilege of the aristocratic institution. But beyond the fact that rational constitutional law has turned away from the democratic abstractions which absolutely reject such an institution, the privilege of this (in any case) given actuality

---

[20] *Staatsbeamte.*   [21] *Concussion* – a Roman legal term, referring to use of threats or violence.
[22] *Staatsrecht.*   [23] *jenen allgemeinen Wahrheiten eines staatsrechtlichen Zustandes gemäß.*

has been distanced widely from feudal rights through further statutes. Here it will suffice merely to point out that the king's Constitutional Charter grants only fifty votes to this element, which has been united into one chamber with the elected deputies, while the elected representatives have seventy-three votes and thus a significant majority. This political balance of power departs greatly from that involved in the dual-chamber system whose considerable authority stems from its age and widespread acceptance.[24] The reason we have bothered to mention the contrast between this voting relation and that incorporated in the provisional Estates Assembly of the Kingdom of Hanover – where the nobility is allotted one vote more than the burgher Estate – is that in the following *Proceedings*, the Württembergian Estates frequently invoke the liberal expressions of the Hanoverian delegation at the German constitutional Congress in Vienna.

Even less expected are the wider scope and almost complete freedom given to the democratic principle by the mode of electing representatives, which allows this element to enter into the order of the state in an almost completely unrestricted form. Among the few tempering factors which appear here, besides the fact that the non-elected members are not in a chamber of their own, are the provisions that the chief crown officials (or, in the good towns, the provincial governors) preside over the election assemblies,[25] and that the persons brought in for the business of the election, such as the district notary[26] and his assistant, are only eligible for election in districts other than the one in which they serve. The eligibility for being elected representative is, as mentioned above, limited by very few conditions. First, all civil servants[27] and clergy, as well as doctors and surgeons, are excluded. The reason why the last two classes are excluded

---

[24] Although Friedrich's 1815 constitutional sketch involved a unicameral assembly, a significant proposal for a bicameral estates was made during that year by University of Tübingen curator Karl August von Wangenheim in an anonymous publication entitled *The Idea of a State Constitution in its Application to Württemberg's Old Estates Constitution and a Proposal for its Renewal.* Wilhelm I, Friedrich's successor, appointed Wangenheim minister of state and took up his bicameral suggestion in the new constitutional proposal he offered to the Estates in March 1817. It is interesting to notice that, although Hegel here certainly indicates a preference for two chambers, his support is limited to this sentence (as Rosenzweig points out in exonerating Hegel of the charge of having tried to curry favor with Wangenheim for a position at Tübingen), whereas in his contemporaneous 1817–18 *Lectures on Natural Right and Political Science* there is an extended justification of bicamerality – in fact, a more extended treatment of the issue than is later present even in the Berlin *Philosophy of Right* (cf. *Lectures on Natural Right and Political Science*, pp. 151–153).

[25] *Landvogten.*

[26] The district notary (*Amtsschreiber*) was a senior position of great influence within Württemberg's peculiar notaries system (*Schreiberei-Institut*). The district notary had a monopoly on all the accounting done in his particular jurisdiction (*Amtsbezirk*) or "district." This is the first mention in Hegel's text of the class of notaries (*Schreiber*), whose official functions (and corruption) are discussed below.

[27] *Staatsdiener.*

may also be the reason in the first case: that their official functions allow them no long absence or other business demands. Yet this reason is certainly not significant enough to justify a provision of such great importance for the main issue. For apart from the fact that the same argument would apply **38** to the non-elected members who have crown positions (as it is hardly to be assumed that they are supposed to be stood in for every time), it loses much of its force in the case of civil servants living in the location of the Estates Assembly, which is of course usually the capital. Yet in the outline of the chief provisions of the new Estates constitution, the drafting of which the king himself had worked on (see supplement of files, p. 5), and which he delivered in an address on January 11, 1815 to the Assembly of the council of state[28] for consideration of a special commission of councillors and senior officials, the provision occurs that the civil servants, insofar as their service allows, should also be eligible for election.

The reviewer wants to enlarge upon this highly important matter. It ought not be overlooked, first of all, that in large states such as France and even more so in England the whole domestic social situation and the far-reaching connections available with foreign countries afford individuals completely different relations – in terms of wealth, education, and the habit of living in and comporting oneself toward more universal interests – than are possible in a country with a greater limitation of its territory, social circumstances, and wealth. In such smaller countries the greater part of those who receive a higher education,[29] or any more universal education at all, see themselves compelled to seek their economic and social existence in some form of public service.[30] If civil servants are out of consideration, there will therefore be disproportionately fewer to be found who possess sufficient insight and experience in universal matters – and even still fewer, in any case, who could be called statesmen. Part of the nobility is already excluded as being non-elected members, and another part of them are in service to the crown. In general, the positions of the elected deputies are not expected to be filled by the nobility. On the contrary. Among the remaining classes, although the class of lawyers might seem specially suited, they are bound because of their concepts and business to the principles of private right and (moreover) of positive right, which are opposed to the principles of constitutional law,[31] namely of rational law, for a rational constitution rules out any other. The spirit of an all-too-famous statesman[32] hit the mark exactly when he declared lawyers to be the most inept advisers and actors

---

[28] *Staatsrat.*   [29] *wissenschaftliche Bildung.*   [30] *Staatsdienst.*
[31] *Staatsrecht.*   [32] Knox says Hegel means Napoleon here; Jamme and Hogemann suggest Burke.

in public matters. The influence which the lawyer's spirit has exercised on the history of the Württembergian Estates Assembly will become apparent in the following.

39   The legal exclusion of this class could well be disputed from the stance of abstract right, but not more so than the exclusion of doctors and surgeons. A state's organization rests on a completely different concrete wisdom than that of a formalism extracted from private right. In what follows we will make acquaintance with a peculiar structure of Old Württemberg which was of the first importance for its Estates constitution: the class of notaries.[33] The contribution which the class of merchants, tradesmen, and other proprietors can make to an Estates Assembly in this regard, as important as it is, can not be in such a heavy proportion as perhaps in England, and cannot by itself make up for the loss occasioned by the exclusion of state officials.[34]

The fact that this exclusion reduces the supply from which capable deputies can be drawn is important enough; yet more important, however, is the effect it has on the basic attitude[35] of the Assembly, which must be the weightiest thing in an Estates Assembly if it is not to fall into the most dangerous evil. This fundamental quality can in general be called the "sense of the state."[36] It cannot be reduced to abstract right, mere rectitude, or a good attitude in favor of the well-being of the whole and the best for individuals. Landowners as well as those individuals who are in trade or who otherwise find themselves in possession of a piece of property or of a skill have an interest in maintaining civil order, but their *immediate* purpose here is what is *private* in their possession. When all that Estates deputies bring with them is the sense of private interest and private right as their chief aim, to which everything else is subordinated, they will try to limit the demands of the state as much as possible, arguing that they are superfluous, and though not purposeless, even so not strictly necessary for their own purpose. In a word, they thus come into the Assembly with the will to give and do as little as possible for the universal. The question is not which attitude the deputies *could* have, from whichever class or

---

[33] *Schreiberstand.*   [34] *Staatsbeamten.*

[35] Hegel uses here the word *Gesinnung*, which refers in general to a person's basic set of convictions or atttitudes. More specifically, Hegel is linking the "basic attitude" which should be represented in the Assembly to the "sense of the state" referred to below – the awareness of the demands of the state as a political whole to which one belongs. The notion of such a *political* attitude or set of convictions is central to Hegel's account of the dispositional or subjective side of an individual's relation to the state in the *Philosophy of Right*. There, he characterizes *politische Gesinnung* as a sort of "patriotism": the *habitual* awareness that the community is "the substantial basis and end" (*PR* §268).

[36] *Sinn des Staates.*

circumstance they are taken; when it comes to the setting-up of the state, or of any rational institutions, it is not the contingent that ought to be counted upon, but the question can only be what the nature of the matter – here, of the class – involves.

The sense of the state is acquired above all in habitual occupation with universal concerns, which gives occasion not only to discover and acknowledge the infinite worth which the universal has in itself, but also to experience the intransigence, hostility, and disingenuousness of private interest and to struggle with its obstinacy in cases where it is posited in the form of right. Since the deputies are elected, it is essential that the electors come from conditions in which this sense of the state must be present and in which it is developed. The previous interior minister in France, Vaublanc, bluntly included in his sketch of a law for the mode of electing the Chamber of Deputies the provision that crown officials of all sorts as well as the clergy should make up the majority of electors in the departments. There is unanimity that the English constitution is maintained only through what are called its abuses – for without the completely unequal and therefore unjust, even at times fully senseless, privileges connected with voting rights, the government could not in general count on the majority of votes. The ill-informed believe that the opposition party is a party that is anti-government or anti-ministry as such. Even when the opposition attacks not merely individual ministerial measures (which happens with individual members who otherwise vote, on the whole, with the ministry) but fights the ministry on each and every point, its fight is only against the individual ministry, not against the government and ministry in general. The reproach that is often made against the opposition – that it only wants to be in the ministry itself – is actually its greatest justification and entirely the opposite of the tendency which is often prized in German individuals and Estates as the courage of freedom and the defense of citizens and their rights, the tendency, that is, to win as many state resources as one can for oneself.

It must be left to German history to show how far the appearance of the former so-called "third estate" in the Estates Assembly had its origin in the former status of city leaders as princely officials in relation to the government's ministry. A similar historical account would be needed to show how the burgher delegates, as they acquired the same status, came to participate in the Estates. Nor can we recount here how the original officials were at first mere advisers and only later came to have a direct say in decisions. In the Tübingen Treaty of 1514, which is regarded as the fundamental law in the constitution of the former Duchy of Württemberg, the princely officials are expressly named along with one from the court

40

and one from the city council as those who should compose the deputies of the Estates to the Assembly. But the Estates were able with the help of the imperial commissioners to root out the officials again only six years later, in

41 1520. The Estates thereby presented a bad example for the unchangeability of treaties so recently and solemnly concluded. The objection is readily made against the eligibility of officials to be deputies that, being in the service of the prince, they will naturally also speak and act in his interest, and along with that objection comes, from time to time, the thought that what is in the interest of the prince is against the interest of the people and the state. In any case service for the *person* of the prince in the royal household is something different from service which is performed for the government and the state, and the opinion that what is done in the interest of the government and the state is *against* the interest of the people differentiates the rabble from citizens. The most recent world events – the struggle for Germany's independence – have imbued German youth in the universities with a higher interest than that of a mere focus on immediate future bread-winning and provision. Some of them have shed their own blood that German states might obtain free constitutions, and they have brought with them from the battlefield the hope that they might further contribute to that cause and go on to play a role in the political life of the state. If higher education[37] has equipped them to have such a role and they are devoted above all to the service of the state, ought they now, along with the entire educated class who share this calling, lose their eligibility to become members of the Estates and representatives of the people?

Here the important circumstance is to be considered, that the change in the relation of what used to be service for the crown was a significant moment in Germany's transition from its earlier crudity and barbarism into the rational condition of the life of a state. Something about this circumstance can be cited from the appendix to the twenty-fifth section of the *Proceedings*. There it is mentioned (p. 25)[38] that, beginning in the thirteenth century, the offices of the chamber were at first usually entrusted only to persons from the nobility with a considerable income from real estate and proceeds from vassals;[39] but the nobles found an excuse to give up an office which had become burdensome to them and to delegate

---

[37] *wissenschaftliche Ausbildung.*

[38] Hegel's further direct references in the body of his text to section and page number of the *Proceedings* – most of which he makes by parenthetical insertion – will be footnoted in what follows.

[39] *Prästationen* (= *Precariae*), a term, originally from Roman law, for what tenants of manors were bound to give their lords for use of the land (Eugen Haberkern and Josef Friedrich Wallach, *Hilfswörterbuch für Historiker. Mittelalter und Neuzeit* [Munich: Francke, 1964]).

its administration to a caretaker from the burgher estate, with orders to manage things with a light hand. Later these offices, such as those of ducal commissioner, judges, and other positions, were simply given over to persons from the burgher estate, who viewed this not (as it was later viewed) as a favor, but as a great burden. Also, this hardship was not imposed on anyone for too long. It was considered a particular favor to remain spared from such positions – of which many examples are cited in the section mentioned.

Now although these ministers continued to be vassals and even perhaps thralls of a sort, it was at least no longer possible for someone to believe that they existed only for the interest of the prince against the people in the sense later believed, namely that those in the service of the prince were virtually the prince's servants[40] and a class excluded from the people. To the extent that they were a class apart from the people, this was because the income which they had to take in and account for, as well as the judicial and police power which they had to exercise in the name of the prince, had more the character of rights stemming from a private possession and of a private power of a third element against the citizens than the character of state income and state duties. But as the domanial possessions and princely family trusts have come ever closer in later times to the character of state property, and as the rights of ducal commissioners and others over their subjects and dependants have begun to take on the rational character of state duty and state power, so the servants of the prince are no longer dependent for their salaries on the prince's arbitrary whim but have rights in their offices and the dignity of officials in service of the state.[41] This transition from the administration of a private possession to the administration of the rights of the state is one of the most important transitions which have been introduced over time. It has also freed officials from the position they were in at the time of the old Württemberg constitution. This is one of the changes that has been solidified and completed by the general transition of a non-sovereign principality[42] into a state.[43]

Since history is the basis of the positive claims of constitutional law,[44] upon which the Estates Assembly in turn based their claims, the general remark can here be made that it is exactly history which teaches us to recognize the conditions under which a particular constitutional provision was rational, and which leads us in the present example to the result that if the exclusion of crown officials was at one time rational, it is no longer

---

[40] The contrast is between *fürstliche Diener* and *fürstliche Bediente.*   [41] *Staatsdiener.*
[42] *Fürstentum.*   [43] *Staat.*   [44] *das positive Staatsrecht.*

so under other conditions. That the Estates Assembly has recalled neither the old relation of the ministries and the explicit specifications of the Tübingen Treaty, nor the difference between former princely servants and state officials, is quite understandable. But what is more striking is that it appears to have been the ministry that occasioned the exclusion of state officials.

The constitution of the former duchy presented another closely related sphere of public business: the courts and city councils, from which the parliamentary deputies were supposed to be taken. Certainly the position of a city magistrate is an appropriate school of preparation for Estates functions. Magistrates live, as do state officials, in the daily activity of handling the civil order and in the daily experience of how laws and institutions function, and of exactly which counter-forces of evil passions must be fought against or endured. Magistrates are, moreover, drawn from the class of citizens; they share in their particular interests and can have their closer trust. From one end of Germany to the other the complaint about incompetence, laziness, and indifference – and even the corruption and wickedness of local administration – had become so loud that a rebirth of their very nature seemed necessary before they would be able to produce men who were capable of taking on a wider spectrum of duties. The right of the magistrates themselves fill positions which have become vacant among them was probably one of the chief reasons for their decay. What otherwise could perhaps be called despotism – that many governments have taken away from city magistrates and other community leaders the administration of community property and of church, school, and welfare agencies – may in light of such incompetence not only prove to have been justified, but to have been an unavoidable duty. Their incompetence is also the reason why the role of the magistrates in the administration of justice has frequently dwindled to a mere formality, leaving the proceedings and the decision in the hands of the crown's judicial overseers and senior officials or making it necessary to take recourse to the legal opinions of counsellors and advocates. The governments in any case saw themselves thereby forced to take out of the magistrates' hands the part of the administration of justice that was formerly theirs.

Now even if the city magistrates, given their previous organization and character, can awaken no great hope of producing competent parliamentary deputies, still this provision of the old constitution should not be completely forgotten. But further modifications would admittedly be needed to alleviate some of the more exaggerated and one-sided restrictions against their service. The other extreme, equally wide-reaching, can be seen in the king's constitution: that, first of all, the eligibility of deputies is almost unlimited, and second of all, that the qualifications for being a voter are **44** equally insignificant. The only requirement besides being 25 years old is that one have an income of 200 guilders from real estate.

This latter sort of condition on voting eligibility has until now been alien to German institutions and has come into circulation only in more recent times. We want to say something about it. The first striking thing is that, on such dry, abstract stipulations as the two mentioned, voters appear otherwise in no unity or relation with the civil order and the organization of the state as a whole. The citizens appear as isolated atoms and the electoral assemblies as unordered, inorganic aggregates, the people in general dissolved into a mass – a shape in which the community, when it performs an action, should never have shown itself. It is the most unworthy of its essence and the most at odds with its concept, which is to be a spiritual order. For age, as well as property, are qualities which concern individuals taken in isolation, not characteristics which make up the worth of an individual in the civil order. The individual has such a worth only by virtue of his office, class, a civilly recognized occupational skill, and the qualifications for the same, for example a master craftsman's diploma, title, etc. This notion of worth is so familiar to common expectations that a man is not said to "be somebody" until he has achieved an office, become a master craftsman, or otherwise gained acceptance in a particular civil circle. By contrast, someone who is only 25 years old and possessor of real estate which yields him 200 guilders or more per year is said to be "nobody." When a constitution makes him somebody – that is, a voter – it grants him a high political right without any connection to the rest of the roles he plays in his life as a burgher, and it creates a situation in which an important constitutional matter is determined more by the democratic, even anarchical, principle of isolation than by the principle of an organic order. The great beginnings of internal legal relations in Germany, through which the formal development of a state has been prepared, are to be found in history, where, after the old monarchical government's power sank in the middle ages, and the whole had dissolved into atoms, the knights, freed peasants, cloisters, the nobility, and those who run trade and industry formed themselves, against this state of disruption, into associations and corporations which were in friction against each other until they found a tolerable co-existence. The highest state power, whose weakness made these corporations necessary, was so loose that these partial communities were able to shape their modes of connection all the more closely and exactly, **45** even pedantically, up to the point of a completely restrictive formalism and guild-spirit, whose aristocratic character became an obstacle and a danger to the formation of state power. With the more complete development of the supreme powers of the state in more recent times, these subsidiary guild-circles and communities have been dissolved, or at least their political position and relation to internal constitutional law[45] has been taken away. But perhaps it would again be time to bring the subordinate spheres back into political order and dignity and to lead them, now purified of privileges and injustices, back into the state as an organic formation, just as previously the circles of the higher-ranking state authorities were also organized. A living connection lies only in an articulated whole, whose parts form the particular, subsidiary circles. But to achieve such a whole, the French abstractions of pure number and quanta of wealth must be left aside, or at least they must not be made the chief determination and represented as the only conditions of the most important political functions. Such atomistic principles are – in science as in politics – death for every rational concept, articulation, and vitality.

It is worth remembering that the exercise of such a completely isolated calling[46] as that of being a voter quickly and easily loses its interest, depending, as it does chiefly, on contingent conviction and momentary whim. This occupation expires with a single action – an action which occurs only once in several years. When the number of voters is large, the influence which the individual's vote has can seem to him quite insignificant – even more so, given that the deputy whom he helps elect is himself only a member of a large assembly in which only a small number can ever gain manifest importance, while most members are also limited to making only a modest contribution with their single vote among many. From the perspective of psychology, it might be expected that the interest of the citizens[47] would drive them to seek eagerly the power to vote and that it would be held as an important honor, exercised disinterestedly and with great circumspection. Yet experience shows the opposite. The huge distance between the importance of the effect which is supposed to follow and the extremely insignificant influence of the individual soon makes voters indifferent to their right, and if the first laws are concerned with the exclusion of many citizens from voting, legal arrangements are soon needed to encourage those entitled to do so to make it to the polls. The often superficially used example of England – of the powerful machinations when Parliament is elected – is not appropriate here, since in this part of the English constitution it is exactly the privileges and inequalities of voting rights that are

46

---

[45] *das innere Staatsrecht.*   [46] *Beruf.*   [47] *Staatsbürger.*

the most influential condition, while the opposite occurs in the atomistic method.

Obviously, however, these remarks against the abstract principles of number, of property amount, and of age are not meant to deny the importance and influence of these features. On the contrary: when voting rights and eligibility are connected with the other institutions of the state, these features exercise an influence of their own, and when for example the law requires that one be of a certain age or own a certain amount of property in order to be eligible to become a member of the city magistracy, a court, or a corporation, or a guild or similar association, such requirements are more fitting than when such dry, merely external conditions are so sharply placed upon the high interest of Estates membership. The guarantee which is sought through such conditions for the competence of voters and those elected is in any case in part merely negative and in part pure presumption, since there is instead a completely different, positive guarantee in the trust the government has in those who serve the state[48] – or in the trust communities and citizens have in those who serve the communities, to be chosen for offices and accepted in associations. Moreover, effective activity and participation in the organic life of the state and the people guarantee that voters will have acquired political skill as well as the sense of the state and of the people, the sense of ruling and obeying, and that they will have been able to get to know and test their attitudes and abilities for such participation.

Stipulations of the sort which assume that the people are not a state but rather a mass, and then divide this mass into smaller masses according to age and one lone property condition, cannot truly be called state institutions.[49] These stipulations are not sufficient to eliminate the democratic formlessness from the people's share in universal concerns, and, more specifically, are not sufficient to eliminate contingency when it comes to finding competent deputies for an Estates Assembly. To earn the right to be called a state institution, it is not enough merely to demand that something should happen, or to place limits on a few conditions which could impede it; to be a state institution is to make happen what ought to happen.

Since the reviewer has digressed on this point, the remarks about other matters must be shorter. The Estates have been given the prerogatives that **47** without their consent no new taxes should be introduced and that existing taxes should not be increased. Württemberg may have been the first German state where the general Estates[50] have been granted this right so early,

---

[48] *Staatsdiensten.*   [49] *Staatseinrichtungen.*   [50] *allgemeine Landstände.*

and in such an open and determinate manner. The Estates which we have elsewhere seen emerge or revive either contain very restrictive elements from the feudal constitution, or their formation and the determination of their influence is still too provisional and indistinct to be compared with the free, frank, and clear form which the monarch of Württemberg wanted to give his own Estates. The bloody struggle of the Tyrolese against forms of state administration which they believed were opposed to their old traditional rights awakened universal interest. When they finally succeeded in reintroducing their former constitution, the monarch reserved for himself the right to determine the total amount of state taxes and left to the Estates only their distribution. Now it may be disputed whether the old Württemberg Estates already had the right which is recognized in the king's constitution or not – and whether their earlier rights were not more extensive. This is a dispute utterly devoid of practical interest, though it is for that very reason all the more suited for a proper *querelle d'Allemand*.[51]

It could well be said that the Württemberg Estates, through the provision that existing taxes remain and that their consent be required only for tax increases, were formally returned approximately to the status of the previous Württemberg Estates. For direct and indirect taxes, which had never stopped flowing into the prince's treasury, and which derive from ground rents, dues, tithes, and provision of labor, are seigneurial rents and the property of the ruler or of the state in the sense of property as defined by private right. They are based on an existing arrangement and are thus not subject to approval by the Estates. The other part of actual, direct, and indirect taxes, the revenue raised in the sense of constitutional law, was determined by treaty under the supreme judicial court's action and the ratification of crown officials, both in terms of its amount and its use for state purposes – namely, for paying off state debts and for paying both local and royal military. The Estates were thus bound to an existing arrangement as to a law. From all the qualification and particular elaboration under which the previous Estates exercised the tax-consent, and not merely in the case of raising taxes, a general perspective and claim can be drawn, that they possessed this right of consent in a broad sense. Yet such a right comes to have a completely new status and an incomparably greater extent and importance in the context of Württemberg's transition from imperial fief to independent state. In its condition as an imperial fief, war and peace were made, not by an individual Estate of the empire, but by emperor and empire. At least part of their military contributions in

48

---

[51] A dispute over nothing.

time of war were fixed, once and for all, by a quota-list.[52] This is not to mention that the formalistic obstinacy of the German Estates, their doing nothing which could be legally or illegally avoided, usually brought on even greater exertions than would otherwise have been necessary, the expense of which inevitably fell to the Estates. Against refusals of the Estates, the prince generally had support and help from the imperial courts. But after Württemberg became an independent state, the Estates' right of consent in matters of taxation attained an independence and a completely new meaning which cannot be justified by appeal to the previous situation. Now the state needed completely new guarantees against private interest and the pretension of the Estates, since the previous guarantees which the government had in the emperor and the empire were no longer available. The Estates were thrust into an essentially new element, that of the political, which had previously been missing.

Germany's special history gives sufficient examples of the earlier Estates' impulse, in their political nullity, toward a passive neutrality. Most of all they would have liked to avoid any intervention into world affairs at all and would rather have endured disgrace than make any decision of their own or undertake any action for the sake of honor. This inclination to neglect honor and refrain from action in external affairs is bound up with a tendency to direct activity against the government rather than against external enemies. Only too often the Estates have used critical situations merely as an opportunity to embarrass the government, an opportunity to prescribe conditions and acquire advantages for themselves against the government and for the efforts which the government made for the honor and well-being of the government and the people. Only too often did they manage to bring immediate misfortune and an affront to the land, and to limit and weaken the government's power in the long term, thereby paving the way for internal and external destruction. A spirit of all-consuming private interest and an indifference or indeed hostility to the very thought of national honor and its attendant sacrifices were the inevitable result of the political nullity to which the German people had been reduced by its constitution, and the result as well of the inability of the many small wholes and the greater part of the imperial Estates to have their own decision and will. When the feeling of national honor has permeated the different classes of the people more universally, as it has in England for example, the right of parliament to give annual consent to taxes takes on an **49**

---

[52] *Matrikel.* The *Reichsmatrikel* was a roster of estates of the empire according to their rank and resources.

entirely different meaning from that which the same right would have in a people brought up to attend only to private affairs,[53] and who, because any political standpoint is alien to them, have been kept in a spirit of limitedness and private selfishness.[54] Even just against such a spirit, governments would need a new guarantee for the preservation of the state, since they have lost the guarantee of emperor and empire which was insufficient to begin with. Now that the Estates have no supreme authority other than their own state government,[55] with which they are at the same time locked in opposition, the right of participating in the determination of state taxes, however it might previously have been structured, has rather become, in-and-for-itself, an infinitely higher, more independent right than it was before, for it grants the Estates an influence on war and peace, on external politics generally, and on the inner life of the state.

Because in the king's constitution existing taxes were regarded as basically determined for the lifetime of the reigning monarch, there was a formal limit to the right of taxation. Materially speaking, of course, this right is limited in any case by necessity – a necessity which should be evident these days in terms of how high taxes are. In all states – and, most of all, in the richest, such as England – the need of recent years has driven taxation to a previously unimagined extent, and France, Austria, and others have been able to help themselves in these financial difficulties only through high-handed, powerful maneuvers. Apart from the consideration of need, whose presence has never been disproved, and apart from the impossibility of basing a financial constitution all of a sudden on any other principles, the Württemberg Estates could have put up with this article out of gratitude to a prince who was the first (and up to now, after two and a half years, almost the only) prince who has given his country such an open and liberal constitution – a prince to whom, as Count von Waldeck[56] said in the first speech given on the part of the Estates Assembly at the opening of the meetings,[57] all the Estates of the country, all the provinces of the empire vie in expressing their feelings of gratitude for his decision to establish a constitution – a prince whom Count von Waldeck goes on to praise

---

[53] *in dem Privatsinne auferzogen.*   [54] *Privateigensucht.*   [55] *Staatsregierung.*
[56] Georg Friedrich Karl, Count von Waldeck (1785–1826), Landvogt of Stuttgart, was the leading representative of the nobility in the Estates Assembly and played a vital role throughout the negotiations with the king. After the majority of the nobles left the Assembly at its first meeting on March 15, 1815, Waldeck was one of four noble representatives who remained (the others being Prince von Hohenlohe-Oehringen, the president of the Assembly, Prince von Hohenlohe-Schillingen, and Count von Zeppelin).
[57] *Proceedings*, Section II, p. 3.

(1) "for leading Württemberg in all the storms of the last decade with rare strength" ("rare qualities," it says in the continuation of the speech,[58] "have for a long time been displayed by the rulers of Württemberg"; for this vague word, a more precise meaning – that of imperious arbitrariness, or weakness of character – is given by the broader historical record, with the exception of Duke Christoph); 50

(2) "for having given Württemberg a considerable expansion" (through the so-called "mediatizing" of Estates that previously stood in a direct relation to the empire – an expansion which Count von Waldeck characterized[59] as an unlawful situation, as a reduction of the rights of mediatized princes[60] and of the subjects entrusted to them by God, and as an expansion which the incorporated part of Württemberg would have sought to avoid had it not succumbed to force);

(3) "for losing no time in cancelling the results of the events of 1806 which ran counter to his will – i.e., the cancellation of the constitution established forever by his lordship's ancestors." (The whole remainder of the *Proceedings* shows that the opposition of the Estates concerned only the point that the constitution the king gave did not bring back the old one, that the results mentioned were not cancelled.)

It is of course well known that the Estates' demand that, even during the lifetime of the king, their right to consent should extend to already existing taxes, was moot because of the early death of the king.[61] It is equally well known that their refusal to accept the king's constitution has blocked the way to negotiations on new taxes at the change of a government, for it was his constitution which conceded the right to such negotiations.

In order to complete the historical details of the chief moments of the constitutional charter, the second part of the *Proceedings* should be cited: "General Provisions in Relation to the Constitution of the Kingdom and of the Rights and Obligations of the King's Subjects." These allow, however, neither excerpt nor assessment – they are simple, organic provisions which speak for themselves and make up the rational basis of a constitutional order.[62] For example:

---

[58] Ibid., p. 4.   [59] Ibid., sect. VI, p. 93.

[60] "Mediatized princes" translates the German term *Standesherrn*, used to designate the nobility who had been mediatized in the years from 1803 to 1806. They constituted the high nobility (*Hochadel*), i.e., that part of the nobility which (until the dissolution of the empire in 1806) had been subject to no lord but the duke or king and the emperor himself. They were thus the highest-ranking nobles within the state and enjoyed special privileges.

[61] Friedrich I had died during the night of October 29, 1816, while the proposed new constitution remained unapproved by the Estates.

[62] *die vernünftige Grundlage eines staatsrechtlichen Zustandes.*

§52. All subjects are equal before the law; they have access to all state officials; they are excluded neither by birth nor by membership in one of the three Christian confessions.[63]

§53. All contribute equally to public costs and taxes, according to the laws.

§55. Every subject has the right to emigrate once he is free of military duties or has satisfied them.

51   §56. Every subject is free to choose his class and trade according to his own free inclinations and to educate himself for it.

These examples allow only the remark that it would never have occurred to the imperial Estates[64] to reject them, and that only contrarian perversity or stubbornness or whatever one wants to call it could cause such an assembly to fail to mention them and to honor the king who expressly made them the fundamental provisions of the rights and obligations of his subjects. However older constitutions were related to such principles, those principles were bound up with, entangled in, and even frequently obscured by particular and external circumstances. Rights were not incorporated in such constitutions on principled grounds – that is, for the sake of rationality or absolute right – but appeared rather as individual acquisitions thanks to particular circumstances and were thus limited to certain kinds of cases, as if through unfortunate circumstances they could be as easily lost. It is an infinitely more important development of culture that it has advanced to the knowledge of the simple foundations of the institution of a state, and knows how to grasp these foundations in simple sentences, like an elementary catechism. If the Estates Assembly had given occasion for the twenty paragraphs which contain these general provisions to be hung on tablets in the churches, for youth to be taught them as they matured, and made into a standing article of school and church instruction, it would have been less amazing than for an Assembly to ignore them and fail to feel the worth of the universal awareness of such principles and of their public recognition by the government.

Because of their generality, however, these principles make up only the outline for legislation to be drawn up, like the Mosaic law or the famous *Droits de l'homme et du citoyen* of a more recent time. For existing legislation and a government and administration that is already in power, these are the permanent regulators upon which a revision or an extension of what already exists must be grounded. The king's Constitutional Charter stops with

---

[63] In Württemberg, these were the Lutheran, Reformed, and catholic communities.
[64] *Reichsstände.*

these universal foundations and contains neither the further development of them nor the inclusion of more precise provisions which could already exist as state institutions. Organic constitutional provisions and actual laws generally verge quite close on one another, and the further work of the development and subsumption of the already existing institutions could have provided a primary object of activity for the Estates Assembly.

[THE ATTITUDE OF THE DIET]

These, then, are the chief aspects of the manner in which the king thought he had supplemented the previous state constitution of his realm by adding the important element of the people's representation and by recognizing and proclaiming the universal principles of justice in the life of the state. And he believed himself to have achieved and perfected the incorporation of that element, thereby creating the basis for the further development and application of the principles of right, namely by actually convening the Estates according to the provisions of the Constitutional Charter, publicly pledging to uphold the charter, and solemnly presenting it to the Estates and promulgating it as the basis of their authority. The expectation was that the further course of history would show how this new creation, the Estates, was active in the sphere given to them and how this important vital element which had been introduced into the organism of the state would influence it. But the story developing before our eyes is not one of vitality and assimilation into a larger whole. Instead, the members called to the Assembly refuse to be taken as members into the state, declaring themselves instead to be Estates of another world,[65] a past time, and demand that the present be changed into the past, and reality into unreality.

What happened at the beginning of that same March 15 meeting, at which the king thought he had completed the inward constitution of his realm, was that both the previously privileged classes and those called to the Estates declared that they were outside the new legal constitution and that they would not accept the constitution given by the king.

To begin with, the male heirs[66] of the royal house declared[67] that they wanted explicitly to reserve the rights of their earlier condition for themselves and all future male heirs, other descendants, and heirs-of-heirs of the royal house. Then a number of mediatized princes declared that they awaited from the Congress of Monarchs in Vienna the determination

[65] I.e., as Estates of the old German Empire, not of the new sovereign state of Württemberg.
[66] *Agnaten*, the specifically male heirs of the king.
[67] *Proceedings*, sect. I, pp. 26 ff.

of their rights and relations and that they could therefore not subordinate themselves in advance to a particular Estates constitution; they thus renounced participation in the proceedings. In fact, a declaration was inserted into the first address of the Estates (without it being exactly clear on what authority) to the effect that the remaining princes and counts and the entire nobility could participate only under reserve of their rights and the decision of the Congress. These reserved rights were given a strikingly broader sense in particular in an appeal directed to the Estates by Count von Waldeck in the name of the House of Counts of Limpurg.[68] It is stated there[69] that the house had never accepted the abdication of the Roman emperor (an abdication which had been accepted by all the potentates of Europe) and[70] that after the dissolution of the Confederation of the Rhine it had returned to the legal possession of all its earlier rights, though it lacks until the present moment the actual possession of them (even if that is unjust). In other words, it formally renounces legal incorporation into the Württemberg state and any subjection to it. It was further stipulated that the count was prepared, when Württemberg became a constitutional state, to give the conditions under which the county of Limpurg would become subject to Württemberg by treaty.

To determine how the king's ministry might have viewed the pretensions of the mediatized princes, which reached the ridiculous level of refusing to recognize the abdication of the Roman emperor, is not the business of this account. It does seem incomprehensible, however, that an Estates Assembly would concede participation and voting rights in its deliberations and decisions to members who have formally declared that they legally do not belong to the Kingdom of Württemberg, and that although they wish to take part in reaching obligatory decisions for the people of Württemberg, such decisions will not be binding on those who help make them until such time when a constitutional state has come about with their help and they have declared the conditions on which they are willing to join it. Even if the pretension of making laws for others but declaring oneself not to be subject to them is a frequent enough phenomenon elsewhere, it may be more difficult to find examples of such a degree of laxity in Estates that allow such participation in deliberations and decisions under conditions which treat the king so arrogantly.

Several days later, yet another Estate – the prelates – made the insignificant move of addressing a petition to the king that they be represented in the Assembly and be accorded their prior rights as a particular Estate,

---

[68] Ibid., sect. VI, pp. 91 ff.   [69] Ibid., p. 93.   [70] Ibid., p. 97.

all the while characterizing the content of their petition merely as a *wish*.[a] Of the two prelates who were already members of the Estates Assembly, the one who was summoned as chancellor of the University of Tübingen declared that he did not know whether he represented the university, the church, or the learned class; the other, summoned as general superintendent of the protestant church, made the naive comment that a good friend had advised him not to endorse the appeal of the other prelates in order to appear impartial and to be able to support their cause all the more.[71]

54

The whole Estates Assembly thus puts itself in a position that is opposed to actual conditions in the world. It rejects the constitution given by the king and therewith the instructions on the strength of which it was convened. It gives itself a determination of its own and, in deciding upon the rejection of that constitution, contradicts the universal constitution of Germany and Europe as so recently founded by all the European powers.

The Estates Assembly did not reject the king's constitution because it was opposed to the right which subjects can demand for themselves in a political constitution on the basis of the eternal rights of reason. One might have expected that their rejection would proceed from an investigation of the Charter, which they did not get involved with, and that they must at least have recognized its universal principles. But they rejected it because it was not the old Württemberg constitution – not merely because it differed from the earlier one (an investigation did not precede this either) but frankly and expressly because it was not this former constitution itself, because the act whereby they would accept it was not the pure restoration and revival of the old one. But the dead cannot come to life again; the Estates Assembly proved in their demand that they had not only no concept of, but no clue about, the nature of the task at hand. They showed that they regarded what was necessary in this task as a wish or private arbitrary choice of the king or his ministry and that they thought it had to do with a contingency and not with the nature of the thing. They granted that several circumstances were new and therefore modifications had to be introduced.

Yet the changed circumstances which they themselves referred to were highly marginal and had virtually no bearing on the essential difference between the old and new political condition of Württemberg. For example, they mentioned the addition of a noble class. But as we noted above, the

---

[a] [Footnote in the original:] In the Assembly of the previous Duchy of Württemberg all fourteen prelates had seats and voted, and were thus not *represented* but participated as non-elected members, as peers.

[71] *Proceedings*, Section II, pp. 64 ff.

nobles insisted that legally and hence constitutionally (since it is only in the context of a constitution that legal conditions apply) they were not yet actually subjects of Württemberg; indeed, they even refused to allow the state with the concurrence of the Estates to give them a determinate constitutional or civil status within the realm. The other circumstance they mentioned was the extension of equal civil rights[72] to subjects belonging to a Christian confession other than the Lutheran faith – a circumstance which had no bearing on the nature of the constitution anyway, just as the first circumstance was supposedly not yet part of the constitution either. A further cause for modifications was thought to be the expansion of the country by more than half its previous size. In fact this circumstance could have provided a very important ground for opposing the mere reintroduction of the previous constitution of Old Württemberg. Instead, the Estates Assembly sought to show, with lawyer's arguments drawn from prior cases and appeals to the old positive right of the state and the formal concept of incorporation, that the newly added part had the same right to the blessing of the constitution that the other part did. At root, however, the whole treatment of this consideration and especially the legal argument was quite pointless in regard to the main issue at hand, something quite close to a *querelle d'Allemand*. For even if Württemberg had not been expanded and had remained in its prior territory, the change in the situation, and the need for and necessity of a new constitution, would have remained the same.

In order to illustrate the necessity of a new constitution, it would be possible to adduce many and various adverse consequences of reintroducing the old Württtemberg constitution under circumstances which had changed in many other ways than those just noted. The culture of the age already demanded at least a collection and review of the constructions and constitutions which had ended, like the German imperial constitution, in an unshapely building. One needs only to consider the commendable collection of chief articles of the original Württemberg state constitution arranged by our ecclesiastical counselor Herr Paulus[73] in order to see that such a condition makes the principles of the constitution into an inexhaustible armory for lawyers' and advocates' deductions but at the same time makes knowledge of the constitution and thus more or less the

---

[72] *Staatsbürgerrechte.*

[73] Hegel's one reference in the *Estates* essay to the theologian Heinrich Eberhard Gottlob Paulus, who was now his colleague at Heidelberg (hence "our" Paulus). It was Hegel's rejection of Paulus' essay on the Württemberg Estates that led to a falling-out between the two (see Introduction, footnote 5).

constitution itself inaccessible to the people. Our age can no longer be satisfied with such a condition of the constitution. That something was achieved in regard to this formality and that what is to all appearances a purely formal business also came to have an influence on more material concerns, will be the subject of discussion below.

To return to the adverse consequences just mentioned, other supposedly beneficial consequences may be weighed against them – especially the law, which is supposed to be made independent of consequences – and this the Estates did to the point of tedium. Such controversies lead to the usual interminable back and forth, because such arguments and counter-arguments are insufficient for a final decision so long as there is no Praetor to render it. What matters is only the nature of the issue at hand, and this is in the present case very simple. The change which has been in preparation for centuries and has only recently been completed is the transition we have already mentioned: that the more important German countries have gone from being imperial fiefs to being sovereign states. In the previous situation the prince on the one hand and the country and people on the other hand (although the latter are subjects, often to the point of bondage) could stand opposite one another with an independence which on both sides verged on rights of sovereignty. Between the two stood the emperor and the empire as an external connection which kept both in their independence and also necessarily kept them together – just as a private individual as opposed to another private individual is an independent person. The relations which bound such individuals to one another were predicated on subjective need and arbitrary choice, yet it is only to the extent that they are within a single state and subject to a common authority and courts that there are contractual relations at all, and only then does making contracts have a complete and actual sense, and only then are the independence and the mutual relationships of individuals maintained. But the less powerful that authority between and over them proved itself to be, the worse the collisions between both parties had to be, because they were bound together in their independence as government and subject and could not break apart from one another.

Such a condition, in which prince and people were bound through such an external power, carried with it the consequence that political rights[74] in the proper sense of that term were found on the side of subjects.[75] To rights of this type belong most of those which flowed from the fief-relationship, yet it would be superfluous to touch here on such rights, because there

---

[74] *Staatsrechte.*   [75] On the side of the subjects rather than on the side of the prince.

was in Old Württemberg an insignificant nobility whose rights were of no great consequence for the state's relations. The right of the previous Württemberg Estates to handle the receipt of taxes is, however, worthy of special mention. Bound up with that was the right not only to enjoy a parliamentary allowance themselves, but also to name officials, advisers, and above all a committee,[76] as well as to order payments from the treasury for their members and other officials. Indeed this committee itself had the management of the treasury, from which it drew the payment determined as a whole by the Estates. Beyond that, however, its administrative right stretched so far that it also decreed allowances and remunerations for itself, and both decreed and made awards and recurring payments to its own

57 members as well as to other individuals for actual or imagined services. It was just this use of the country's monies for personal ends, for themselves – something honor most disdains to hold secret – that was removed from all control. The inner destruction and ethical decay inherent in such private plundering and in such a condition more generally is very closely related to the formal destruction of the state, in that the Estates use their control of the treasury to pursue their own ends and become a kind of sovereign power standing in relation to foreign powers. There is only a small step between having one's own treasury and maintaining one's own troops, and it would be simply laughable to place a legal prohibition on the Estates' maintaining their own troops but to give them the power and means to do just that, by letting them have their own treasury. When the previously mentioned power of the emperor and empire over and between its subjects was still present, such consequences could be prevented in individual cases – when, that is, this power was effective and also when it desired to act; but it remained a contingency whether this consequence was prevented or not. Indeed, the German Empire did not lack for cases in which Estates were authorized to keep their own troops – as, for example,

---

[76] A central feature of the politics associated with Württemberg's Estates was the standing committee (*Ausschuss*) which met and made decisions in the absence of plenary meetings of the Assembly. There was a smaller (eight-member) and a larger (sixteen-member) version of the committee, but over time the positions in both tended to be drawn from a very narrow circle of families and, given the infrequency with which the Assembly met during long periods of Württemberg history (in the 100 years after 1699 there were only four plenary sessions), real power – especially over financial matters – shifted to the committee members. The committee was not only authorized to assemble at its own discretion, it also possessed the right to petition the sovereign independently of the plenary assembly and to elect its own members; it even had separate finances. The smaller committee established itself as a virtual oligarchy within the state, co-opting new members without need of the Assembly's approval and taking on all the rights and responsibilities of the Estates Assembly itself. (Cf. Hartwig Brandt, *Parlamentarismus in Württemberg 1819–1870. Anatomie eines deutschen Landtags* [Düsseldorf: Droste, 1987], pp. 21 f.)

the city of Emden in East Friesland. It was in this country, which was more distant from the reach of the empire's power, that the Estates themselves recruited troops in opposition to their princes, concluded treaties with foreign powers, and called armies into the country and paid them. It is hard to find in this connection a more instructive history than the splendid history of East Friesland by von Wiarda. We see in it a coherent picture of the most shameful, oppositional, and destructive ruin emerging from the relation between prince and Estates, in whose hands lay rights to which the sovereign was entitled. On a larger scale, we find the same thing in the history of France and England (not to mention Poland), for example, before these countries had completed their development[77] into states, only that these histories are also free from the nauseating aspect of the rights- and paper-formalism of Germany.

The archives of the East Friesland Estates were open to von Wiarda, who was in their service and on whose commission he wrote his work. The Württemberg Estates have not arranged for such a history. The famous Moser, who was qualified to do it and who was also the Estates' adviser, was driven out of their company. Yet among other particularities put before the public, a brochure stands out that allows at least a glimpse into one aspect of the matter we have touched on: the independent administration of the treasury by the Estates during a certain period. The title of this brochure is: "The Administration of the Württemberg Treasury by the Former, Now Cashiered Committee of the Württemberg Estates; Drawn **58** from the Accounts, Acts, and Articles of the Estates" (1799, no place of publication given). The Assembly, which in 1796 was convened again for the first time in twenty-five years or so, investigated the accounts of the committees that had been in power; the brochure relays at least part of the results of this investigation. The preface says summarily: "the results of these accounts contain not only many tons of gold which had been spent against the law but run into the millions, and, from the last Parliament of 1771 until the opening of the present one in March 1797, when the trouble was put to an end, amount to the enormous sum of 4,238,000 guilders: that is, four million, two hundred, thirty-eight thousand guilders of state funds to whose trustworthy administration and use the committees were bound by oath and duty."

It is perhaps sufficient to mention this result. A detailed picture, drawing out how deeply independence has been allowed to sink the Estates' admin- istration, does not belong here. In particular there would be the manifold

---

[77] *Bildung.*

forms of remuneration to dig up which the committee members allotted themselves for every significant and insignificant task outside of their
usual salary – for example, a clerk inquiring after the health of the duke –
and so much that can rightly be called fraud, in which these same family
names come up particularly often. Noteworthy also are shining examples
of diplomatic attempts and embassies, and above all their remuneration. In
the account from 1778–81 there appears a sum of 5,000 guilders which was
paid to a foreign councillor in 1770 for a trip to St. Petersburg to pursue
the concerns of the country that had come to "embarrassment" (??);[78] a
trip to Munich on commercial affairs at 8,700 guilders, etc. It does not
help to say that the squandering and plundering of the state treasury were
abuses and illegalities; when the sum of illegally spent national funds can
run up to 4 million, certainly the laws that make such illegalities possible
are no good. A good constitution is indeed only one through which illegal
actions are punished and moreover prevented. If they do such things in
the green tree, one could ask, what shall be done in the dry?[79] Such plundering and squandering, after all, occurred at a time when emperor and
imperial courts stood above the Estates, when the Estates themselves ended
a lengthy, extremely costly suit against their prince because of extortions
and illegalities, and a huge mass of debt had been taken on which has not
been paid off in fifty years to this very moment. This is a time one hears
praised as a time of German honesty, a time when the Estates were worthy
and happiness was brought about through the constitution – all this in
contrast to the ruin, luxury, and wrong of more recent times!

The deplorable fact that the Estates' independence made it possible for
them to plunder the state treasury may have been a natural consequence
or it might have been possible to stop it by laws and altered institutions.
Yet be that as it may, there remains the greater social evil in relation to
the state, that the independence of the Estates in the arrangement and
management of a state treasury makes it possible to impede and hinder the
progress of the state both in its internal affairs and particularly in its political
relations with other states. It is the latter set of relations which in any case
is distant from the concern of the Estates – indeed, it is often odious to
them, and, for the Germans up to now, has been a completely alien matter.

---

[78] Hegel's question marks are occasioned by what is probably a solecism in the German original from
which he is quoting. There reference is made to the "*dort verlegenen Landesangelegenheiten*," literally
"the land's business which is embarrassed there." A more likely reading would be "*die dorthin
verlegten Landesangelegenheiten*" ("the land's business which had been transferred there"). Hegel's
point seems to be to draw attention to the Assembly's poor command of German – yet another jab
at the Estates.

[79] Cf. Luke 23:31.

The notion of putting military power and an army independent of the government into the hands of the Estates or some corporation in the state would be universally viewed as a provision that destroys the state, but there would be no great difference if the arrangement of the whole or of a part of the state treasury and the authority to allocate payments and pensions should be granted to such a corporation. It might seem that the Estates of a former German country which had and then lost such control over the treasury would thereby lose much of their authority and power. Yet it has already been observed that through a country's transition from imperial fief to sovereign state the authority and power of the Estates were infinitely increased and, if only for that reason, they must not retain their earlier authority. The state would cease to be a state under such provisions and would be destroyed by the two sovereign powers it finds in itself. Or rather the unity would be restored, either by the so-called Estates' bringing down the government and seizing it, as we have seen in recent history, or, as we have likewise seen, by the government's throwing out such Estates and thereby saving state and people. The greatest guarantee and security of the Estates lies precisely in their not possessing a power opposed to their nature. By contrast, the greatest folly is to seek in such a power a protection for themselves and for the people, since such a power makes it right and (sooner or later) necessary to annul such Estates.

It remains to be added that with the qualitative change from fief to state 60 there has also been a complete change in the more precise formal relation between prince and subject that had obtained in the former. Since prince and land stood over one another as owner and holder of particular rights in the manner of persons bearing private rights, they thus were subject to a third party, the power of emperor and empire. They were therefore able, under a praetor, to conclude contracts with one another and to relate to one another in the mode of private right. Even in more recent times, when truer concepts have emerged in place of the idea – previously accepted without thought and reason – that governments and princes rest on divine authority, the expression "contract of state" has still seemed to contain the false thought that in the state the concept of contract truly suits the relation of prince and subject, of government and people, and that the legal provisions of private right which follow from the nature of a contract could and even should find here their application. It does not take much thought to see that the connection between prince and subject, between government and people, has an original, substantial unity at its basis, while in the case of a contract one proceeds rather from the opposite assumption, namely the equal independence and indifference of both parties with respect to one another. Any agreement into which they happen to enter is a contingent relationship, emerging from subjective need and the arbitrary choice of both. The connnection involved in the state differs essentially from such a contract in that it is an objective, necessary relation independent of arbitrary choice and pleasure. Rights depend on what is a duty in and for itself; in the case of a contract, by contrast, arbitrary choice grants reciprocal rights between parties, and duties follow from these reciprocal rights. When a country undergoes the transition from being a fiefdom under the empire to being a state, the previous independence of the two sides, mediated by a third power between and over them (and therewith also the whole relation of contract), has fallen away.

The fundamental error of the position taken by the Württemberg Estates lies in their beginning from a *positive* right, believing themselves still to have it as a standpoint and to be demanding their right only on the ground that they had previously possessed it. They have acted like a merchant who lost his fortune in a shipwreck, yet who wanted to continue his same mode of life and demanded the same credit from others, or like a landowner who, after a flood has covered his formerly sandy field with fertile loam, wanted to till and cultivate his field in the same manner as before.

The attitude of the Estates that have been convened in Württemberg is precisely the opposite of what began twenty-five years ago in a neighboring realm and what at the time had resonated among all spirits: that in a state constitution nothing ought to be recognized as valid except what can be recognized according to the right of reason. Some were worried that the leavened dough of the revolutionary principles of that time – the abstract thoughts of freedom – had not yet risen and been digested in Germany, and that Estates Assemblies might take the opportunity to make similar experiments and to cause confusion and danger. To that degree, Württemberg has provided the admittedly comforting example of that evil spirit having ceased its haunting. At the same time, however, it has also shown that the incomparable experience which took place in France, and outside of France in Germany as well, was lost on these Estates – the experience that both the extreme of fixed insistence on the positive constitutional law of a defunct state and the opposite extreme of an abstract theory and shallow prattle were equally the entrenchments of selfishness and the sources of unhappiness in that land and outside of it.

The Württemberg Estates wanted to begin again on the basis of the standpoint at which the previous Estates had found themselves: they refused to consider the content of the king's Constitutional Charter, and neither asked what rational law was nor sought to prove that anything was in accord with it, but insisted instead on the formalism of demanding an old positive right on the ground that it is positive and in accord with contract. The beginning of the French Revolution must be considered as the struggle of the rational right of the state against the mass of positive rights and privileges which had oppressed it; in the *Proceedings* of the Württemberg Estates we see the same struggle between these principles, except that the positions are reversed. If at the time the majority of the French Estates and the people's party claimed and demanded back the rights of reason while the government was on the side of the privileges, in Württemberg the king placed his constitution in the realm of the rational right of the state. The Estates, on the other hand, are casting themselves in the role of defenders of what is positive and of privileges; indeed, they present the perverse spectacle of doing so in the name of the people against whose interests, far more than against that of the prince, those privileges are directed.

One could say of the Württemberg Estates what has been said of the French émigrés who returned to their country: they have forgotten nothing and learned nothing. They appear to have slept through these last twenty-five years, the richest that world history has perhaps had, and for us the most instructive because our world and ideas[80] belong to them. There could scarcely be a more terrible mortar for pulverizing the false concepts of right and the prejudices about state constitutions than the trial[81] of these twenty-five years, but these Estates have emerged unscathed, just as they were. "Old right" and "old constitution" are such grand and beautiful words that it sounds like a sacrilege to rob a people of its rights. However, whether that which goes by the name of the old right and constitution is right or wrong cannot depend on its age. The abolition of human sacrifice, of slavery, of feudal despotism and of countless infamies was also always a cancelling of something which was an old right. It has often been repeated that rights cannot be lost, that a hundred years of wrong cannot make a right. One should have added: even if the hundred years of wrong had been called right for those hundred years; and moreover that a hundred years of actual positive right is rightly destroyed if the basis falls away which is the condition of its existence. Those fond of empty phrases may insist that one spouse retains his right toward the other even after the other's death, or that the merchant whose ship was swallowed up by the sea yet retains his right to it. The Germans' sickness has always been to hang upon such formalisms and waste time arguing about them. Thus also with the Württemberg Estates Assembly almost the entire *content* of their

[80] *Vorstellungen.*   [81] *Gericht.*

activity has been limited to fruitlessly asserting their formal right with the stubbornness of a lawyer. There were some, among others the Assembly president, the Prince zu Hohenlohe-Oehringen,[82] who attempted in vain to lead them to the real issue and to deter them from their litigious path. For the mortar in which our age has been crushed for the past twenty-five years was clearly powerless to change them.

[COURSE OF THE PROCEEDINGS]

The Estates' insistence on the formalism of positive right and the standpoint of private right, when what was at issue was a matter of rational right and the right of the state, has had the effect upon the history of their one-and-a-half year proceedings that they are extremely empty of thoughts, and for such a great object as that which was presented – the free constitution of a contemporary German state – they contain little or almost nothing instructive. Instead of a fruitful work, what is almost only a superficial history presents itself, to whose main thread we now turn.

As we mentioned above, after the king had solemnly opened the Estates Assembly on March 15, 1815, presented the Constitutional Charter, and then left the Assembly to itself, Count von Waldeck (who was neither from Old Württemberg nor even a non-elected member of the Assembly, but only a substitute for one) made a speech that began with the previously mentioned praise of the king, the "sublime monarch, who demonstrated rare power, enlarged Württemberg considerably, and is now restoring the constitution eternally founded by his lordship's ancestors, pure princes of rare qualities."

It could not perhaps have been otherwise than that the first statement on the side of the Estates Assembly, while not acknowledging the fact that the king had just given his realm a constitution, nevertheless contained a vague encomium intended to preserve appearances. This praise is, like the whole speech, so pretentiously and ambiguously given, the stamp of subtlety so pressed upon every word, that the Estates Assembly could enjoy the skill of their speaker, proving outwardly due devotion but inwardly committing to nothing; the king and his ministers, on the other hand, could take these twisted and concealed expressions as scorn, the more so particularly as the decision is ascribed to him to restore the bond between ruler and all

63

---

[82] Friedrich August Karl, Prince of Hohenlohe-Oehringen (1784–1853), was a non-elected member of the Estates Assembly from 1815 until 1819 and its president from 1815 till 1816, a post the king had commanded him to accept after Christian Friedrich Karl, Prince of Hohenlohe-Kirchberg, originally appointed as president, had failed to appear at the Assembly.

Estates of the state that has been recognized for centuries as beneficial and a constitution that is satisfactory to all parts of the state, and to cancel again the cancellation nine years ago of the constitution founded for all time by his lordship's ancestors. One could take this assurance for a bold presupposition, if they had only and immediately acted in accord with that; but, as we said, it could only appear the more spiteful and scornful as the vexations of the Estates Assembly had from the beginning stemmed from the very fact that the king did *not* want to restore the old constitution, and that no single Estate of his state, no part of it (except for the king himself and his ministers), was satisfied with his constitution.

The further course of this speech is an historical compilation of the fortunes of Württemberg under its constitution; in general it appears that the condition of the land had been miserable, dejected, and unhappy for as long as it had had that constitution. From these premises, the highly surprising conclusion is drawn "that the old Württemberg constitution made the country happy for centuries, that it has the most decisive merits in comparison with all other constitutions of other lands, and has without doubt always been the best constitution of any German country, being the object not only of admiration in Germany but even repeatedly drawing attention in England."

64

For these reasons and for the reason that in the old constitution everything had been settled by contract, that nothing in it was open to doubt, that it was guaranteed and sworn to by all the rulers, that the people had not waived their right to it etc., the Estates insisted that it alone must be recognized as the fundamental law[83] and the fundamental compact.[84] Any modifications made necessary by the aforementioned change in circumstances would, they said, have to be grounded on the old constitution. The petition proposed by the speaker and accepted by the Assembly expressed these thoughts not in a direct style but inappropriately put them in the form of the following indirect hypothesis: if the people had elected representatives only on the assumption that the old, bequeathed, confirmed, beneficial etc. Württemberg constitution would have to form the foundation of any modifications, and if furthermore the majority of mediatized princes were forced to reserve their rights and await the decision of the Congress,[85] then the Estates must recognize with most humble gratitude that by opening the Assembly the king has given them occasion to deliberate on how to apply the new conditions to the former conditions of the

---

[83] *Grundgesetz.*   [84] *Grundvertrag.*   [85] I.e., the Congress of Monarchs at Vienna.

land. Thus although the Assembly could not at this point tell the king what the outcome of their deliberations would be, they do not doubt etc.

In its very next meeting and in a style altogether different from these hypothetical and cryptic formulations of "reserving the right to further deliberations," "informing the king of the outcome of their deliberations at some future date, in case they should reach a conclusion," and so on, the Assembly expresses the meaning of its petition in an explicit way, saying that they have declared that the newer modifications brought about through particular conditions could be negotiated only on the basis of the old Württemberg constitution.

After Count von Waldeck's speech and the verbatim reading of his previously prepared petition to the king, a single deputy made a few remarks encouraging the Assembly to endorse the petition, whereupon it was silently and unanimously accepted.

We have already remarked on the content of the speeches and petitions and their carefully balanced style, laced with a boldness that could be called contempt and yet nevertheless obfuscatory, cryptic, and stilted. In all their carefulness, level-headedness, and balance of expression, the diplomatic proceedings of recent times nevertheless reveal an open, direct, dignified attitude, and in their great astuteness are anything but complacently clever. How much more ought one to expect from a German Estates Assembly a frankness, liveliness, and dignified openness in their first declaration, and not the sickening obfuscation and crypticism and then the silence with which the rest of the Assembly hid itself behind that obfuscation!

65   What they prided themselves on most as time went on was the unanimity of their decision to accept the petition. The following meeting and the further course of the proceedings reveal the reason for that unanimity and for the external manner in which the petition had been accepted in the meeting. For in that meeting (on March 17), six nobles protested against the petition's statement that the present group of nobles were reserving their rights. By way of explanation they point out that the reports of two members which led to the petition were given so quickly and with such a weak voice that they could not be heard; and they go on to remark that not everyone knew that standing up from one's seat was supposed to represent a formal vote.

Above all else, formal voting procedures must be determined in an assembly and must be made known to the members. Even if they were only going to be tentative, they ought to have been accompanied by an expression and declaration whose meaning could be subject to no doubt. The picture of silence is completed by the mention of the quick reading of the reports and of the soft voice in which they were read. Is this a picture worthy of the first appearance of an Estates Assembly, an appearance with which they make the most decisive, even their only, resolution? Those six members straightforwardly declared that they gratefully accepted the constitution given by the king. This explicitness contrasts with the phrases of the petition, for one could not have known that it was supposed to signify the non-acceptance of the constitution if one had not been prepared and instructed to this effect in advance. It would have been more open and worthy of an Assembly of German men and representatives of the people if it had declared its non-acceptance of the king's constitution as straightforwardly as those six nobles gave their acceptance. In what follows, we will occasionally mention the delicacy which was observed toward the king; genuine delicacy, however, lies without doubt in a cultivated frankness, and the indelicate behavior and tone toward the king and toward the Assembly itself is precisely the obfuscatory attitude mentioned above.

More importantly, however, the Assembly's main resolution should not have been preceded by just two written statements, which were moreover tangential to the issue; and the unanimity of their decision, far from being a virtue, is rather occasion for reproach and criticism. What we see is an Estates Assembly, the overwhelming majority of which has already agreed **66** in advance about their decision and settled the matter in silence. Although later on another group mounted partial opposition, what they really showed was complete indifference toward the real thrust of the decision, namely the old constitution; this group neither made appeal to formal right nor to its content, but only wanted a good and thus a better constitution than that of Old Württemberg. Thus we see an Assembly which is still new to its role, an assembly which has been made restrained and silent by its ignorance of constituent parts, its uncertainty about what ought to happen, and its lack of habit and practice, and which is intimidated by the obfuscation and concealed resolve of a few members. If the Assembly could have grasped its status and concept more clearly and more courageously, they would have made a rule of the greatest openness and fullness, rather than remaining silent, and they would have had to agree that the greatest thing was to have a say now that they had been given one. Whether their unanimity corresponded to their genuine intentions or whether it was the result of intimidation and a lack of self-confidence, in either case they should have felt obliged to appoint an *Advocatum diaboli*, if one can call it that, as this name does not appear too inappropriate in light of the animosity they demonstrated toward the king's constitution. It would have been the duty of their office to look into all the grounds which could be given for the acceptance of the king's constitution and put those in the brightest light, and then to have an equally straightforward statement of their actual opinion and a detailed discussion of their motives precede their resolutions. Yet such deliberation neither preceded nor followed their resolutions, whereas it is the purpose of an Estates Assembly not only not to act without deliberating, but to deliberate about the interests of the state before the eyes of the people and of the world.

When several months later Herr Gleich, the representative of Aalen,[86] delivered a speech which was completely opposed to the previously undiscussed assumptions of the Assembly, the committee in charge of making a report on it impressed upon him that such appearances were bound to occasion displeasure and general disapproval in the Assembly, where up to now harmony and patriotic sincerity had kept any alien, dishonest influences at a distance. What? Is a deputy to be exposed to insinuations of having bowed to "insidious influence from outside the Assembly" merely for having shown the courage of voicing his dissent from that silent and dead unanimity? In any case the direct accusation of dishonesty, or else complete abstention from mere insinuation, would have been worthier.

67   In the beginning of the committee's report, Herr Gleich's speech is ascribed the purpose – or rather it is said that he *appears* to have the purpose – of forming an opposition party in the Assembly that until now has most gloriously been characterized by harmony. It cannot escape anyone who has reflected on the nature of an Estates Assembly and is familiar with their appearances that without an opposition[87] such an Assembly will lack external and internal life, that such an opposition[88] belongs to its essence and justification, and that it is not actually constituted until an opposition[89] emerges within it. For without an opposition,[90] the Assembly has the shape only of a *party* or even of a clump.

The reviewer has spent so much time on the behavior of the Estates Assembly not only because it is noteworthy in its own right but also because it is characteristic of the whole of what follows. Regarding the purely formal

---

[86] Heinrich Maximilian Gleich (1776–1859) joined the Assembly on March 15, 1815, as a representative from Aalen, but left his post seven months later in September of 1815. As indicated in the text, the reason for his brief tenure was his openness to accepting the royal constitution and his sharp criticism of the Assembly's manner of proceeding. The unfavorable response to his proposals moved him to resign, and he later refused any candidacy as a deputy in the *Landtag*. For a further account of Gleich's criticisms and the Assembly's response to it, see Joachim Gerner, *Vorgeschichte und Entstehung der württembergischen Verfassung im Spiegel der Quellen (1815–1819)* (Stuttgart: W. Kohlhammer, 1989), pp. 149–160.

[87] *Opposition.* In contrast to *Gegensatz*, also used in this passage, *Opposition* has primarily political connotations.

[88] *Gegensatz.*   [89] *Opposition.*   [90] *Opposition.*

aspect of the proceedings, it is useful to highlight two further circumstances. The course of their proceedings within the Assembly was in general that the committee was appointed for a matter that had come up, a report was given by the committee, and then debated, and a decision about it reached. In the selection of the committee, most frequently, particularly at the beginning, when it is most crucial to stake one's claim and intimidate rivals, it was invariably the vice president who suggested the members by name. This executive committee,[91] chosen by the Assembly, suggested members for the first committees at a point when only two members of the Assembly had shown up, exactly those who were forever distinguished as the heads of the Old Württemberg party. The result was that they had all the say, even more so when one sees the further delicacy of the members of the Assembly toward one another. This delicacy extended so far that in one case, where eleven members on a committee of twelve had received a majority vote, whereas for the twelfth position four members had the same number of votes, the Assembly did not choose one of these four (which would have meant excluding the other three), but contrary to their original decision named all fifteen to the committee of twelve members.

In the case of the very next committee up for appointment, they managed, by way of a conspicuously obfuscatory maneuver, to bring it about that the four leaders named to the first committee would not miss out on being members of the second. Given the great influence of a committee in general (for every matter that comes forward must be prepared by such a committee), it is essential for the freedom of an Assembly that the same individuals not occupy all committees and that the same hands not be responsible for preparing everything. This influence is almost completely unrestricted in an Assembly where almost the only or at least the main **68** statement on any issue is presented by the committee – and, so to speak, is actually not even discussed.

The other notable item is the mode of speeches. One does not find in the proceedings any extemporaneous speeches but rather for the most part only lectures read from prepared scripts,[92] fewer and only brief oral expressions, and no spontaneous exchanges of opinions at all. Only once, toward the end of the Assembly, when, instead of the matter itself, the personality of a dissenting member, Dr. Cotta,[93] was made into an issue,

---

[91] *Vorstand.*   [92] Hegel contrasts here *freigehaltene Reden* with *abgelesene Vorträge.*

[93] Johann Friedrich Cotta (1764–1832) is famous as one of the most distinguished German publishers of his times. Works by Goethe, Schiller, Hölderlin, Schelling, and Hegel appeared in the prestigious *J. G. Cotta'sche Buchhandlung.* Cotta represented Böblingen in the Estates Assembly from 1815 to 1817 and was active in almost all the major committees. Though he remained a staunch opponent of the royal constitution, he came to be a moderate supporter of Wangenheim's constitutionalism.

were statements made (among them rather offensive personal slurs), and then extemporaneously and in close succession. Instead of the usual *vota scripta*, statements were delivered on this occasion without preparation, blow by blow, and although they displayed the natural eloquence which has remained in common use in our marketplaces for cases such as this, the eloquence which dominated the Roman forum was not on view.[94]

It is natural that committee reports were drawn up in writing and read aloud. But the so-called *debate* that followed consisted mostly of one or several members reading a prepared *votum scriptum* several days and weeks afterwards, and again perhaps days and weeks later another member producing another such *votum*. Thus in one and the same meeting, several papers might be read aloud in succession, each related to a completely different issue, even very frequently having no further consequence than that of having been read aloud. This method of doing everything in writing almost entirely does away with the living element that results from an assembly of men confronting each other in order to make face-to-face assertions, proofs, disputes, and motions with the living presence of the spirit.

One cannot call the reading aloud of various treatises a discussion. The English Parliament rightly prohibits by law the reading aloud of written speeches, in part because such a paper can very easily be the work of another and especially because the whole nature of such an assembly is thereby altered. Outside of a very few speeches which, though composed with a sense of vivacity,[95] were likewise read aloud, the present volumes of the *Proceedings* make up, above all, a collection of legal reflections, stillborn briefs by lawyers, and closely reasoned arguments larded with citations, not merely from the litany of parliamentary bills that have been passed, inheritance settlements, princely wills, and so forth, but also, for example, from the *Corpus Juris, Montesquieu, Zonaras, Cramer* (in the Abb. *de tacente dissentiente* in *Opusc.* T. II and in *Usus philosoph. Wolf. in jure spec* XII), and other such weighty products of scholarship.

If an Estates Assembly represents the people, are such proceedings the way in which the people express themselves? Is this the way to influence **69** an assembly and the people itself? Treatises composed in a scholar's study are also only addressed to the scholar's study or destined for the files of

---

[94] Hegel's contrast between the *marketplace* where German eloquence can be heard and the eloquence associated with the Roman *forum* underscores the contrast, central to this essay and Hegel's contemporaneously emerging political philosophy, between the economic realm of civil society (represented by the Estates) and the distinctively political world of the state.

[95] *mit lebendigem Sinn.*

businessmen. Estates assemblies, however, have their essential audience in the people itself; how can the people take an interest in and thus make any progress with such paper-proceedings and pedantic deductions?[96] Rather, the people's representatives isolate themselves in this manner from one another and still more so from the people itself, and (even if the meetings were public) pursue the business of the people by excluding the people. The physiognomy of the *Proceedings* of the Württemberg Assembly is thus not much different from the activity of a society of young people who come together to compose essays for practice and the progress of their education, and swap them with each other to hear them read. Apart from the material, it was perhaps this written mode, with the consequences which it inevitably had for the whole course of treating business, which occasioned the utterance (declared, of course, to be "unseemly") of one representative,[97] quoted as saying that "if the submitted petitions had not provided matter for conversation, no one would have known how to fight off the boredom." In any case, if the debates of the Estates were supposed to consist mainly in the communication of written arguments, meetings in person would be rather superfluous and much expense could have been spared; the whole could be accomplished through the circulation of papers. Those accustomed to reading prefer to read such papers themselves, anyway, rather than having to listen to them; and they would also have had the choice of having the papers read to them by their wives or by a good friend, and they could have sent in their *vota* in written form as well.

To pursue the history further, the great political event of Bonaparte's arrival in France from the island of Elba occurred right at the beginning of the meetings of the Estates Assembly. It was only two days after the Assembly convened that the king informed them of the measures Vienna had threatened to impose. An event of this sort was suited to illuminate the whole attitude and character of a German Estates Assembly through its behavior and manner of action. If it had been possible for a German people to respond to this event with joy and hope, it might have seemed dangerous for Estates who were (as already mentioned) opposed to the will of their king to be meeting at this moment in time. But since that was impossible, such an Assembly was bound to seem even more desirable, to be able with united energy to provide the means demanded by such an important event, which appeared to threaten the peace of Europe anew, particularly in those countries near France.

70

[96] *Deductionen.*   [97] *Proceedings*, sect. VIII, p. 20.

All too often it has been the ruinous, unpatriotic, even in a higher sense criminal ploy of Estates Assemblies to use the pressure of the political circumstances to win advantages for themselves from the government and at the same time create an awkward situation in internal and external affairs, rather than making open and common cause with the government to ward off the trouble facing the state. They have thus weakened the power of the government, instead of expanding it, and made common cause with the enemy both in essence and in deed. On March 28 a member, filled with conviction of the importance of the present circumstances, made the motion[98] that the Assembly should make a declaration of their own to the king. It would state that they were prepared to give the last drop of their blood, the last gift from their soil for him and for the good cause; say how the Assembly intended to achieve this arming the population and granting a loan to the government; but that they were only able to do so on the basis of the old constitution. In an address to the Estates,[99] a part of the nobility recognized that great dangers demand strong measures, and they urged the Assembly, without adding conditions, to suggest that the king order both a general mobilization[100] of the country and weapons training. Similar petitions were received from many districts of the land. One petition from Esslingen on March 29[101] (the others have remained unpublished) expressed a worry that the king's provision for a regional battalion of 500 men from every district was too sparing and could hinder and delay the defense measures; a general summons was requested instead. A report added by *Schultheiss*[102] Reinhard of Oberesslingen likewise is printed as a "bold declaration"; it says:[103]

The attempt to get formerly discharged soldiers to re-enlist as sergeants appears to be in vain. The feeling for love and defense of the fatherland is too dull with these men, as it is with many or indeed most of the common people. Whoever is healthy and between the ages of 18 and 40 should reach for a weapon. If the Swabians are summoned *en masse*, they go and fight with might, but when they have free will, nothing happens!

71   Since this *Schultheiss* speaks of his people as one of its common members, the Estates Assembly presumably did not want to charge him with

---

[98] Ibid., sect. II, p. 41.   [99] Ibid., p. 14.   [100] *Bewaffnung.*   [101] *Proceedings*, sect. II, p. 48.
[102] Although often translated as "mayor," the *Schultheiss* was (at least originally) not a popularly elected local official but rather one who reported to the ducal administration. According to Vann, however, most mayors by the late sixteenth century were elected for life by a council of village elders (James Allen Vann, *The Making of a State: Württemberg 1593–1793* [Ithaca: Cornell University Press, 1984], p. 40).
[103] *Proceedings*, sect. II, p. 50.

slandering the people – a popular expression in recent times – when they distinguished his letter by printing it under the description of a "bold declaration."

But the Estates Assembly had already tied its own hands in this and other matters by assuming that if they made offers and suggestions, these could be interpreted as an exercise of the right of petition acknowledged in the king's constitution and thus, as a consequence, as a de facto recognition of this constitution. As if the very Assembly of the members of the Estates were itself not a fact rooted in that formal framework and as if the people's representatives, brought together under such circumstances and under whatever title, form, and authority you wish, were not obliged to ban all other considerations from their minds – in particular the fear of actions having consequences – and to devote all their energy to acting and thinking for the salvation of their people!

At first, the Assembly read aloud the petitions it had received and then placed them *ad acta*. The city of Tübingen was credited (rather prematurely) with having called for a general mobilization before the conditions in France were even known. Though at a time of external threat patriotism is quick to hit upon the notion of a general mobilization of the people, we should have expected the Estates Assembly to display more mature and better insight into the military and, what is more, the political advisability of such a measure, especially at a time when the new Assembly of the Estates itself caused manifold machinations and internal tension. Think how the call for mobilization could have been interpreted if it had been made even earlier, before the events in France gave occasion for such a measure! The experience of twenty-five war-torn years in Württemberg had shown anyway that such a mobilization as provided for in the constitution had never had the least effect; indeed, it never once even took place, which is hardly surprising in light of the whole purpose and condition of the constitution. Thus it is faintly ridiculous even to think of what such a general mobilization could have achieved in the face of the danger of the times. When the Estates brought forward a proposal upon which they must in all probability have assumed that the king would not act, and when they then went on to fail to co-operate in measures which the king thought appropriate and which he had ordered, the faith in their seriousness and good will became yet more doubtful. Of those measures, the main one was the raising of emergency wartime funds. The king had presented the Estates on April 17 with an estimate of those costs. According to it, the costs of outfitting and maintaining an army of 20,000 men – provisions the king was obliged to his allies to make – went beyond the peacetime budget of $3^1/_2$ million.

72

There were also the costs of the marches of the allied armies which had likewise been settled by agreement. If we ask what Württemberg's Estates (whose co-operation had been explicity requested by the king and by those on whose behalf they were acting, and who were thus authorized to do their part in the European cause) did to turn away that danger, which was of a unique sort and an entirely extraordinary character, the answer is: they did nothing. Whatever contribution Württemberg made among the ranks of all the European powers in those days is due solely to the king, the erstwhile crown prince, the ministry, and the army. The government pursued its course with honor and glory to the fulfillment of its universal, moral, and positive obligations, and as it appears, found itself hindered not in the least by the refusal of the Estates to co-operate. The Estates by contrast achieved nothing besides having shown their own ill will, their failure to appreciate their lovely position, and the dispensability of their co-operation.

Further, several of the petitions directly relating to this matter were given by the Estates to the ministry, petitions which no longer spoke of the readiness for sacrifice but proposed to provide relief to an admittedly exhausted land by demanding that the king's domain treasury, church property, and so forth be used to pay for the expense of the war. For that purpose the king had already effectively negotiated with his allies and the appropriate army commanders; the answer which the Estates received to their demand was simply this, that whatever was chipped in from other state revenues would have to be repaid into the budget from other sources in turn, and that the present issue was one of *emergency*[104] relief funds in the first place. The spirit of the former relation, where prince and land each had their own private treasury, led both sides to try to shove the burdens as much as possible onto each other. Since the Estates in general recognized nothing of the existing relation of a state, and since in particular the exclusion of a civil list (about which the king had already declared his openness in the constitution) had not even been discussed yet, let alone been settled, the old ideas of the opposition of country and state interests, of a country's treasury and the state's treasury, taken as they were from 73　the conditions of the past and more confused than ever in the altered circumstances of the present, had no meaning and even less application and effectiveness.

---

[104] *außerordentliche Hilfsmittel.* The sense of *außerordentlich* here is to denote that these are *irregular*, that is, non-recurring, expenses, not part of the Estates' regularly recurring contributions to the budget.

But the Estates' main response to the king's request for co-operation in the extraordinary conditions of the fatherland was that their co-operation depended on whether the king agreed to revoke his constitution and re-institute the old one. That part of the nobles who on April 4 thought they were able to speak both for themselves and for the whole nobility on this matter, declared in a petition to the Estates that they recognized their duty to fight in any military action and with the other Estates to sacrifice blood and property for the fatherland, yet they qualified their remarks the following day to the effect that the submitted declaration was appropriate only for the Estates Assembly and in no way for the king's ministry of state, since texts which flowed from the heart were easily susceptible to various construals.

In point of fact, this explanation was itself the most immediate example of how something can be susceptible to multiple interpretations. They thus made their willingness to contribute with blood and property to the defense of the fatherland contingent upon the initiative of the Estates Assembly. The Assembly's initiative, though, consisted in a petition to the king on the same date in which they combined both the issue of the constitution and the measures which the present situation demanded, in spite of the fact that the king had already announced that he would post-pone a definitive decision on the first matter until the return of the crown prince. This momentarily evasive reason was an *argumentum ad hominem* directed toward the Estates, since the latter had proven by involved arguments drawn from constitutional law[105] that any matters concerning the constitution had to be submitted to the male heirs for approval; hence the Estates could infer from the king's consultation of the crown prince that he had in fact recognized this right.

More precisely, the Estates declared in their petition that nothing was more pressing than putting the people, through the united leadership of monarch and estates, in the position of defending the fatherland, and that the will of the honest people, in their enthusiasm, was prepared to do anything that seemed to them necessary. But they could only base their actions upon the foundation of the inherited constitution of the country, and the restoration of the state's credit would be possible only through a constitutionally guaranteed loan – that is, by transferring responsibility for the collection of taxes and the disposition of this part of the state trea-sury to the Estates. Something similar occurred in an address on April 18, 74 in which they say that "for all subjects, for new and old, the name 'old

---

[105] *staatsrechtliche Deduktionen.*

constitution' has a magic power." The submitted petitions and addresses, however, showed that the universal indignation at Bonaparte's reappearance, the feeling of the threat it posed to the fatherland, proved to be a magic power in itself, and it had the effect of an electric shock. When the petition states in the passage immediately prior to this one that the fruit and wine harvest was ruined by frost and thus a great part of the subjects were literally struggling with despair, it is hard to understand how the old constitution could have demonstrated its magical power in this case, or how the Estates could abstain from trying to effect a unified relief when the internal and external circumstances were so hard. It has moreover become sufficiently evident that the Old Württemberg constitution exercises utterly no magic power on the new subjects – more than half the land – and that to the extent that they have had the pleasure of getting to know it first-hand, they view it as a kind of plague and the worst scourge of the land, as will be shown later. Otherwise, though, the whole course of the Estates proceedings can be seen as a story of the magic power of the name to which the Assembly had surrendered itself right from the beginning without bothering with what it was (or rather *had been*) a name for – for our discussion of the Estates' treasury budget above already intimated what that name concealed, and our later description of a certain plague on the land will reveal yet something further in this regard. In the present case it is due to the black magic of that word that nothing more came of the words "being ready to sacrifice blood and property for the good cause" than that they remained mere words. The Estates go on to declare that the fatherland has had no more certain protection against the poison of the dangerous principles which now again, as twenty-five years ago, are emerging from France, than the magical power of that word, though we already remarked that that power has protected the Estates not only from the poison of the bygone twenty-five years, but also, so to speak, even more from the rational concepts of those twenty-five years.

As to the more specific aspects of the position in which the Estates had placed themselves, they were in uncertainty as to whether they existed at all or not since they had rejected the king's constitution, upon whose basis they were gathered. To be consistent, they should have dissolved and separated after the king opened the Assembly – or rather, since even the mode of election was not in accordance with the old constitution, they should not have let themselves be elected in the first place and the voters ought not to have voted. Since it had become a fundamental maxim of their activity to do nothing from which their factual recognition of the king's constitution could be inferred, they continued to tread on eggshells even in

the most trifling formalities. Even in their first address on March 15, they 75
prudently abstained from signing themselves as the "Estates Assembly."
Instead, they signed themselves as "Those Called to the Estates Assembly."
It was made clear to them in the king's resolution of the 17th of the same
month, that the king awaited motions and petitions not from such an
entity, but only from the Assembly constituted by him in the appropriate
form, since only the Assembly is entitled to the rights determined in the
Constitutional Charter; for the rest he assured them that he would not
waste time with formalities and hence for the present would ignore the
bad form – and the resolution did in fact go on to discuss the content
of the Estates' petition. The initial reaction of the majority was that the
signature "Estates Assembly" was an inconsistency, since it presupposed
the constitution's validity, until the representative from Marbach, Herr
Bolley,[106] remedied this scrupulousness by the clever expedient of signing
their next petition (of March 22) as the "Estates Assembly," but at the same
time adding a protest below the signature! In this petition it also says that
overscrupulousness about formalities (namely in relation to their mode
of election and their appearance at the convocation) would have been an
offense against their only purpose, the well-being of the monarch and the
subjects. Why, then, are they so scrupulous when it comes to the other
formalities? Have they not thereby offended against that single purpose, as
they say? Despite that *conclusi* and the protest appended to it, the secretary
announced in the meeting of the 28th that it had occurred to him only
after the issuing of the petition (which by the way in the meeting of March
23 had once again been publicly read in the Assembly and signed by the
president, vice president, one non-elected member, and an elected deputy)
that the closing phrase "Estates Assembly" was still missing. This fault was
then removed through a later petition. In the next resolution from the king,
the Assembly was ordered to adhere to protocol and remove the mistakes
in outward form which had marked their previous petitions, and also to

---

[106] Heinrich Ernst Ferdinand Bolley (1770–1847), an advocate president of the superior court in
Stuttgart, represented Marbach in the Estates Assembly from 1815 to 1817. From the first meeting
of the Assembly on March 15, 1815, Bolley asserted himself as perhaps the single most important
leader of the *Altrechtler*, i.e., the majority faction that vehemently demanded restoration of the old
constitution of Württemberg. His draft for the petition of March 22, 1815, justifying the Estates'
demand for the restoration of Württemberg's old constitution, was perceived as having formulated
the *Altrechtlers'* "credo" (cf. Gerner, *Vorgeschichte und Entstehung*, p. 119; cf. 85–90). He was a
leading member of numerous committees, among them the examining committee entrusted with
compiling a legal report on the royal edict of March 17, 1815, the committee for the preparation of
the constitutional negotiations with the royal commissioners, the committee for the revision and
abridgement of the grievances of the country, and the committee for ensuring the recognition of
the "Estates principle," i.e., the validity of the old constitution as the sole basis of negotiations.

get on with the election of a vice president, secretary, and other Estates officials as prescribed by the Constitutional Charter.

To follow the pedantic course of these precautions any further would be too dull and digressive. The president repeatedly summoned the Assembly to elect the officials for whom the king had already prescribed oaths **76** of office[107] and sought to dissuade its members from their continual and "otiose repetition of statements long since made" and from their overly "legalistic" behavior. He admonished them not to jeopardize the good cause "for the sake of mere formalism and empty words," seeing that the election could be held without prejudicing the further course of proceedings. Nevertheless, the Assembly's overscrupulousness won out, and they refused to be moved to what they considered insignificant actions. If only their own actions had had more content and significance!

[THE ESTATES' MISGUIDED APPEAL TO THE "WILL OF THE PEOPLE"]

More specifically, the Estates Assembly claimed that, in legal terms, the old constitution had never ceased to be valid, so that when the king decided to give Württemberg a constitution as soon as circumstances permitted, the Assembly and the people naturally took him to mean that the old constitution was to go back into effect. They also demanded that the king make no decrees while the Assembly was in session without first seeking their counsel and express approval, which was tantamount to their demanding the exercise of the rights they would in fact have had as Estates under the old constitution. Similarly, they refused to appoint a vice president[108] on the grounds that there had been no such office in the Estates Assembly of Old Württemberg, although they did accede to the presidency of the Prince of Hohenlohe-Oehringen and the voting rights of the mediatized princes, neither of which had been provided for under the old constitution. The restoration of that constitution was their sole and simple demand, and they justified it by appealing to the *will of the people*, which, they said, had been expressed at the elections and in numerous petitions submitted to the Assembly. The "will of the people" – a solemn word which the people's representatives in particular must beware of profaning or taking in vain. We have already mentioned what the will of the people of New Württemberg was like. As *Schultheiß* Reinhard, himself a man of the people, said, the sentiments of most of his fellow people for the love and defense of their

---

[107] *Proceedings*, sect. III, p. 151.
[108] The royal edict of January 29, 1815 had specified that the Estates Assembly elect a vice president in the opening meeting of the session.

fatherland were excessively dull. Quite apart from that, however, to say of someone that *he knows his own will* is a term of rare praise. Thus not just anyone is chosen to be the people's representative, but only the wisest among them, for it is not the people, but their representatives who must *know the people's true will*, that is, they must know what is truly good for the people.[109] The Assembly sorely misconstrued their own dignity and vocation as the people's representatives when they followed the loud yet empty calls to restore the old constitution and even appealed to written statements and petitions as the source of their authority.

Moreover, the Assembly's appeal to the will of the people as the *sole* basis of its authority, along with its refusal to recognize the authority of the king in constitutional matters, effectively placed the Assembly out- 77 side the government as an independent and opposed power whose basis very nearly contained the poison of a revolutionary principle. In keeping with this relation between government and Assembly, the Estates referred to their proceedings with the government as "negotiations"; they spoke of their written exchanges with the sovereign as "notes" and saw the petitions they sent to the various ministries as expressive of "diplomatic relations"[110] – relations that can only obtain between sovereign states. Both the vulnerability of the government (due in part to the troubled times and in part to the tension caused by the very existence of an Estates Assembly under the given circumstances) and the king's own resolve to see his initiative through to the end may have contributed to his restraint, but the king is to be praised nonetheless for overlooking the Estates' impropriety and presumptuousness. In spite of the Assembly's contemptuous refusal to recognize the king's constitution, the monarch continued to treat them as legitimate Estates according to the principles of his constitution.

[THE ESTATES' POLITICAL OPTIONS. BASIS
OF CONSTITUTIONAL LEGITIMACY]

So much about the formal aspect of the Estates' relationship to the king. As to the essence of that relationship, however, it should be noted that once the king had presented his constitution, the Estates had three options. For one, they could refuse to recognize the constitution as binding until it had been submitted to their scrutiny, and then proceed with an examination, at the conclusion of which they would announce their final decision. Alternatively, they could provisionally accept the constitution, amend and adapt

---

[109] Cf. *PR*, §301.   [110] *Proceedings*, sect. VIII, p. 81.

it, and then initiate appropriate legislation. Or thirdly, they could reject the royal constitution outright, produce one of their own, and demand that it be recognized by the king.

It might be thought not only unobjectionable, but absolutely just that a people first examine and approve the constitution given to them, for what other source of legitimacy is there for a constitution except its conscious and willing acceptance by the people? Otherwise, one might add, despotism, tyranny, and infamy could throw the people in whatever chains they pleased. Yet even so, if historical experience be our guide, we must admit that oftentimes even peoples who loved their freedom above all else have confessed their incompetence to frame a constitution on their own and entrusted a Solon or a Lycurgus with the task – men who moreover resorted to deception to get around the so-called will of the people and the necessity of submitting their constitution to it for approval. Moses and Louis XVIII both established constitutions on their own initiative and appealed not to the will of the people, but to divine or royal authority as the basis of their legitimacy.[III] As for Württemberg, the dictum of *Schultheiss* Reinhard of Ober-Esslingen says it all: *When Swabians have free will, nothing happens.* – Concerns over despotic constitutions being set up without consulting the people's will may sometimes be based on sound suspicions, but they can also stem from shallow wisdom and a faint-hearted underestimation of the true power inherent in the spirit of the people and the times. We are speaking of a particular case, and not of an hypothesis. These lessons of experience can as easily be learned by reflecting on the nature of the matter itself: no one could be less suited to setting up a constitution than what is commonly referred to as the common people or than an Estates Assembly, unless one means to say that the very existence of a people and an Estates Assembly presupposes a constitution, an organic condition, an ordered life of the whole people.

The third option and the one chosen by the Württemberg Estates was the most untoward, inappropriate, and unpardonable of all, namely to reject the king's constitution out of hand without prior examination and without any indication of what they found acceptable and unacceptable, and of how it might be amended. For by doing so they effectively demanded that the king in his turn unconditionally accept whatever constitution the Assembly and the people happened to believe they wanted. They even refused him the act of acceptance, since he was in any case forced to acquiesce. It

78

[III] Louis XVIII had decreed his *charte constitutionelle* in 1814; it provided for a chamber of peers and a chamber of deputies with the right to approve taxation, but not to introduce legislation. The *charte consitutionelle* was the model for Friedrich I's original draft of a new constitution for Württemberg.

is beside the point that the Estates were at least not so arrogant as to presume to frame a constitution on their own. It was the old constitution of Württemberg they opposed to that of the king, and in demanding its restoration they were appealing to the authority of a constitution that lay in shambles and which later on they would naively admit they were not even able fully to present. And why not? Because they were barred from using the old Estates archive![112] That a scholar of books is lost without the key to his library is to be expected, but that the Estates are incapable of presenting their constitution without consulting an archive – what dust pile of a constitution can that be?

To answer that question, let us consider the sources on which "the number and the development of the basic articles of the constitution are to be based." Their enumeration is characteristic enough to warrant being quoted in full. The constitutional laws are not to be based merely   79

on Württemberg's budget regulations, government regulations, the resolutions of the *Landtag*[113] and its committee, and the testaments of the rulers... but also on the various statute books such as Württemberg's Code of Law and administrative regulations, the so-called miscellanies, church regulations, forestry regulations, local administrative regulations... and on innumerable (!!) individual decrees and above all on the many resolutions formulated in response to grievances, petitions, and requests by the Estates... Some important articles can only be deduced[114] by

---

[112] *Proceedings*, sect. XI, p. 282. "Estates archive" translates the German term *Landschaftsarchiv*. *Landschaft* is a collective term signifying the union of all the Estates as a single party to negotiations with the duke or king. (The difference between *Landschaft* and *Landstände* is one of nuance only, and both are rendered here as "Estates.") Friedrich I had confiscated the Estates treasury and the Estates archive on December 30, 1805, when he dissolved the Assembly.

[113] In pre- and early modern Württemberg, as in other regions of Germany, the *Landtag* was an Assembly of the Estates convened by the prince in order to deliberate on matters of importance to the state, but especially to approve special taxation. Although "state parliament" recommends itself as a translation in the case of the corresponding institution in modern, federalized Germany, we have chosen to leave the term untranslated here. The reason is that in the dual system that characterized the pre-modern and early modern German state, or rather fiefdom, *Land* (and hence also *Landtag*) carries special political and institutional implications in contradistinction to the *Regierung* (the sovereign or government), which would not only be lost, but also rendered confusing by an English translation.

[114] In eighteenth-century Germany, juridical deductions formed a special genre within the legal literature. They were intimately bound up with the non-constitutional nature of the laws of the Holy Roman Empire and consisted most frequently of genealogically supported derivations of territorial rights. Associations with the logico-mathematical concept of deduction are therefore misleading. Johann Stephan Pütter was the author of a widely used primer for the composition of such deductions. See his *Anleitung zur juristischen Praxi wie in Teutschland sowohl gerichtliche als aussergerichtliche Rechtshändel oder andere Kanzley- Reichs- und Staats-Sachen schriftlich oder mündlich verhandelt, und in Archiven beygeleget werden* [*Introduction to legal practice, concerning the manner in which in Germany suits both in and out of court, as well as other matters pertaining to the chancellery, the Empire and the state are to be handled orally or in writing, and how to document them in archives*], 4th ed., Göttingen, 1780.

combining different sources of the law of Württemberg, others only by induction, and still others only on the authority of tradition as confirmed by law.[115]

Earlier in the same petition they worry that if the positive constitution of Old Württemberg lost its binding power, they would have to stray into the "labyrinth of the natural law of states."[116] Yet can there be any labyrinth worse than their hodgepodge of legal sources? Such an armory of implications, combinations, inductions, and analogies may thrill the heart of an advocate making legal deductions, but if reason itself, the source of the so-called natural law of nations, strikes fear into the heart of the Estates Assembly, how could its members possibly hope to find shelter and safety from it in such a paper labyrinth? If the Estates had the temerity to demand that the king accept *in advance* as Württembergian law the implications, combinations, inductions etc., which by their own admission it would take years to produce, neither did they shrink from claiming that the restoration of this web of a constitution, with which the people could not possibly be acquainted and even the Estates themselves were by their own admission unable to provide in full, was *the will of the people*!

[SINCERITY OF THE ESTATES' MOTIVES FOR RESTORING THE OLD
CONSTITUTION. THEIR TREATMENT OF "POPULAR PETITIONS"]

One might have thought that the Estates were not really serious about restoring the old constitution after all, and that they were merely pursuing the sensible goal of achieving a revision of various points in the royal constitution (especially a more comprehensive development of the basic principles) and were simply in need of an effective means to that end. Admittedly, they could hardly have hit upon a more primitive method than the revival of the "magic formula," as they themselves termed the old constitution of Württemberg. We have already spoken of the Assembly's much touted unanimity on this point. Some among the high and low nobility persisted in claiming rights for themselves that were inconsistent with the rights and interests of the people and the government; they repeatedly cast doubt on whether they as nobles even belonged to the state of Württemberg and spoke of the conditions under which the nobility would condescend to enter into a relationship of subjection. These elements must

80

---

[115] *Proceedings*, sect. XI, p. 282.
[116] For an overview of discussions surrounding the ambiguous term "natural law of states" in the first half of the nineteenth century, see Michael Stolleis, *Geschichte des öffentlichen Rechts in Deutschland 1800–1914* (Munich: Beck, 1992), pp. 121–186.

have found the magic formula of the "good old law"[117] very opportune. The people of New Württemberg did not at first see how the royal constitution could ease the various hardships they were straining under; thus, in the initial unclarity of the situation, they too rallied to the call of the old constitution. Petitions from the towns and districts poured in from all sides; deputations appeared with demands for the restoration of the constitution of Old Württemberg, and a large part of the Assembly's meetings was taken up with reading them.

Popular petitions[118] had generally lost their credibility as a political means, but no one hesitated to make use of them now, and the immense influence that the caste of notaries had on the common people (of which more later)[119] made it even easier to manage. For that very reason, though, the popular petitions had virtually no substance or authority in the eyes of knowledgeable observers and tended rather to cast a shadow on the Assembly. The natural purpose of an Estates Assembly is to mediate between the monarch and the people. But under the prevailing external pressures (namely the renewed civil unrest in France),[120] and in light of the fact that here a people with absolutely no historical experience of constitutional government was in the midst of a transition from political nullity to hitherto unheard-of participation in and influence on the whole of the state, it was imperative that the Assembly not play on the preconceptions of the common people, who with all due respect are consistently lacking in judgment when it comes to the constitution of a state. In the fifth meeting Count von Waldeck deemed it necessary to reassure the people, who, as credible sources had informed him, were alarmed by the publication of the royal constitutional charter. In order not to cause a sensation, von Waldeck suggested that the representatives announce to the people that they had

---

[117] "The good old law" (*das gute alte Recht*) became a watchword among the opponents of Friedrich I's constitutional draft when the Swabian poet Ludwig Uhland put the phrase in verse in his poem of the same title, which begins *Wo je bei altem, gutem Wein, der Württemberger zecht, da soll der erste Trinkspruch sein, das alte, gute Recht* ("Wherever Württembergians sit down to enjoy a good old wine, their first toast should be to the good old constitution").

[118] The popular petitions (*Volksadressen*) were petitions demanding that the king provide a constitution and formulating recommendations as to how such a constitution was to be framed. Unlike the petitions by the Estates, the popular petitions were written by one or more persons not belonging to the Estates Assembly and they were signed by groups of citizens. The popular petition movement in the years from 1815 to 1819 involved prominent democratically inclined intellectuals such as Fries and Kotzebue; it came to an end with the repressive measures codified in the Carlsbad Decrees in August of 1819.

[119] See the lengthy account of the abuses of the notary system below.

[120] Napoleon had landed on the French coast on March 1, 1815, and begun his march to Paris, where he arrived on March 20, beginning his reign of the "One Hundred Days" that ended with his defeat at Waterloo.

"made themselves the spearhead of the people's prejudices." What kind of reassurance is it when the Estates Assembly announces to the people that they are the supporters of the peoples' unrest against the king?!

Despite the many petitions that were read and although the Estates Assembly prided itself on the attention they devoted to them, it is easy to see that for the most part they were ignored. From the minutes of the proceedings it is impossible to tell why some petitions were read and others not even mentioned. Just a few examples: in the meeting of December 20, 1815 it was suggested that a number of received petitions "at least be noted in the minutes, considered as read, and then filed away."[121] On February 21, 1816 a petition from the town of Riedlingen is read before the Assembly; the petition had been received on April 12, 1815. In another case, a representative requests permission to transfer a petition that had ostensibly already been transferred to another section a year previously, on June 11, 1815. However, the Assembly did not convene on that date and on the 12th, when they did convene, the petition was not mentioned. There are many more instances of this kind showing that the Estates Assembly had no *objective* respect for the petitions of the people, treating them rather as a means to their own ends.

To return to the question of the Estates' seriousness about the old constitution, the proceedings reveal that the Assembly was not just using the "magic formula" to gain public support. The majority consistently demonstrated their seriousness about the old constitution, not least by insistently demanding recognition of a formal principle of right.[122] Since time immemorial, the spirit of formalism and particularism has determined Germany's historical fate, and that spirit is manifest here in all its strength. If that spirit be called *Germanness*, then nothing could have been more German than the attitude of the deputies from Old Württemberg, including the nobility. But if we define Germanness as a concern for what is essentially universal and rational, then in spite of the differences in territorial rule, it will be difficult to find anything more *Un-German* than that attitude.

The immediate effect of the Assembly's rejection of the royal constitution was to render the Assembly incapable of any organic life-activity. For now,

---

[121] *Proceedings*, sect. XVII, p. 49.

[122] For a determination to be *formell* means in Hegelian parlance that the form can diverge from the substance or content of the determination. An example would be an unjust law: although it has the form of law (*Recht*), it is substantially unlawful or an injustice (*Unrecht*). Similarly, the will of a particular individual is formally free, i.e., the individual chooses freely among alternatives, yet to the extent that the individual makes choices which are incompatible with reason, he may prove to be substantially unfree.

instead of forming an opposition on common ground with the government, the Assembly was in a stand-off with the sovereign and hence in no position to undertake and accomplish effective work on the institutions of the state. When, after three months of waiting in vain for some sign of progress, Mr. Gleich of Aalen finally lost patience and reproached the Assembly for wasting time with trivialities and losing sight of the main business,[123] it was explained to him that he was quite mistaken, for the Assembly had "passed a resolution" requiring every member to "prepare himself" for a draft of the constitutional charter. As though not every deputy should have come fully prepared in the first place, and as though the passing of such a resolution was to count as work and as an answer to the question of what the Assembly had been busy doing for three months! But as we said before, on the following October 26 the Assembly would realize that it was impossible to provide the basic constitutional laws anyway, since they had not as yet been able to visit the Estates archive.

Even so, it would be wrong to say that the Assembly had been idle. In the course of its "diplomatic relations" it had been occupied with its various formalities. Since, however, such formalities are confined within the contingent limits of the positive law, which had ceased to have any reality anyway, the harder the Assembly tried to enforce legal formalism, the harder it became to find a rational content for it that could stand on its own. Thus, having already touched upon the most important aspects, nothing is left for this account but to present the main points of an historical series of events already familiar to the reader.

[THE ESTATES' BEHAVIOR TOWARD THE GOVERNMENT AFTER REJECTING THE CONSTITUTION FRAMED BY THE KING]

The king's reply followed two days after the Assembly's first petition, in which they had announced their rejection of the royal constitution in a manner intended to be "tactful" but which was in fact merely roundabout and stilted. The king simply notified them of their rights under the new constitution and reminded them that should they find anything lacking in this regard, the constitution also provided ways for them to enter requests. He also assured them that any requests and desires that proved consonant with the interests of the kingdom as a whole were sure to find favorable attention.

---

[123] *Proceedings*, sect. VIII, p. 20.

How else could the king have replied to their indistinct declaration? He had asked that they submit matters of substance, but in their reply on March 23, they persisted in formalities without content. Mr. Bolley composed a more detailed draft of their petition containing critical remarks on many points of the new charter (despite the fact that he begins by saying he will **83** refrain from a complete examination). The Assembly held this draft back, retaining it as a record of their political creed and as justification of their behavior which might, if necessary, be submitted to the ministry of state at an appropriate time.[124]

Surely nothing could have been more pressing than to submit an account of their reasons for rejecting the royal charter, and to do so precisely on the basis of a complete examination. Nor were mere "remarks" suited to furthering the cause, even if they had been submitted. Remarks are answered by *counter-remarks*, and quite apart from any concrete results, what the Assembly's so-called "diplomatic channel" would ordinarily have required were *arguments* and *counter-arguments* by the parties to the negotiation. Ignoring the fact that such exchanges cannot take place between parties whose relation is that of a government and its subjects (a relation into which admittedly the high nobility claimed not yet to have entered), the real business of an Estates Assembly is something quite different, namely the internal examination and discussion of its own issues. The proceedings might conceivably have taken a different turn from the very beginning if the ministers of state had attended the meetings and taken the floor, as provided for in §26 of the royal charter. The style of royal edicts precludes remarks, refutations, and the amplification of reasons; instead of written statements against written statements, we might have found the content of speeches delivered during the meetings by ministers and councils of state. These too could have been submitted to scrutiny and been made the subject of development and discussion. Perhaps they would even have roused the Assembly from the mute speechlessness of its paper proceedings.

In the closing plea of the Estates' petition of March 22, Count von Waldeck repeated his contrived ploy (which was neither honest nor sensible) of omitting any direct demand for the restoration of the old constitution and taking it for granted instead. Though it may seem brave and dignified not to beg in such a matter as the constitution and instead to

---

[124] Ibid., sect. I, p. 67. Upon joining the Confederation of the Rhine, Friedrich I completely reorganized the system of government. Among other things, he dissolved the *geheimen Rat* (or privy council), which had been at the heart of the old government, and replaced it with a ministry of state consisting of six sub-divisions: the foreign ministry, the ministry of the interior, ministry of justice, ministry of war, ministry of finance, and a ministry devoted to ecclesiastical matters.

create an air of indubitability, the ploy could never have succeeded. For sooner or later it would become necessary to discuss the matter directly. For the time being, the closing plea subtly refrained from making any request except that the king extend the constitution of Old Württemberg to the whole kingdom. To this end, they appended to the application a deduction of the rights of the incorporated regions to be included under the constitution of Württemberg's original territories.   84

The royal resolution had asked that the Estates make any further wishes known to the government. Now the Estates turned the tables and demanded that the government make its wishes known to them. In private legal affairs, reticence may be a sound legal tactic; rather than being the first to speak, one forces the other party to make the first move and thus reveal his claims and intentions. Thereafter the attack can be mounted without danger of losing face or exposing a weak flank. For an Estates Assembly, however, no model could be less appropriate than the tactics of advocates. Nevertheless, instead of indicating what they would have changed or added to the articles of the royal charter, the Estates entered a second subtle request for a list of modifications necessitated by the present conditions, ostensibly to the end of reaching a common understanding (as though that were all that was needed). If such a request, uttered with such confidence, is not to be taken as mockery, then it can only be an unfathomable lack of good sense. Were the Estates altogether incapable of reflecting on the fact that they were dealing with the king? How could they go their merry way without once considering that to reach any understanding at all – not to mention an understanding with the monarch and his government – it is necessary to take account of the views and the desires of the party with whom the understanding is to be reached?

The ministry responded on April 4 by announcing that the king would postpone his answer to the Estates' application until the return of the crown prince, whose voice also should be heard in the matter. On April 17, however, the king enjoined the Estates to help raise emergency war funds, and at that time he also sent them a further response in which he presented the point of view that had guided his framing of the constitution. Namely,

that in light of the state's independence from superior rule, the relations between the head of state and the Estates had been modeled after the example of other sovereign states in order to ensure the establishment of a permanent condition and to guarantee the rights of the people and the stability and efficacy of the government. No consideration was given to the question of whether the Estates' rights had been more or less extensive under Württemberg's constitution while it was still a territory of the empire, though in fact those rights proved to be greater in several substantial points under the new constitution than they had formerly been, particularly in regard to the independence of the Estates' proceedings, the extent of their participation in legislation, and even in regard to taxation, which in the days when Württemberg had been part of the empire had never been subject to approval by the Estates.

The king also announced his intention of initiating oral negotiations by authorized representatives from both sides in order to reach a common understanding as to the applicability of the Estates' motions.

As stated above, the Estates refused to help raise emergency war funds unless the government agreed to meet their demands. They saw a state bond as the means to this end. In order for the government to obtain favorable terms, a guarantee by the Estates would no doubt be instrumental. The Estates could have seized upon this situation as an opportunity to make good on their constant declarations of devotion to the fatherland, for which they were ostensibly ready to sacrifice both life and property, and to prove the truth of their good will, for such proof can only consist in deeds. Such a proof by deeds would also have facilitated a general agreement with the government and contributed toward establishing a fund for the amortization of debts. However, the Estates refused to extend the guarantee required of them; instead, on April 18 they sent the king a couple of the written statements they kept in stock, repeated their monotonous complaints, and agreed merely to elect their authorized representatives.

[THE ESTATES ASSEMBLY'S NEGOTIATING COMMITTEE AND ITS SECRET ACTIVITIES]

On April 24 the Assembly appointed a twenty-five-member committee to "prepare" for the negotiations and four commissioners to negotiate directly with the king's four councils of state. The four commissioners all appear to have been from Old Württemberg. The present turn of events seemed finally to promise more substantial developments. It immediately became evident that the committee which had been entrusted with preparing the negotiations intended to lead the negotiations themselves and instruct the Estates' commissioners as to how to proceed. The result was a de facto exclusion of the plenary assembly from the negotiations. When a member of the Assembly complained of this on April 28, saying that the committee needed to be more forthcoming about its activities, Mr. Bolley (the district notary and one of the most active members of the committee) assured him that the committee would undertake "nothing dangerous" without first consulting the Assembly, but reminded him too that negotiations required certain things to be kept "secret." Hereupon the **86** Assembly formally transferred responsibility for appointing commissioners and leading negotiations (pending ratification by the Assembly) to the committee.

The real business of the Assembly – drafting a constitution – was thus placed in the hands of the committee. We now find mention of meetings between Estates commissioners and those of the government. On April 28 and May 2, two unpublished reports by the committee are read to the Assembly; after that we hear nothing more until May 29, at which time Dr. Cotta presents a royal resolution on six articles of the constitution which had been communicated to the Estates commissioners.[125] To form a more accurate idea of the spirit and behavior of the committee, we may refer to a remarkable speech given by Mr. Gleich of Aalen on June 23,[126] from which we learn that instead of accepting the king's charter in its present form as a basis for further negotiations, the committee set down without further ado six preliminary articles. These articles were in effect, as Gleich correctly observes, fragments lifted in part from the old constitution of Württemberg and in part from the royal constitution. The supposedly "tactful," but really rather absurd, intention behind this action was apparently to pave the way for the government to acquiesce in the Estates' wishes without losing face. Equally strange is the fact that the committee kept these six articles secret from the Assembly, as can also be gathered from Gleich's speech, for it was only after several members threatened to resign in protest against the committee's secretiveness that they were *confidentially informed* of their existence. The Assembly's characteristic muteness has been remarked on above; but now, at the hands of its own committee, the Assembly was in danger not of becoming deaf, since to be deaf is not to hear when one is spoken to, but rather of having nothing to hear in the first place, since no one spoke to it! At this point it becomes impossible to imagine what the Estates Assembly's purpose and activities were supposed to be. As Gleich tells us, "no one even thought of discussing these six articles" (a fact confirmed by the *Proceedings*), and yet if anything were indispensable for an Estates Assembly, certainly such a discussion would have been! And so the proceedings went on lacking any material upon which substantial work could have been done.

---

[125] *Proceedings*, sect. VI, p. 79.   [126] Ibid., sect. VII, p. 81.

[THE SIX PRELIMINARY ARTICLES]

87 The six preliminary articles which the committee had kept secret were not made public until June 26, in a written statement by the Estates.[127] This was a turning-point in the whole affair. Since they contain matters of real substance, it is appropriate to relate the content of the articles here along with the king's resolution of May 29, which contained concessions of great importance.

[1. Estates' participation in taxation legislation and state finances]

The commissioners awkwardly referred to their first demand as "self-taxation," which they defined as including prior submission of the state's budget for the Estates' approval, an account of the royal chamber's income, and access to relevant financial records, oversight of expenditure of allocated funds, as well as the administration of funds belonging to the Estates.[128] The king had rescinded the limitations he had placed on matters requiring the Estates' concurrence and agreed to submit not only tax raises, but all taxes whatsoever, direct and indirect alike, for approval by the Estates, with the exception of the period from 1815 to 1818, in which no current tax-laws were to be repealed. Although the king refused to grant the Estates the right to levy taxes and did not agree to their having their own treasury, he did grant them oversight over state revenue and expenditure, and complete control of how revenue was to be used (with the exception of revenue from the king's private and domanial property). The king stressed that he was not opposed to a civil list on the basis of the domanial properties. Furthermore, an office for the payment of debts was to be called into existence with an equal number of deputies from the Estates and from the government.

---

[127] Ibid., sect. VIII, p. 89. Weishaar had formulated the six preliminary articles on April 24, 1815, in a meeting of the instruction committee. See Gerner, *Vorgeschichte und Entstehung*, pp. 119 ff.

[128] The following explanation of the difference between chamber income and the income of the Estates sheds light on the issues involved in the Estates' fiscal participation and oversight: "According to the constitution of most German states, especially of those in which the land estates still have a say in the determination of contributions and taxes, the state's income is divided into 'fiscal' or 'chamber income' and the income of the '*aerarium*' or the Estates. Each kind of income is destined to be used in its own special way. So-called *fiscal income* is reserved for the maintenance of the ruler's person and his family, the court and its servants, as well as for all matters concerning the ruler's sovereignty and his ability to maintain himself in a condition appropriate to it. The income of the *aerarium*, on the other hand, is intended to be used to maintain the security of the population and such measures as necessary to increase the welfare of the state. The chamber income consists of the income from the ruler's domanial properties, royal monopolies, and sovereign rights [*Hoheitsrechten*], while the Estates' income mainly consists in taxes and contributions" (translated from Johann Georg Krünitz, *Ökonomische Encyclopädie, oder allgemeines System der Staats-, Stadt, Haus- und Landwirtschaft*, 1773–1858, entry "Journal").

The liberality of the king's concessions need hardly be emphasized. We have already stated that the Estates may control the treasury in a fiefdom but not in a state. As is well known, neither the French Chambers nor the English Parliament have any such administrative rights; the French Chamber of Deputies appoints full deputies from among its members to administer cash for the amortization of debts. The Estates commissioners' use of the term "Estates' assets" instead of "state assets" served to denote the Estates' right to administer the funds as their own. By contrast, the expression "state" is incompatible with the distinction between the government and the Estates, which is characteristic of a fiefdom to the empire. Such a distinction plays no role in a state, for here private funds belong exclusively to the state once they have become taxes, i.e., public funds.[129]

[2. Restoration of church property]

The second demand was the restoration of church property. The king conceded it in whole, refusing only to restore a separate administration as had formerly been the case.

[3. Special representation of the nobility]

The third article was a form of representation in which all classes of subjects were to be represented in equal proportions. We went into some detail about the very democratic form of representation above. To this very indefinite, cryptic demand, the king replied that he expected further proposals in the matter, stating merely that he would not accede to separate representation of the nobility if that was what was intended. On the same June 23, Mr. Gleich remarks in this connection, "It is not easy to guess the commissioners' intent; it would have been only fair of them to state their

88

---

[129] What is at issue here is the contrast between the pre- or early modern and the modern state. In the pre-modern state, there is a distinction between the government (*Regierung*), frequently identified with the state as such (*Staat*), and the Estates Assembly (*Land* or *Landschaft*). In a pre-modern political entity such as Old Württemberg, the government or state is to be identified with the ruler and his court with its various administrative organs, whereas the *Land* and its representatives is essentially a body outside the state and with its own source of funds. What is lacking in such a state, Hegel is implying, is the existence of a public sphere encompassed by the state itself, such that the administration and the Estates Assembly are elements within a unified and centralized state. In the pre-modern context the distinction between funds belonging to the *Land* and those belonging to the state makes sense but, as Hegel rightly remarks, in the context of taxation by a modern state the distinction is anachronous.

intentions more plainly before the Assembly itself."[130] As late as June 23, therefore, the meaning of this article was still a secret.

[4. Payment of the members of the Assembly and its committees]

The fourth article was such as to be particularly dear to the hearts of all those members of the Estates prone to miss the old familiar committee system: it called for uninterrupted exercise of the Estates' rights by a permanent committee. The king replied that the period of four weeks set aside in the royal constitution for the committee's annual session could easily be extended and the session even be repeated if necessary. He also called the Estates' attention to the attendant increase in costs. The question of costs had been particularly important to the old committee system as well, though it might well be said that under the old system the costs were more of a tacit reason *in favor of* the extension and even the uninterrupted duration of the sessions whether they were necessary or not, but never a reason against them. Yet such considerations were probably superfluous under the old system. For in the brochure entitled *Administration of Württemberg's Estates Treasury* quoted above,[131] we find instances of the inner committee (which controlled the cash and had the right to convene the larger committee) ordering financial recompense to be made to the committee as a whole precisely *for not having convened*. In other words, the inner committee was well versed in increasing costs without there being any business to attend to and without any sessions taking place.

The public was only recently informed that the proceedings of the Estates Assembly cost the government 260,000 florins. In the published minutes we occasionally find references to a committee on members' salaries and other costs, but nothing more definite is ever quoted from the committee's reports or decisions, and specific sums are never mentioned. If there was anything that the Estates Assembly should have been absolutely open about, it was this. They should have made a point of publicizing any recompense they received for their work – or at least, that is, for their having convened. Though they ignored the other articles, the Assembly accepted this one as to their own advantage. The very fact that members of an Estates Assembly should receive salaries or allowances is highly unfavorable, and the importance of the issue should not be underestimated, for the whole character and status of a representative body can hinge on it. Salaries to

89

---

[130] *Proceedings*, sect. VII, p. 130.
[131] The German title is *Die Verwaltung der Württembergischen Landescasse.*

members of the Estates contribute to the predominance of the propertied class at elections, not to mention their bearing on the honor of such an Assembly. As long as the Estates receive a salary, they will never be above the suspicion or reproach that perhaps not all, but many or at least some of their members make their decisions with an eye to their pay. Yet in the proceedings of the Estates we never find any trace of scruples when it comes to receiving a salary. Apparently they considered it a matter of course that the deputies be salaried or at least that they have their costs reimbursed, which happened on at least one occasion. If the author remembers correctly, reproach of the practice was indeed publicly voiced. However, the most bizarre demand that an Estates Assembly could possibly have made was the right to appoint a committee with separate salaries and other regular payments – indeed to establish and decide over consular positions as they had in the old days, with the effect of legitimating the laziness and incompetence of its members in advance.

Though the Estates' leaders doubtless considered themselves to be the most qualified members for such a committee, they did not claim the full status and former rights to a secret fund. Even so, that hardly excuses them. Regular payments were to be made to those who (in the formulation of the draft for the restored constitution of Old Württemberg)

had dedicated themselves completely to the service of their fatherland and been called upon to take up residence in Stuttgart (what dedication!), but who had failed to be reappointed to the committee at the end of the three-year term and who were therefore to be paid annual recompense for their sacrifice to the fatherland until which time they should be reappointed.[132]

If the Estates' leaders had succeeded in introducing salaries for committee members and especially such regular payments, they would have restored a state of things, the abolition of which the people and the Estates themselves (with the exception of the committee members and those with prospects of being appointed to the committee) had every reason to view as the greatest single step toward a free and popular constitution in recent times.[133]

That the Estates Assembly itself would have been rendered somewhat superfluous by such a permanent committee is a consideration of perhaps even greater importance. When abuses of this kind are anchored in the very nature of the institution, the creation of laws is not sufficient to 90

---

[132] The parenthetical interpolation is Hegel's.

[133] The oligarchy of the inner committee was finally broken in 1796 as a direct result of the crisis into which the state was plunged by Württemberg's defeat in the War of the First Coalition and its consequent loss of extensive territories on the west bank of the Rhine.

prevent them. Even disregarding the spirit that would inevitably come to predominate in such a well-paid committee, historical experience with the Estates of Old Württemberg should have been sufficient: if the present Estates had reflected on the matter or given their own past experience even a moment's thought, they would have seen that the establishment of a permanent committee, far from being the talisman they took it to be, could very well turn out to be the downfall of the independent existence of the whole Assembly.

[5. The revision of legislation since 1806]

The fifth preliminary article provides for the Estates' participation in legislation from 1806 onward, i.e., it provides for a revision of all laws decreed since 1806 by a bilateral deputation consisting of representatives of both the government and the land estates. The king replied by reminding the Estates that such a revision had already been provided for in the right to petition. (The fact that the Estates demanded a revision of legislation *only since 1806*, when the old Estates Assembly had been dissolved, can be interpreted either as blind prejudice in favor of the conditions under the old constitution and blind animosity against everything that originated later with the king's initiative, or as the need to demonstrate their faith in the former and dissatisfaction with the latter.)[134] Moreover, it was strange and formally unacceptable that the revision was to be carried out only by a deputation of royal counselors and members of the Estates – in reference to whom incidentally the well-worn terms *herrschaftlich* ("of the sovereign") and *landschaftlich* ("of the Estates") are again employed. For in the case of actual legislation, the concurrence of the *whole* Estates Assembly is required, though of course it remained in the power of the Assembly to entrust committees with any preparations that might be necessary.

[6. Right of subjects to emigrate]

The sixth article pertains to liberality in the old sense of the term. The king granted anyone who wished to emigrate the right to do so at any time

---

[134] Friedrich had dissolved the Estates Assembly late in 1805, a step made possible by the imminent collapse of the Holy Roman Empire and by his own new status as the monarch of a sovereign state. When the War of the Third Coalition broke out in 1805, Friedrich had sided with the French, sending ten thousand soldiers to fight against the coalition forces; in recognition, Napoleon made Württemberg a kingdom and, soon after, a state within the Confederation of the Rhine. For the decade preceding the Assembly's constitutional proceedings, Friedrich ruled Württemberg without an Estates Assembly.

(rather than having to wait a year after giving notice of his intention, as the old constitution had required), extending this right even to serfs, who were no longer required to purchase their freedom. Since, however, emigration involved relations with other states, the king insisted on the principle of reciprocity in respect to the supplementary tax.[135]

[THE ASSEMBLY'S INTRANSIGENT REFUSAL TO ENTER DEBATE]

The Estates' negotiating commissioners submitted these articles with a peremptory statement to the effect that failure to grant them legally binding recognition would wreck any hope for a positive outcome to the negotiations and make it absolutely impossible for the Estates to co-operate in view of the troubled times. They declared that in order to reassure not only the Assembly, but the people as well and even the international public, the king would have to make a satisfactory declaration right now, or else negotiations could not be continued. It was glaringly tactless of the Assembly to refuse to co-operate in urgent affairs of the state and to block further negotiations unless the king immediately submitted to their will, but the king turned a blind eye to the fact and also overlooked the poor style of negotiating on the basis of disjointed, vague, and often sketchy preliminary articles. Instead, he graciously accommodated everything of substance in their demands, adding only that his decisions were based on "unalterable" principles and that it was on the basis of these same principles that negotiations with the Estates' deputies would continue in hopes of reaching an understanding.

The Estates did not, however, continue with negotiations. If at this point they had agreed to discussions, their previous insistence on formalities might have seemed justified by the important concessions they had wrested from the king. Even if the negotiating committee had continued to ignore the royal constitution, which either already contained most of their articles or in some cases even worked out their contents in greater detail, still it was time that the Assembly began to make up their minds about what exactly they found acceptable and what they did not. At least that might have resulted in preliminary articles of an *agreement* with – as opposed to

91

---

[135] *Freizügigkeit* was the right of a subject to emigrate without purchasing his freedom and without paying a tax to the sovereign. According to the *Deutsches Rechtswörterbuch* (ed. Eberhard, Freiherr von Kunßberg, Preussische Akademie der Wissenschaften, 1938 [Weimar: H. Böhlaus Nachfolger], vol. III), the "supplementary tax" was a contribution paid by a subject upon leaving a sovereign territory. The amount of the contribution was usually either three times the amount of the annual wealth tax the subject would have owed or a tenth of the assets which were withdrawn from taxation due to emigration, sale, gift, or inheritance.

the *subjugation* of – the king. The committee had not presented the six articles for discussion by the Assembly before submitting them to the king as non-negotiable, and neither were they discussed now that the king had responded. Rather than devote attention to the articles and the king's reply to them, three or four members of the Assembly read written statements intended as drafts for a response to the king's resolution. Their utter fixation on the goal of restoring the old constitution led the Assembly naively to believe that the king's constitution had nothing to do with them and that they need not involve themselves in discussions of it now, either, but could rest content in drafting "diplomatic notes."

In a committee meeting on May 1, Dr. Cotta read a written statement on the establishment of an Estates treasury. The matter was then brought before the Assembly and occasioned a written statement by Mr. Weishaar[136] in the meeting of May 27.[137] Cotta followed up with a further written statement on June 23, in which he argued that such a treasury, like all the other privileges of the old constitution, must not be carried to the point of interfering with the rights of the monarch, and hence that the treasury should be limited to an extent consistent with the state's credit and the dignity of the Estates. Cotta's ideas, to which he was later to return, were highly suited to a debate preparatory to passing a resolution on the king's declaration. Nonetheless, their only effect was that three weeks later and long after the Assembly had already sent answer to the king, first the district notary Bolley and eight days later Dr. Weishaar read written statements criticizing them. No vote at all took place on the matter itself.

Mr. Bolley had (as he phrased it) put his thoughts down on record, and these were read before the Assembly, who received them with warm expressions of gratitude.[138] Notably, he refers to the well-known work *The Idea of a Constitution* by the minister of state von Wangenheim,[139] which he justly praises, saying "that the rights of the people, especially in

[136] Jakob Friedrich Weishaar (1775–1834), lawyer, represented Kirchheim in the Estates Assembly from 1815 to 1817. Together with Bolley, Weishaar was a leading figure among proponents of the old constitution and served on numerous committees, among them the examining committee entrusted with compiling a legal report on the royal edict of March 17, 1815, the committee on the question of whether it was permissible to elect a vice president, the committee on the reply to the royal edict of April 16, 1815, the committee for the preparation of the constitutional negotiations with the royal commissioners, the committee for the revision and abridgement of the grievances of the country, and the committee for ensuring the recognition of the "Estates principle." From November 1815 onward he was an authorized commissioner at the constitutional negotiations.

[137] *Proceedings*, sect. VI, p. 38.   [138] Ibid., sect. IX, p. 114.

[139] Karl August, Baron von Wangenheim (1773–1850), had been called to Stuttgart in 1806 to preside over the royal financial authority; since 1811 he had been acting as a high court official and curator of the university in Tübingen. After Friedrich I adjourned the Assembly on June 26, 1815, Wangenheim intervened with the (anonymous) publication of *The Idea of a State Constitution in*

Württemberg, have found a passionate defender in this noble author."[140] Bolley's remark concerning the Estates' provisions for tax revenues are also noteworthy. He gives his word that "when the vital interests of the state demand the speedy raising of funds in extraordinary circumstances, the Estates, conscious of their urgency, will surely never fail to help the sovereign in every way they can."[141] That "surely" is rather naive: is giving *his word* a guarantee that the existence of *two* independent powers of government will not endanger the state? And when we ask what interest could have been more vital, which circumstances more extraordinary than Napoleon's reappearance in France, that "surely" will sound very naive indeed, for we have seen the manner in which Württemberg's Estates came to the aid of their sovereign and dedicated themselves to the cause of Germany and Europe just a few weeks before Bolley read his written statement and gave his word before them.

We have already had several occasions in these pages to quote Mr. Gleich's spirited and eloquent speech of June 23, so excellent in thought and spirit. Gleich presents the Assembly with more comprehensive reasons for entering into serious discussion of the six articles. He admonishes the Estates that they should be concerned not so much with Württemberg's old constitution as with framing a *good* constitution, less with legal formalism than with the substance of the laws; and instead of taking up random fragments from this or that constitution, he proceeds to give a reasoned

---

its Application to Württemberg's Old Estates Constitution and a Proposal for its Renewal [*Die Idee der Staatsverfassung in ihrer Anwendung auf Württembergs alte Landesverfassung und den Entwurf zu deren Erneuerung*], in which he adapted Montesquieu's doctrine of the separation of powers to suit conditions in Württemberg. Wangenheim was influenced by Schelling's philosophy of nature, and organicist metaphors abound in the work, which develops the idea that the various Estates are representative each of a peculiar form of life all of which are meant to flow together in the integrated life of the state, creating a harmony of functions. Wangenheim recommended a bicameral system with separate representation of the nobility in an upper house. When Friedrich I reconvened the Assembly on October 15, he appointed Wangenheim to negotiate with the Estates. Wangenheim won the loyalty of a small group of moderate constitutionalists within the Estates Assembly, notably Friedrich Cotta, the publisher, and Ludwig Griesinger, a prominent Stuttgart advocate. After Friedrich I's death in October of 1816, he was succeeded by Wilhelm I, who made Wangenheim and Karl Friedrich Kerner ministers of state. This very liberal administration was, however, short-lived. Wangenheim lost his post in June of 1817, after negotiations had once more ground to a halt, and his recommendation of a plebiscite on the royal constitutional draft failed to produce results. Wangenheim was replaced by Theodor Eugen Maucler, a conservative bureaucrat who was destined to be the architect of the agreement between crown and Estates that paved the way to a constitution in 1819. (Cf. Rolf Grawert, "Der württembergische Verfassungsstreit 1815–1819," in *"O Fürstin, der Heimath! Glükliches Stutgard." Politik, Kultur und Gesellschaft im deutschen Südwesten um 1800*, ed. Otto Pöggeler and Christoph Jamme [Stuttgart: Klett-Cotta, 1988], pp. 126–158 and especially Dieter Wyduckel, "Die Idee des Dritten Deutschlands im Vormärz. Ein Beitrag zur trialistischen Verfassungskonzeption des Freiherrn von Wangenheim," ibid., pp. 159–183.)

[140] *Proceedings,* sect. IX, p. 124.   [141] Ibid., p. 135.

account of the essential principles of a constitution. The Assembly was taken aback by the tenor of Gleich's speech, which was foreign to their fixed ideas, their incessant self-congratulation, and the praises heaped on them by the papers. His courage certainly did not endear him to the Assembly, as was noted above; his voice died away in the desert while half a dozen written statements were written rebuking him for his plea "at least to take the royal resolution into serious consideration and not simply throw away the offers made by the king, some of which were acceptable." From this point on, Gleich disappears from the meetings, with no further explanation in the minutes of why he left; some time later he is replaced by another representative from Aalen. Such irregularities are typical of the Assembly: deputies resign their posts and are replaced by others, and there is never an indication of the authority to which the resignations were submitted or on which the new deputy assumed his post. In Gleich's case, more than a year later we find a dubious remark by a member of the Assembly, in which he warns another deputy with an opinion different from that of the majority not to forget what happened to Mr. Gleich.

By rejecting Mr. Gleich's motion, the Assembly also rejected the opportunity which the king's resolution had offered to them of acknowledging their agreement on substantial points and thus of laying a sound foundation for further negotiations. They discussed neither the issues themselves nor the question which of the king's decisions were acceptable and which were not. Instead, they spent several meetings debating which written statements they should append to their reply and under which titles to compose them, and similar formalities. On June 26, four weeks after receiving the royal resolution, they were finally done writing a reply.[142] Yet again, this reply contained no instructions to the Estates' negotiators on how to respond to the king's decisions, for it was another petition to the king. Thus the Assembly fell back into their old litigious ways, though they had led nowhere and should have been given up in favor of oral negotiations with the royal commissioners.

The king's concessions are not even mentioned in the petition. It is filled instead with grandiloquent expressions of the "utter disappointment" of all the Assembly's hopes, their "unspeakable pain" and "consternation," their dearly held "convictions," and self-congratulatory avowals of their unadulterated love of truth and the purity of their motives, to which they would one day bear witness before the throne of God, and so on. As far as the royal resolution itself was concerned, their position was

---

[142] *Proceedings*, sect. VIII, pp. 58 ff.

as straightforward as it was naive: the royal resolution was incompatible with the principle of the Estates. The petition concludes dramatically by requesting, nay beseeching, the king in the name of God and all that is holy and venerable, and for the sake of the royal family's own happiness, to refuse no longer to restore the old constitution. (Mr. Gleich had abstained from any admixture of such empty pathos in his speech, displaying that much more reason; but reason had failed to achieve the desired effect, and perhaps Gleich would have had more success if he had resorted to such pathos, though he could not have achieved more than merely to prevent the insinuation of ulterior motives.) In the rest of the text, the Estates bring forth the usual arguments based on positive law and contractual relations. They especially draw the king's attention to the fact that he had "solemnly sworn" to uphold the constitution upon becoming head of state, just as all rulers before him had done. They add that in spite of diligent efforts to determine whether any change had taken place that would legally free him from his obligations, they had been unable to find any. That they should have been more conscientious in their search ought to have been clear to them, for as things stood they were on the verge of arrogating the authority to charge their sovereign with perjury against his whole people – an authority from which they ought better to have recoiled.

94

[THE "GRIEVANCES OF THE PEOPLE"]

The petition was notable for its appendix which, in addition to two written statements, contained as a third supplement what was in effect a book of 162 pages in small print containing the "grievances of the people."[143] The members had worked on this book for many weeks and stockpiled grievances of all kinds and from every quarter. The book is revealing if only because the Estates considered it to be their most important work, the one by which they believed themselves to have fulfilled their most sacred duty and incontrovertibly justified their behavior toward the king. It is hardly possible here to go into the details of this lurid specimen of pressuring and complaining. Without even beginning to question the accuracy of the factual claims made in the book, one might at least have distinguished between real grievances and the merely putative ones obviously based on the authors' judgment of the utility and harmfulness of government institutions. And then there would be the task of deciding how much of the burden of taxation was the government's fault (to the extent that

---

[143] Ibid., pp. 91–252.

the complaints were at all based in fact) and how much was due to the general hardship and misfortune of the times. For not to mention the unreasonableness of many of the complaints, there was hardly a region of Germany that was above blaming the government for what was in reality the consequence of the unprecedented events and developments of the past twenty-five years. The list of grievances compiled by the Estates goes to show how ill-informed they were as to the financial needs of the state and the condition of its finances, for the grievances were lodged without troubling to compare the level of taxation with the extent of the state's needs. Furthermore, in the case of those grievances which were at all justified, one should have determined whether it was the demise of the old constitution of Württemberg that had actually caused the problems, since that was the claim that the book was supposed to prove in the first place or, to be more precise, the truth of which it assumed from the outset. Finally, there was no trace of an argument showing that the royal constitution with its concessions to the Estates was incapable of adequately redressing the grievances, much less that they were bound to continue if that constitution was accepted. Such an argument would have formed the only possible backbone to all the remonstrations this mass of grievances was intended to substantiate, and yet it did not even occur to anyone to make it.

The investigation of all these issues, however, though justice might seem to demand it, proves superfluous as soon as we recognize an inherent flaw in the Estates' book of grievances that rendered it utterly inconsequential. Not to digress, the *gravamina of the people* or *cahiers de doléances* were a familiar article in the business of the Estates under the Holy Roman Empire. Equally familiar is their ineffectualness. Every new *Landtag* and *Reichstag*[144] found the mass of grievances left unfinished by the last and piled new ones upon it. The Estates or parliaments were in the habit of indulging themselves in the name of duty and conscience in endlessly digressive formulations of grievances; and the governments were in the habit of receiving such lists from the Estates, together with the notices of budget approval. Thus the lists of complaints finally grew to such an extent and both sides became so inured to them that the sending and receiving of these masses of paper finally sank to a mere formality. The author recalls reading somewhere how during the legal conflict between Duke Carl of Württemberg and his estates in Vienna in 1768 the imperial court council in Vienna passed on

---

[144] The *Reichstag* was the Imperial Diet of the Holy Roman Empire. It became an official institution in 1495, meeting at intervals in Regensburg. From 1663 until the demise of the empire in 1806, it remained permanently in session.

the Estates' collection of grievances to the duke's commissioners.[145] The commissioners replied that the court council should not be surprised at the quantity of the grievances, for the authors of such *gravamina* had been competing with each other for generations to exceed and outdo each other in the severity of their descriptions, and that if one were to believe their exaggerated accounts, the country would have been completely ruined a century ago.

The royal constitution had opened new avenues for the Estates Assembly to work toward actually ridding Württemberg of its problems instead of simply filing grievances, but the Estates, stuck as they were in the legal principles and protocols of the old constitution, preferred to continue on their well-trod path and compile their list of disputes. They could not have reconciled actually improving things with their conscience, since to have engaged in any kind of productive work would have been tantamount to recognizing the new constitution. In any case, it is easier to amass grievances than to come up with constitutional and legislative initiatives, which alone could have improved conditions in any substantial way. The merit to be gained by actual legislation is meager and hard-won, and it was by far the easier course for the Assembly to ease their conscience by telling themselves that what they were doing was their duty. Minor problems caused, say, by the excessive protection of wild game and hunting (which seem to have been bad enough, anyway) can perhaps be solved by mere complaining, since all that is needed is an order from the king to shoot the animals. Indeed, the transactions show that the king gave orders to deal with the problem, "for the solution of which he was immediately responsible," as soon as it was brought to his attention in March.[146] Later on, when the Estates came to doubt the effectiveness of the king's measures, they rightly renewed their complaints. But since they treated everything else they deemed unjust or harmful about the institutions and the administration of the government in the same way, namely by lodging formal complaints, it looked as though they expected the king to solve these problems, too, by giving orders to shoot.

Drawing attention to abuses and misgovernment is not completely without merit; it is liable to reproach, however, when divorced from positive

---

[145] Duke Carl Eugen had dissolved Württemberg's Estates Assembly in 1763 after they refused financial support to his plans for enlarging the army. The Estates successfully appealed to the imperial court council in Vienna, the highest court in the Holy Roman Empire, to force Carl Eugen to grant the Estates Assembly renewed formal recognition. In the so-called *Erbvergleich* of 1770, the court council found Carl Eugen guilty on all counts.

[146] *Proceedings*, sect. II, p. 57.

efforts to contribute to their improvement by making considered suggestions for corrective legislation. In one session of talks on the written
statements appended to the petition of June 26,[147] someone even expressed
the worry that the king might really act on the grievances and thus divert
attention away from their main goal of restoring the old constitution. In
response to this doubt, Count von Waldeck moved that the petition be
modified in such a way as to ensure that the government would not act on
it, whereupon Mr. Bolley came up with appropriate phraseology: the petition was to state "that the Estates will not permit themselves to be diverted
from their highest goal and only concern by negotiations over individual
grievances, though it was in the way of fulfilling their most sacred duty that
97   they lodged the grievances." Had the grievances been dealt with through
negotiations, they would have been enough to keep negotiators busy for
years, or rather indefinitely, since there was no longer any imperial court
council to intervene and end the proceedings. Yet what was the point of
the whole ballast of formal grievances if the Estates had no intention of
getting involved either in the business of legislation or in so-called negotiations? The fact was that this ballast served no other purpose than to
give the Estates an opportunity to fulfill their "sacred duty," as they called
it. They had another duty, as well, more sacred, albeit less comfortable,
namely the duty to take steps toward legislation that would remedy present
conditions; but of this duty no one spoke. On July 21 the king replied in
the only way he could have, by saying that he had no choice but to base
his decision regarding the complaints on the information given him by his
ministries.[148]

[THE ABUSES OF THE NOTARY SYSTEM]

One among the many grievances touches upon what was referred to as
the abuses of the notary institute. Von Forstner's[149] untiring admonitions
served to single out the subject within the "melancholy litany of grievances"

---

[147] Ibid., sect. VIII, p. 8.   [148] Ibid., sect. X, p. 14.

[149] Georg Ferdinand Forstner von Dambenois (1765–1832) represented Gerabronn in the Estates
Assembly from 1815 to 1817. Together with Bolley and Weishaar he served on the examining
committee entrusted with compiling a legal report on the royal edict of March 17, 1815 and on
the committee for composing a petition in response to it. He was especially active in the inquiry
into the abuses of the notary system, introducing seven motions for its reform. In 1816–17 von
Forstner was co-editor of the journal *Württembergisches Archiv*; from 1817 on he was professor of
state economy (*Staatswirtschaft*) at the University of Tübingen.

and to illuminate it from its various sides. His report introduces us to an institution peculiar to Württemberg, the notary institute, and exposes legal, moral, and intellectual conditions that can only be described as a swamp and which shed light on the nature of the Estates' interest in restoring the "good old constitution."[150]

Since the notary system exercised wide-spread influence it is worthwhile to consider it more closely here. As early as May 15, von Forstner criticized the influence of the so-called notaries on the running of the government as a "plague upon the land" and declared the evil to be rooted in the very heart of Württemberg's old Estates constitution, which left the notaries "wide margin for unprincipled behavior, oppression, and swindle."[151] A committee was formed and entrusted with compiling a report with recommendations for the improvement of the institute. When six weeks passed without further mention of the matter, von Forstner repeated his motion on June 28, remarking that even if the one or other honorable principal among the notaries happened to deplore the abuses, he would still not be able to prevent them and would not dare to express a desire for reform, knowing that that would desecrate the old constitution, into whose very fabric the abuses were woven. He adds that the people of Württemberg would never (and that means even if the old constitution were restored – indeed, especially if it were to be restored) experience any relief as long as these abuses continued, for they were insufferable and more than enough to drive the common man to desperation. He adduces unimpeachable evidence that those abuses had always been the cause of the frequent emigration of Old **98** Württemberg's subjects (for there had been a constant departure of emigrants under the regency of all the different Württembergian monarchs even during the flowering of the old Estates constitution). What else but the constitution, he exclaims, could have caused them to leave the country? What was it about the constitution that was so insufferable to them? What made them so desperate? Nothing but the extortion by the caste of notaries. And it was the constitution that authorized this caste to oppress the subjects as they did.

---

[150] As Hegel will later remark, in many cases the leaders of the Estates and members of the inner committee were themselves either notaries or were linked to notaries by familial or professional relations, so that they stood to profit directly or indirectly from the abuses inherent in the system and thus in the constitution in which it was rooted. In 1815, of the roughly seventy-one elected deputies (their number varied slightly), nearly half were advocates (thirty to be exact) and roughly a quarter notaries (eighteen in all): cf. Gerner, *Vorgeschichte und Entstehung*, pp. 49 ff.

[151] *Proceedings*, sect. V, p. 58.

When von Forstner later renews his motion for a third time,[152] he cites a passage from a report by the former governor von Gemmingen[153] to the effect that "in comparison with other states, Württemberg has the sorry distinction of nourishing a race of people unknown to the rest of Germany since the times of Dr. Faustus, the notaries."

"The burden this race presents for the working class of people," he goes on, "is made heavier by the impudence with which they vie for the highest offices of the state when opportunity presents itself, and the malice with which they deprive the poorest class of nourishment when confronted by misfortune. Either way, they live only from the labor of others." In a most remarkable and detailed report from the superior district of Horb,[154] we read that the annual income of the notary institute was on average as much as six or seven times higher than the annual tax.

This account of things naturally stood in stark contrast to the tone of the Assembly with its talk of Württemberg's three hundred years of happiness under and by virtue of the former Estates Assembly, and with its constant assurance that restoring the old constitution was the simple remedy for all the many complaints. To many, this one single "plague" must have seemed to outweigh all the others together. The contrast between von Forstner's account and the Assembly's enthusiasm for the old constitution is even stronger, for we must not forget that a good many of its members (including leading personalities such as Bolley) held high positions in the dynasty of the notaries, while most of the other elected deputies either had brothers, sons, or other relatives among the notaries, or at least could have hoped that their sons and family members might some day enjoy the privileges of this "plague upon the land."

Nevertheless, the Assembly had agreed to examine the matter and appointed a committee to do so. The reader may therefore find it surprising – and then again, he may not – that the manner in which the committee prosecuted the matter was altogether dilatory. Von Forstner's second motion resulted in nothing more than an admonition to the committee to speed up its work. After the Assembly was adjourned on July 27,

---

152 Ibid., sect. XVI, p. 84.
153 Ludwig Eberhard Freiherr von Gemmingen (1750–1829) was a non-elected member (*Virilstimm-berechtigter*) in the Estates Assembly.
154 *Proceedings*, sect. XIX, pp. 26 ff. As part of his sweeping reforms of government and administration, Friedrich I had reorganized Württemberg into sixty-five administrative units of approximately twenty thousand inhabitants, each called superior districts (*Oberämter*). They replaced the former districts (*Ämter*) and differed from them in that superior-district lines were drawn with an eye to geographical features and administrative need exclusively, with no consideration of historical or social bonds.

no more was done in the matter until it was reconvened on October 16.[155] Von Forstner was persistent, though, and on December 5 other deputies gave him their support. At one point two district notaries, against one of whom serious charges were brought soon after,[156] petitioned the Assembly to better provide for their class, which, they claimed, had had the most beneficial influence on the state of Württemberg and its people for centuries past and to have set it apart from all other lands.[157] Other unpublished petitions, however, which were sufficiently numerous as to fairly represent the general opinion of New Württemberg,[158] implied that of all the grievances of the people the caste of the notaries was the worst (they gave ample evidence in support of this), so that "the Assembly ought to establish institutions that will make it unnecessary for the caste of the notaries to spend night and day thinking up ways of pillaging the citizenry and to make their living by extorting and impoverishing the subjects of Württemberg." All these petitions contain shocking accounts and condemn the oppression by the notaries in the strongest possible terms.

At the time these petitions for help against the notaries' exploitation, cheating, and pillaging started to come in, the Assembly's main occupation consisted in writing remonstrations against the king's collection of the yearly tax of 1815–16. The complaints about the insufferable plague and pillaging wrought on the desperate people by the notary institute came in the midst of the Estates' campaign to lower their financial contributions to the government, creating the impression that the government's taxes were getting in the way of the notary institute's collecting the separate taxes it imposed on the subjects. On April 24, 1816, after nothing had happened in the matter for nearly a year, von Forstner again recalled it to the Assembly in an unpublished written statement. A report had been promised by the speaker of the committee entrusted with investigating the notaries' abuses; it was to contain a list of all the relevant grievances. However, although the Assembly had needed but a few weeks to bring together their mass of grievances about every single branch of government, after more than a year the promised report had never yet appeared.[159]

---

[155] Provoked by the Assembly's insistence on a separate Estates treasury and the establishment of a permanent committee, and not least by the Assembly's claim that the old constitution had not been rendered defunct by the events of 1805 that led to Württemberg's promotion to a kingdom under Friedrich's rule, the king adjourned the Assembly on July 26, 1815, only three months after it had been convened. When Prussia, Hanover, and Austria exerted pressure, however, he agreed to reconvene the Assembly on October 15, 1815.

[156] *Proceedings*, sect. XIX, p. 27.   [157] Ibid., sect. XVIII, p. 27.   [158] Ibid., pp. 95 ff.

[159] *Proceedings*, sect. XXII, p. 7; sect. XXV, appendix, p. 54.

What did appear was an assessment by Consul Griesinger,[160] published separately as an appendix to the twenty-fifth section (pp. 192 ff.). In the course of several meetings from June 11 till July 15, this assessment was read to the Assembly one piece at a time. Apart from an objection by Dr. Weishaar on August 6 to a motion in the previous meeting (of which no mention whatsoever is to be found in the minutes of that meeting) and a few isolated remarks here and there, the Assembly undertook nothing more in this important matter for the remaining duration of its existence.

Consul Griesinger begins his detailed assessment with the remark that he will refrain from painting the sorrowful picture of the "scandalous and almost incredible facts concerning the notary institute that have been amassed in the petitions and written statements received by the Estates, since another member of the Assembly has already taken this task upon himself." (As noted before, the said depiction never saw the light of day.) Nevertheless, Griesinger's assessment, together with the handful of published petitions, still contains enough to illustrate the truly "extraordinary and almost incredible" nature of this famous Württembergian institution and its relation to the constitution of the Estates. Since the author takes an historical approach, the office of the court notaries, which is very old, gives him occasion to speak of the courts of Old Württemberg and offer his opinion of them. These are of sufficient interest that the present author cannot forbear presenting some part of the history of the courts before coming to the matter of the notaries themselves.

Chancellor Naucler,[161] who lived at the end of the fifteenth century, composed a chronicle, from which Consul Griesinger cites the following passage on the constitution of the courts:

---

[160] Ludwig Friedrich Griesinger (1767–1845), chancellery advocate and director of the superior municipal court of Stuttgart, represented the district of Stuttgart in the Estates Assembly from 1815 to 1817. He served on numerous committees, including the committee for the preparation of the constitutional negotiations with the royal commissioners, the committee for the revision and abridgement of the grievances of the people, the committee for ensuring the recognition of the "Estates principle," and the committee for the examination of Heinrich Maximilian Gleich's criticisms of the Assembly. Together with Cotta, Griesinger was for a time a proponent of Wangenheim's constitutional proposals, and on June 2, 1817, he voted to accept the new constitutional draft. The assessment discussed by Hegel is to be found in the appendix of section 25 of the *Proceedings of the Estates Assembly of the Kingdom of Württemberg* under the title "Report by Representative Griesinger" ["Vortrag des Repräsentanten Griesinger"].

[161] The reference is to Johannes Naucler (1425–1510), the young Count Eberhard's supervisor and the first chancellor of the University of Tübingen, famous among sixteenth-century humanists for his *World Chronicle*, published posthumously in 1516.

In each city, market town, and village, twelve men who have distinguished themselves by their integrity and honorable conduct are selected as judges regardless of whether they are literate, and those who take the office of a judge upon themselves do so purely for the sake of honor, for they receive no remuneration or wages. For the sake of the common good they sit in judgment on the appointed days, putting their own affairs last, and each swears to act according to that which he deems better and more just. They hear the cases in the presence of the local magistrate and after hearing both sides until they are satisfied they pass judgment, not by applying the laws (that is, what used to be called *leges imperatorum*), of which they have no knowledge at all, but rather as reason and the customs of the courts dictate.[162]

But do not *ratio* and *consuetudo judicorum*, and the *coutumes* (or customary right) contain laws? Importing foreign rights also meant importing learned   **101** consuls into the courts, and thus in the course of time the courts in which *equal* and *honorable* men had administered justice *for the sake of honor* and *not for money* were so far reduced that it ultimately became necessary to abolish them.

For Griesinger, Naucler's noble account is nothing more than a "vivid portrayal of the ignorance" of Württemberg's courts in those days, and he goes on to explain that

in courts with judges like the ones just described, the business of the court notaries could only consist in recording crude and foolish judgments by the ignorant judges of a barbaric age, for today the many (many indeed!) reasonable extensions and limitations of the laws render anyone who has not studied law (such as the members of the jury in England and France, where this institution is revered as a hallmark of freedom)[163] incapable of finding a verdict in a complicated law-suit.

Evidently, the resurrection of the glory of early German history and of authentic national institutions is not to be expected from a legally educated member of a German Estates Assembly who has views such as these. The triumph of the new laws, "of the young and courageous Ulpians and the defeats of Württemberg's judges," are recounted in more detail on p. 31.[164]

---

[162] Hegel quotes this lengthy passage in the original Latin: "In singulis urbibus, oppidis et villis duodecim *viri, vitae integritate ac honestate praecipui*, eliguntur in judices, nullo habito respectu, *an sciant literas, nec non*, qui munus judicum necessario subeunt, *licet remunerationem seu mercedem nullam habeant, propter honorem. Sed pro bono communi*, suis posthabitis negotiis, statutis diebus judiciis intendunt, *jurantque* singuli, se *facturos* secundum *quod eis visum fuerit justius ac melius*, et praesente magistratu loci causas audiunt, partibusque ad satietatem auditis sententiam dicunt, non ut leges censent [that is, what used to be called *leges imperatorum*], quorum nullam notitiam habent, sed prouti *ratio et consuetudo judiciorum dictat*."

[163] The parenthetical interpolations are Hegel's.

[164] The "new laws" refers to Württemberg's first general code of law, decreed by Count Eberhard im Bart in 1495. Eberhard reorganized the administrative structures of the state, including its court

"The early German legal system and customs were in no way comparable to Roman law. The simple-mindedness of a crude and uncultivated people of the dark ages cannot help but seem laughable and even despicable when compared to the wisdom of the greatest and most sublime jurists of Rome and the ancient world." Is the spirit of traditional German customs[165] alive and revered in tones such as these? Griesinger ridicules the *Landtag* of 1515 for its bitter complaints against the learned "who are making such inroads into the courts throughout the land that someone in need of an advocate must pay ten florins today for what cost ten shillings twelve years ago. If this goes on, soon every village will need one or two learned doctors to administer justice." Futile complaints, for "death had been sworn to the old German mores." Instead of one or two learned doctors, however, it was 102 the notaries who were sent to every village in Württemberg, and we need not look far in order to decide whether the citizens profited from these new mores which were so different from those of old Germany.

Griesinger defines the notaries, who are the proper subject of this account, as legal and economic practitioners, the peculiarity of Württemberg's notaries being that they did not have a university law degree. As far as that goes, however, the case was more or less the same in other states, since the duties of a notary do not for the most part require a university education. As Griesinger's assessment shows, it was actually something else that set Württemberg's notaries apart. Every area of jurisdiction had either a town notary or a district notary (larger towns had a notary of their own, while the rest of the district had the usual district notary) whose monopoly it was to record all the legal and otherwise official business conducted in the district. For the administration of a superior district, especially the departments of justice and the police,[166] the economic administration

---

system. As a result of the greatly increased use of written documents a special office was created, called the *Kanzlei* and directed by legally trained specialists. It is no doubt to these legal specialists that Griesinger refers eponymously as "Ulpians." Domitius Ulpianus was one of the last great Roman jurists, assassinated in 228, likely as a result of his plans for a reform that would severely restrict the privileges of the praetorian guard. Ulpianus wrote encyclopaedically on all branches of the law (nearly 280 books) and was a major source for the compilers of Justinian's *Digesta*. (Cf. the *Oxford Classical Dictionary*, ed. N. G. L. Hammond and H. H. Scullard [Oxford: Clarendon Press, 2nd ed., 1970], p. 1103.)

[165] In the German original the phrase is *Geist deutscher Volkstümlichkeit*. *Volkstümlichkeit* is derived from *Volk*, "the people," and can, in the context, perhaps best be understood as signifying a national identity rooted in popular tradition.

[166] *Polizei* in early modern German usage has a much wider meaning than the corresponding term in modern German or English. In addition to security and law enforcement, early modern German police were responsible for matters as diverse as maintenance of public thoroughfares, public health issues, canalization, and the navigability of waterways – in short, all things implicated in the welfare of the *polity*.

and the forestry department, the employment of notaries is a necessity they have in common with other states. What was peculiar to Württemberg was that here such assistants were never recruited from among those who had studied law, economy, or forestry at the university; the notaries' only education consisted in learning the routine, and they were never destined to head the department in which they were employed. The department of forestry, for instance, had always been in the hands of the nobility, and so a burgher assistant could never aspire to the office of the forester.

On the other hand, whereas in other states university graduates with a law degree were required by law to gain practical skills as interns for one or more years before taking on a permanent position in a department, Württemberg had no such legal requirement. Indeed, Griesinger's assessment frequently mentions that jurists with a university degree were far too haughty ever to work as assistants to a government official. A petition from the town of Urach, lodged with the Estates Assembly, contains the complaint that the (unusually large) territory of the superior district, whose seat had previously been Urach, had been reduced. Among other similarly brilliant thoughts, the petition expresses the idea that the use of the many smaller superior districts lay in providing inexperienced jurists from the university with preparatory training. And training for what? Why, for the administration of larger superior districts! As though there were any difference besides mere quantity; in terms of quality, the tasks are the same. By that reasoning, the citizens of smaller jurisdictions would be the *animae viles* destined to be practiced on by inexperienced staff for the sole reason of their belonging to a geographically smaller superior district. Considering that in Württemberg it was the notaries who were responsible for the legal practice which elsewhere was overseen by university-educated jurists being trained under seasoned officials, it is hardly surprising that they were so important both for their inexperienced superiors and in their own right: in a district of twenty thousand and more, their educated superior, who was the police force, administrative branch, and legislative power in one person, had no one but notaries on whom to rely.

The monopoly granted to the town and district notaries is the most prominent subject in Griesinger's portrayal of the notary system – or rather the *abuses* of that system, for in the grievances and petitions the term "notary abuses" practically takes on the status of a recognized, technical expression for the notary institute. In order to exercise this monopoly, they employed anywhere from ten to twenty notaries, some of whom worked in the main office, while others were sent out to the townships and villages in order to work there. For a detailed list of their various duties, Griesinger's

103

assessment should be consulted. In any case, these included the distribution of taxes, filling out tax forms and tax receipts, the calculation of the taxable assets of individual citizens, recording transfers of title due either to the sale of houses and estates or to marriage, and also the distribution of local expenditures due to the so-called town and district "damage."[b] However, there were two kinds of duties which seem to have been the special focus of the notaries' oppression and abuses.

First, they were in charge of the files of the non-contentious jurisdiction and of contracts, marriage agreements, here especially wills, inventories of the assets brought into the marriage by newly wedded husbands and wives, estate auction inventories, divisions of inheritances, and so on. Regarding divisions of inheritances we read for instance on p. 65 that the value of most of them was less than the fee for the notary's paperwork. Thus the best piece of the property was often publicly sold to raise cash money [sc. to pay the fee]. Newly-weds fared no better. Either the inventory fee consumed the money they had managed to save before they were married or the couple had to go into debt at the outset of their marriage or sell a piece of land etc. The effect of such procedures was the general impoverishment of the lower class. An unwed married couple,[167] for example, is forbidden by law in Württemberg to take inventory themselves or to have a person of their choice do so and then have the list notarized. Only the notary-monopolist is authorized to take their inventory. We shall soon see how lengthy and expensive such inventories can be. The petitions and other documents are filled with complaints unanimously criticizing both the relevant legislation (whose very nature entailed endless accounting and unspeakable costs) and the swindling and other abuses that multiplied the legally permissible costs ten times over.

The notaries' other occupation was keeping the accounts for the office of the chief accountant and the municipality, the accounts of the charities, ecclesiastic assets, and asylums, in short all the accounts pertaining to the church and to endowments for the poor, as well as being responsible for probating and reviewing the accounts of the municipalities and legal guardians. Here we find a very peculiar situation in which the chief accountants and others in charge of managing the various assets of the local government, charity, and so on were not permitted to keep their own

104

---

[b] [Footnote in the original:] According to this terminology the building of a bridge, town hall, and the like would be referred to as "damage."

[167] Literal translation of *unverheiratetes Ehepaar*. Hegel appears to be referring to a couple engaged to be married.

financial records or to have someone of their choice do so; they had to have it done by the district notary's book-keeping factory. The costs were borne by the municipality, and here for once the term "district damage" seems quite appropriate.

Shocking examples of these costs are adduced in the assessment. In one case, a municipality in New Württemberg was charged 50 florins for an account which would have cost only 30 crowns before the introduction of Old Württemberg's notary system. The notaries were artful enough to find sufficient accounting to run up a bill of 56 florins and 20 crowns to a hamlet which, lacking revenue, had formerly had no need of any accounting at all.[168] These and many other examples would make for entertaining reading if only they were not at the same time such outrageous cases of cheating and swindling. Just one more example: the town notary of a place called Mögglingen had entrusted several different of his notaries in turn with the municipal financial records. The local municipality ended up paying these various notaries a sum of 900 florins just for reading the files, without their having yet written a single word. That was the price of the account before ever a line of it had even been written, and naturally the man who finally actually wrote it also had to be paid. One of the most striking complaints of all those filed with the Estates Assembly concerns the steep rise in the cost of managing the municipalities' assets, the endowment for the poor, and so on. What is striking is that the rise in costs is attributed to the demise of the old constitution. To judge from the information brought together about the notary system, these complaints were mainly lodged in the new regions of Württemberg, and the detailed municipal accounts (which are reproduced in the assessment) also show that the enormous rise in costs was due solely to the introduction of this Old Württembergian nuisance.

Many more instances of such unlawful service charges and of the excessive length and unnecessary detail of the accounts could be cited – among others the fact that, since the accounts for the municipal charity had to be filled out in duplicate and triplicate, the notaries charged the full fee for each copy, counting even the craftsmen's bills two and three times over. This habit of milking the citizens for all they were worth by every possible means, be it legal or not, is the basis for the shocking picture of the notaries' mores, their ignorance, brutality, ruthlessness, and arrogance painted on pp. 9 ff. On p. 40 we read "that the profession had never at any time been respected in Württemberg. Implicit in the admiration occasionally shown for one or the other deserving individual was always the disdain for the profession as

105

---

[168] *Proceedings*, sect. XVIII, pp. 99 f.

a whole, for a virtuous notary was always a rarity." The harsh tones in the very first chapter of the assessment are not so much Griesinger's own as they are the unanimous testimony culled from many sources old and new on this peculiarly Württembergian profession. Among those sources are even authors who themselves belong to the profession and so presumably knew it best. Nothing worse can be said of a class of people than what is contained in these depictions.

Most drastic of all, however, is the fact that the principal (i.e., the town or district notary) had to be paid the same amount again that the notaries he sent abroad had been able to earn or extort by their own work. Here we have a situation in which the principal not only has the monopoly on all accounting done in his district, but also has to be paid the same amount again that his notaries earn for themselves – prices which in themselves had already been cause for bitter complaint. Thus the very man supposed to be supervising the actions of his subordinates was exacting payment from the citizens not as wages for his labor, but as a kind of tribute to his dynasty. The duty paid to the town or district notary was separate from the tax placed on accounting documents by the sovereign, and it went into his private pocket. As Griesinger correctly states (p. 137), "The subaltern notaries are the town and district notaries' money makers and the latter have everything to gain by the illegal and incommensurate actions of their subordinates. A worse arrangement than this can hardly be imagined." One is reminded of a fiefdom or dynasty in which town and district notaries exact duty from the citizens as though they were their subjects or indeed *vassals*, as they might be termed. The analogy seems especially apt in cases like the one described on p. 57. Last year a district notary charged a tenant who had inherited the estate of his brother, a catholic priest, 200 florins, although the man had been exempted both from filing an inventory and from dividing the inheritance. The notary was able to do this because the exemption did not legally free the man from the obligation of paying the *fees* for the division of the inheritance. We are told that the heir actually paid the amount and that the district notary pocketed the money without ever having spilled a drop of ink. We do not hear, though, of this act of extortion ever having been punished by forced recompense, prison, or any other penalty. In the feudal system the duties owed to the lord are based on his prior rights to the land, but they also oblige the lord in turn to protect his vassals. By contrast, the fees of the town and district notaries were unencumbered by any such obligations. If Württemberg's citizens were really afflicted by this bondage or serfdom to the notaries (as seems de facto to have been the case; the Estates were in any case unable to deny it), it would at least have been more practical (and more just) to

106

have given the state the advantage of this subjection and to have leased the monopoly to the notaries in the name of the sovereign[c] instead of allowing private citizens to pocket what was essentially a duty and not wages for labor. Indeed, some of the notaries amassed fortunes that put them on the footing of a bishop in France or Austria![169]

We have already mentioned that the chief accountants and other heads of local councils, those in charge of charity funds and so on, did not keep their own accounts since this was the privilege of the notaries. This significantly hobbled local officials and trustees. However, more significant and even more important than the increased expense to the municipalities and their various charitable funds was the fact that the heads of local councils were thus thoroughly dependent on the town and district notaries. This state of things presented a serious interference with the organism of the state. In a petition from Gmünd[170] we find a depiction based on official documents revealing how egregious the notaries' abuses were in this regard as well.[d] In reference to a particular notary we read the following account:

107

In the case of the municipal accounts, the notary took possession of all the documents of the journal,[171] and the deposits and receipts of the accountant, without giving any receipt of his own for them. From that moment on, the chief accountant was his slave. He could no longer sleep, for the thought that his credit, honor, and reputation were in the hands of a stranger tormented him continuously. There were some who demanded pay advances and then left the country for another part of the empire. If the notary handed over the files to a successor, a period of suffering ensued for the accountant. Funds suddenly seemed to have been used improperly, receipts came up missing, a deficit opened up. The accountant's future lay in the dungeon or the prison. When the innocent man had come to this point of desperation and offered appropriate remuneration, the notary would give in, receipts would turn up again or be written anew, and so on. The chief accountant and the others involved in the documentation would sign their names to accounts that were utterly incomprehensible to them and find the fact that they now had a credit as mysterious as the fact that before they had been accused of having a deficit.

---

[c] [Footnote in the original:] On p. 64 it is reported that "in 1760 Duke Carl used the notaries' excessive earnings as a pretense for forcing them to purchase an obligatory bond of 50,000 florins to finance military spending." What is here called a pretense could just as well be described as a legitimate *reason*, and Carl's supposed act of despotism as easily be considered *just*, as the tribute and salaries of the town and district notaries themselves.

[d] [Footnote in the original:] This detailed account of how the notary system preyed upon the local government is astonishing. We find townships in which the notaries' fees run to $6\frac{3}{4}$ and 7 times the tax.

[169] Ibid., p. 111.   [170] *Proceedings*, sect. XVIII, p. 97.

[171] In German book-keeping practice of the time, the term *Journal* (also *diarium*) refers to the chronologically ordered list of *cash* payments received and rendered, kept by an accountant.

These are the clutches into which local authorities and the common people had fallen! In the words of the prophet, "O my people, they which lead thee cause thee to err"[172] with their talk of the *good* old constitution! Though we are far from generalizing on the basis of this one individual notary's personal traits, it is also obvious that the dependency of the local councils, the municipalities, and (when we take the notaries' other activities into account) individual citizens was not the effect of individual personalities but of the notary system as such.

Formerly, the local councils nominated deputies for the main Estates Assembly only, while the majority of members in the committees were 108 notaries. On p. 72 of his assessment Griesinger writes,

> In spite of the flaws of the notary system, which were often felt and as frequently criticized, plans for improvement or even total reform were bound to find their staunchest opponents among the Estates' representatives, for they were mostly either notaries themselves or exposed to the direct influence of notaries, so that any significant improvement was plainly contrary to their interests.

That says everything. Yet, what is presented here in the past tense as merely historical facts about previous Estates Assemblies – are they not facts about the Estates Assembly's own history? Had the present Assembly done anything useful to clean out those Augean stables? Wouldn't that have meant tearing into their own entrails? Did von Forstner's repeated and unflagging efforts bring about the publication of even so much as a committee report on the notaries' abuses after more than a year, or at least some deliberation or even a resolution on the issue?[e]

It is telling that the majority of the complaints came from New Württemberg, as though Old Württemberg were actively and passively so enmeshed in the abuses that they had grown unconscious of or insensible to them or had perhaps resigned themselves to desperation on the one side and soothed their conscience on the other with the conviction that they were within their good, old, guaranteed rights. It may have played a certain role that since the new region was forced to rely on them as experienced professionals, Old Württemberg's notaries wreaked their havoc there as though it were a conquered land. These new countrymen, brought up in

---

[e] [Footnote in the original:] The events of November 1816 will be mentioned below. [Editors' note: Friedrich I died on October 30, 1816, and was immediately succeeded by his son, Wilhelm I. The new king at once began to reorganize the government and replace his father's privy council. Wangenheim was entrusted with the draft of a new constitutional charter, and the Estates Assembly adjourned until mid-January 1817, at which time the draft was to be presented.]

[172] Isaiah 3:12 (King James Version): "O my people, they which lead thee cause thee to err, and destroy the way of thy paths."

the customs and laws of Old Württemberg, thus did little to recommend either themselves or the old laws and constitution to the people of New Württemberg.

The ministry could be reproached for having convened an Estates Assembly whose elements it must have known, rather than advising the king first to improve the miserable state in which the old constitution had placed the majority of the people, and only then to embark on reform of the government's upper stories. For as long as Württemberg's peculiar burgher aristocracy existed, commanding a duty that put its members on equal footing with wealthy bishops and exercising power over the municipalities, their authorities, and private citizens; and until local authorities and their **109** municipalities were freed from the clutches of this privileged caste and until this element of moral and intellectual decadence that threatened to ensnare the minds and the purses of the common people was destroyed, no true concept of right, freedom, and constitutionality would be able to take root, and the ministry could expect nothing other than that the appointed deputies would continue to come from this element.

On the one hand, it was commendable of Württemberg's king to be the first among German princes to give his people Estates organized so as to represent the rights of the *people*, rather than those of a specific class. For he thus salvaged the Estates from the indifference and alienation, indeed contempt, with which the previous Estates in Germany had come to be regarded by the people.[f] On the other hand, there had been no significant nobility in Old Württemberg; in place of such, the less prominent,

---

[f] [Footnote in the original:] *In his Collection of Documents and Records of Württemberg's Recent History* [*Sammlung einiger Urkunden und Actenstücke zur neusten Württembergischen Geschichte*, Göttingen, 1796], [Ludwig Timotheus von] Spittler says in his *Draft of a History of the Inner Committee of the Estates* [*Entwurf einer Geschichte des engern landschaftlichen Ausschusses*] [part 2, pp. 359 f.], "In some countries a well-framed constitution providing for collegiate bodies of appointed counselors [*Kollegien-Verfassung*] has been a better guarantor of the general welfare than even an Estates constitution. Thus the entire public often honors one or other of the ruler's colleges with universal respect, while the Estates Assembly sinks into a disregard that should have been nearly impossible considering its original vocation, but which is unmistakable in every instance." Though much could be quoted from that article that is applicable to present circumstances, let this suffice: on p. 444, we read that there could hardly have been worse oversight of the administration of the Estates treasury than that by the inner committee, but that apart from a few human weaknesses business had on the whole been properly conducted. (In those days the administration of the Estates treasury described above had not yet been exposed.) Spittler's remark on pp. 445 f. is also noteworthy, where he says that the city magistrates' familiarity with and comprehension of the laws dwindled to such an extent that "in their ineptitude they could assert no rights and in their ignorance assert no authority against the members of the committee" – which of course was inevitable, since affairs of general import were no longer dealt with popularly [*volksmäßig*], but legalistically [*advocatenmäßig*] and were moreover conducted in secret. Spittler also describes the relations between the committees and the rest of the deputies during assemblies, at which the members of the committees presented their report and then listened to the opinions of the others "just to pass the while, as it were."

but more oppressive, aristocracy of the notaries had established itself. As long as the people were not freed from these shackles, there could be no genuine popular representation. Though the concept of a monarchic state necessarily entails the existence of estates,[173] it would have been better not to have any at all than to tolerate the continuation of such privileges and the oppression, deception, and demoralization of the people, and certainly better than having Estates that are the representatives of the privileges of such an aristocracy.

The ministry must also have been familiar with the principles of the aristocracy who had just been incorporated into Old Württemberg or (to the mind of some of the nobles) was at least on the verge of being so incorporated. They should therefore have been able to foresee that the aristocrats would try to hold on to their former rights – rights which were so broadly defined as to make an open question of the nobility's status within the state and which, if maintained in their former extent, were inconsistent with the organism of any state. In the majority of cases of great political upheaval and reform, the monarch and the people have been of one mind and will, but only too often an intermediate class (such as the aristocracy and clergy in France or the nobility and burgher aristocracy of the notaries in Württemberg) has insisted on its privileges and monopolies instead of forming the link between the monarch and the people as would have been its true purpose, thus hindering the realization of the principles of rational law and the common good. It falls to that intermediate class to be the intellectuals of a people and to be immediately involved in exercising the people's rights and fulfilling their duties. However, this also places them in a position to deceive the people and seduce them into taking their side when in reality they are busy protecting their own privileges against the people.[174] A sad and revolting drama then unfolds in which injustices which for a century paraded as law and drove the common people to desperation come to be defended by the people themselves, who have allowed themselves to be taken in by the mere name of law.

[THE KING ADJOURNS THE ASSEMBLY]

Now that the principles, the spirit, and the interests of the Assembly have been made apparent, the rest of the story, which is a plain and simple

---

[173] Cf. *PR*, §§301–302.
[174] For related remarks on the special role of the educated middle class (*Mittelstand*) in a constitutional monarchy cf. *PR*, §§297 and 302.

consequence thereof, is of less intrinsic interest and can be told more quickly.

Our account of events left off at June 26, when the Estates refused to discuss any potentially acceptable points in the king's important concessions which might in turn have been connected with other acceptable points in the royal constitution. Instead, they insisted on an attitude of stubborn dissatisfaction. It was a novel idea, though in keeping with the style of the proceedings hitherto,[175] that in the meeting *following* the decision to reject the royal resolutions, an individual member of the Assembly, Dr. Weishaar, suggested in a written statement that the rejected resolutions now be examined. Hereupon, a committee was appointed to examine Dr. Weishaar's written statement. The committee reported back on June 28 but neglected to mention either its examination of Weishaar's statement or any result thereof, and instead offered only to pass the statement on to the royal commissioners. This decision, which fell on June 28, is nevertheless recorded in the main petition dated the 26th. Similarly, the decision taken on the 26th to mention the noble guarantors of the old Württembergian constitution – namely the three powers England, Denmark, and Prussia[176] – in the main petition bearing that date was overturned on the 28th.

The content of the royal resolution that followed on July 21 was predictable.[177] The king adjourned the Assembly from July 26 onward, giving as his reason that the grievances of the people that had been lodged with him were necessarily of far greater importance than the present disceptations on constitutional issues, and that he intended to subject them to a strict examination and investigation by the government ministries and authorities. He added that since the Estates' written statements had surely exhausted everything that they could possibly have to bring before the king, there was nothing left to be discussed by an Assembly. For the rest, the king bade them to name representatives who might continue negotiations in the interim and to give them instructions suited to bringing about a

---

[175] *Proceedings*, sect. X, p. 3.

[176] In 1565, Württemberg's Estates Assembly had declared the Lutheran faith as the state religion and obliged the duke and his successors to relinquish all claims to a *ius reformandi*, i.e., the right to change the state religion to suit his own. In 1733, the catholic line of the succession, represented by Duke Karl Alexander, came to power and insisted – unconstitutionally – on making catholicism into the state religion. This attempt to overturn the constitution, as the Estates saw it, was thwarted by the intervention of the protestant states of England, Denmark, and Prussia, which were thus perceived as "guarantors" of the constitution. Cotta made the letter to the guarantors public in his journal, the *Allgemeine Zeitung*.

[177] *Proceedings*, sect. XX, p. 13.

timely agreement. One must admit that in regard to the two issues at hand the king's resolution was appropriate to the situation.[178]

In a petition dated July 24, however, the Estates avowed that the complaints did not mean nearly as much to them as the constitution and that they were much disheartened that the king had resolved to adjourn the Assembly before they had been able to give the people any consolation, any reassurance.[179] Apart from denying the king's concessions of so much they themselves considered essential – and he had indeed granted them everything essential – they also announced that they had authorized a twenty-five member committee, chaired by the acting president of the Assembly, to carry on negotiations "and attend to the interests of the Estates." Beyond that they professed themselves unable to give any other instructions to the committee than they had received from the people and carried in their heart, and added that they would reserve the right to approve the result of any negotiations. The Estates were thus on their way back to a committee in the old style, authorized to "attend to the interests of the land as a whole." The king protected his people from such a committee and – though it was against their will – saved the Estates from themselves. In a resolution from July 26,[180] he rejected the Estates' ridiculous proposal, saying that it would be incompatible with the very concept of an adjournment to retain a body representing the whole assembly. (Though, as we have seen over and over again, many things were compatible with the ideas of the Estates which were incompatible with reason.)[181] They were instead to appoint the same number of interim representatives as they had had negotiating commissioners.

In the same meeting of July 26, during which the king's resolution was read, Bolley argued in a *votum scriptum* that the Assembly could under no circumstances appoint only four representatives.[182] Hereupon it was

112

---

[178] The two issues to which Hegel refers were the Estates' insistence on a separate treasury of their own and the establishment of a permanent committee to represent the Estates both during and between sessions of the Assembly.

[179] *Proceedings*, sect. X, p. 15.   [180] Ibid., p. 50.

[181] In the original, the passage reads, *Aber mit den Vorstellungen dieser Stände vertrug sich ... vieles, was mit dem* Begriffe *nicht vereinbarlich ist.* Hegel plays here on two meanings of the word *Begriff.* On the one side, he is using it according to more common usage as meaning the concept of something; on the other side, however, he shifts to his own more technical, normative usage in which *Begriff* denotes, inter alia, reason or rational thought as such. In this latter usage Hegel frequently contrasts the term *Begriff* with *Vorstellung*, that is, the *"mere" idea* of something as taken outside its connection with reason. This contrast is explicitly present in the passage at hand.

[182] The king later agreed to the appointment of twelve commissioners instead of the original number of four.

suggested that a deputation be sent to the king to repeat their demands orally and in person, though this idea was immediately rejected on the grounds that such a deputation would be no more effectual than the written demands they had already sent. They argued moreover that such a course would not be in keeping with traditional norms and that a ruler had so many ways of sending those who came before him away in embarrassment that such a plan could end up causing troubles for the Assembly. (Were they worried that their deputation would be tossed out on their ears?) In view of the urgency of the situation, and while the committee was busy composing their petition, the rest of the Assembly had nothing more pressing to do than to listen to petitions from occasionally remote towns and their districts dating from the previous day and sent by messenger to the Assembly, in whose interest and manner they were written. In the case of further petitions concerning other matters, only the long list of where they had been sent from was presented – without, however, indicating the dates when they were written and received. Among other written statements, one in particular was read that had been "specially requested by several members of the Assembly," concerning the allowances the district cashier had refused to grant them! For it had been noted in a previous meeting that the members refused to accept their allowances from the state treasury and demanded to be paid out of the municipal treasuries; the administrators of the municipal treasuries, however, were not all willing to make the unauthorized payments.

The petition ultimately approved by the Assembly reiterates their previous demands and concludes with great pathos and with the usual self-praise and avowals of their good conscience, as also with the assurance that they had done nothing but their duty, that the people had offered them moving evidence of their gratitude, and all of Germany demonstrated its esteem for them, and so on. – The king had convened them, presented them with the constitution whose foundations we considered above, agreed more than once to concessions, and persisted in negotiations in spite of the Assembly's contemptuous attitude; the meetings of the Assembly itself were pointless; and the Estates reserved the right to instruct their authorized negotiators 113 and to ratify the results of talks between them and the sovereign. Yet despite all that, the authors of the petition and with them the whole Assembly had the effrontery to say to the king that if he failed to approve the transfer of the Estates' rights to a committee, they would have no choice but to conclude that he intended to give the people no constitution at all! In this desperate situation, when all seemed balanced on the razor's edge, the

Assembly resorted to the dire remedy of appealing directly to the guarantors. Mr. Bolley expressed the view that if the king failed to comply with the demands formulated in the petition, not only would there be no possibility of addressing the *Bundestag* as an Estates Assembly, but the cause itself would be utterly lost.[183] It is strange indeed to see the Assembly work itself up to such a fever pitch. Their exaggerations could have had no other purpose than to make it appear that the king's own intentions were aimed at "losing the cause," where that "cause" in fact was the reduction of the Estates to the committee of yore.

As for the Estates' appeal to the guarantors of the *old* constitution, all that was lacking was for them to send letters to the *Reichstag* in Regensburg, too, and the imperial court council in Vienna. The powers they called on as guarantors were the very ones who had but lately reaffirmed the dissolution of the empire and the promotion of the Duchy of Württemberg to a sovereign state at the Congress of Vienna; powers which, as was only reasonable, stipulated *Estates constitutions* for the new German states, not *old* Estates constitutions; powers who had with this article[184] extended the only possible guarantee for a new German state, assuming any was necessary to begin with, and who had spared even the French nation the humiliation of such a guarantee for their *charte*, despite the fact that they had only just done them the service of returning their king to his throne for the second time[185] – not that the French would ever have sunk to the depths of asking them for such a guarantee! Nor of course did Württemberg's Estates ever receive an answer to their letter to those three powers.

In his decree of July 27, the king made the Estates feel how incongruous their behavior was and left it at their disposal, should it comfort them, to appoint two or three times as many deputies as they had had negotiating commissioners. He postponed the adjournment of the Assembly until the 28th in order to give them time to take possession of themselves. On the day of the 28th, the Assembly drafted another long petition like the ones that had preceded it, full of an opinionated spitefulness and bitter ill-temper that contrasted sharply with the composure, calm simplicity, and focus of the king's resolutions. The petition's conclusion, which stated that the

114

---

[183] *Proceedings*, sect. X, p. 37. The *Bundestag* (federal diet) in Frankfurt am Main (established in 1815 at the Congress of Vienna) was the highest political organ of the German League.

[184] Article 13 of the Articles of Confederation stipulated that every member state was to have a constitution providing for an Estates Assembly.

[185] Hegel is referring to Napoleon's defeat at Waterloo and the end of his reign of the "Hundred Days," at the end of which Louis XVIII returned to the throne.

king had caused an irreparable division between himself and the land, was unforgivable for an Estates Assembly. They disbanded.

Are we to imagine that this bitter ill-temper was cause for the people's "moving evidence of gratitude" (consisting among other things of a *Nachtmusik* performed at one of the last assembly meetings)?[186] It would seem rather that only the rabble could have taken pleasure in such sentiments and drawn a sense of self from them. The king in any case proved immune to them, for by announcing that the Assembly was to reconvene on October 16, he refuted the Assembly's propensity to act on the basis of the intentions they themselves imputed to him, rather than on the basis of the facts of the situation and the king's own express intentions.[187]

Given the material available in Württemberg for an Estates Assembly, the ministry might from the outset have known it to be highly improbable that anything useful could be done with it; yet actual experience must have convinced them that it was indeed impossible, and in the eyes of the world they would surely have been justified had they never reconvened the Assembly again. Such an Assembly, however, is of infinite importance for the political education that a people and its leaders require when they have hitherto lived in a condition of political nullity. Unlike a people untouched by political experience, in which case political education could begin afresh and from the beginning, the people of Württemberg had lived enchained by an oppressive aristocracy and the inner constitution erected upon it, with all the resultant perversion of the concepts of constitutional rights and civil liberties.[188] As we have seen, those concepts had become closely entwined with the vested interests of the ruling caste, and in such a case it is hopeless to combat misapprehension by means of argument alone or to expect it have any immediate effect. Though less obvious, the indirect effects of giving rein to such a mindset and allowing it to come fully to

---

[186] This so-called *Nachtmusik* took place when the deputies resolved to remain in assembly until midnight of July 26, 1815 (the deadline set by the king for their adjournment) as a demonstration of their political will. Apparently, the musicians had been hired for a quite different engagement very nearby. When the crowd that had assembled to support the Estates deputies began calling out cheers for the individual Assembly members, the deputies came out to acknowledge them and mistakenly assumed that the musicians had also come to honor them. The ensuing coincidences and misunderstandings (which nearly had dire legal consequences for the unwitting musicians) are described in Gerner, *Vorgeschichte und Entstehung*, pp. 183, 206–208, as are the flyers containing poems and other expressions of gratitude that were in circulation at about the same time.

[187] In fact, the Estates had appealed to Hanover, Prussia, and Austria as powerful members of their German League to intervene on their behalf. It was under their pressure that Friedrich agreed to reconvene the Assembly in October.

[188] *Freiheitsrechte.*

light and to tire itself out in the process are ultimately more lasting. The effect on public opinion is that the people cease to have any sympathy for such perversity as soon as it takes on explicit form. The disclosure of the privileges at the base of the notaries' abuses and the more enlightened and wide-spread awareness attendant upon it was one such consequence of far more lasting effect than the character and actions of the sovereigns or passing circumstances, and we shall soon have opportunity to observe the consequences of an education at least of their understanding.[189] Given the situation in Württemberg, the a priori introduction of a constitution could not have been, and indeed was not, successful.[190] Thus there was

115 no alternative but to set the Estates on the path of educating themselves – a path which humans admittedly have every right to take, and it does honor to the king and his ministers to have opened that path in the faith that although the Assembly began at the opposite standpoint, it would eventually (whether consciously or not) be led to reason.

[THE KING RECONVENES THE ASSEMBLY. NEW CLIMATE
OF NEGOTIATIONS]

In the royal decree of October 16, 1815[191] which opened the new session, the king clearly outlines the state of the negotiations. As he sees it, the Estates hold that prior to any further proceedings the right of both Old *and New Württemberg* to the old constitution must be laid down, whereby the king would be obligated to carry over what he sees as the faults of the constitution

---

[189] The phrase "education of their understanding" renders Hegel's expression *formelle Bildung*. Comparison of several passages written at about the same time as the *Estates* essay shows that by *formelle Bildung* Hegel means an education or development of the cognitive ability to form distinct concepts of the various aspects of things by abstraction, differentiate between essential and non-essential characteristics, and to apply the concepts gained by abstraction in novel situations. (See *Werke*, ed. Eva Moldenhauer and Karl Markus Michel [Frankfurt: Suhrkamp, 1970], vol. IV: *Nürnberger und Heidelberger Schriften*, p. 348; cf. Hegel's draft for his inaugural speech as professor at the University of Berlin on October 22, 1818: ibid., vol X, p. 414. See also the somewhat later formulation in section 525 of the second edition of the *Encyclopedia* (1827), which Hegel carries over with slight modifications in the same section of the 1830 edition: ibid., p. 322.) These are clearly aspects of what Kant referred to as the power to judge (*Urteilskraft*; cf. *Critique of Judgment*, XXVI).

[190] Hegel's talk of introducing the constitution "a priori" is not untendentious; many contemporary observers and later historians were apt to describe Friedrich I's actions as an attempt to impose from above a constitution suited to his own autocratic propensities. The biographer Rudolph Haym was particularly critical of Hegel's portrayal of events, referring to Hegel as a "Napoleonist" who was drawn to "despotic natures" and also stood to gain a prestigious post as chancellor of the University of Tübingen by flattering the king. (See Rudolf Haym, *Hegel und seine Zeit. Vorlesungen über Entstehung und Entwicklung, Wesen und Werth der Hegel'schen Philosophie*, pp. 352 ff.) Haym later withdrew the latter allegation.

[191] *Proceedings*, sect. XI, p. 26.

of Old Württemberg to New Württemberg as well; such an obligation, however, would be contrary to his firmest convictions. If he believed Old Württemberg to have a legitimate claim to its former constitution – which he does not – he would willingly restore that constitution *within the older territories*; nor is it his intention to disregard the former rights and laws of the newly acquired territories. There could, however, be no question of organizing these very different parts of the kingdom according to their peculiar norms. Rather, one constitution suited both to the former and to the present state of affairs must be established on the basis of mutual agreement.[192] Furthermore, the decree contains no mention of a "royal constitution"; instead, there is only talk of individual modifications which the king thinks necessary for the welfare of the state and which are subject to negotiation. He also declares his willingness to retain any elements of the old constitution that prove compatible with modern times and a good administration of the state. The recognition of the principle of the old constitution in its whole extent would have been senseless and contrary to the nature of the enterprise, and the promise to retain everything in it that was of any use exhausted all that was of true value.

As to the composition of the Estates at the time the Assembly was reconvened, most of the non-elected members had either joined the Assembly personally (among them six princes) or transferred their vote to those who had.[193] In a petition dated May 3, twelve members of the nobility had informed the Assembly of their limited expectations and desires regarding the maintenance of their former privileges within the new organism of the state.[194] Their demands were moderate, and, more importantly, they were formulated precisely, in detail, and in an open, frank, and yet appropriate

---

[192] Until 1805–06, Friedrich had governed the newly granted territory of New Württemberg as a political entity separate from the traditional territory of what at that point came to be known as Old Württemberg. From 1805 till 1815 Old and New Württemberg formed a unified kingdom within the Confederation of the Rhine, and Friedrich ruled it without an Estates Assembly.

[193] Of the thirty-one noble non-elected members who had appeared at the first meeting of the Assembly on March 15, 1815, twenty-seven had departed immediately after the opening statement by Prince Maximilian Wunibald von Waldburg-Zeil-Trauchburg (1750–1818), who announced that it would not be possible for the nobility to participate in proceedings until the status of the former mediatized princes within the new German League had been settled (Gerner, *Vorgeschichte und Entstehung*, pp. 71 f.). By the time the Assembly was re-convened in October, the Articles of Confederation had been signed into effect in Vienna (on June 8, 1815). Article 14 reaffirmed the status of the former mediatized princes as the most privileged class in the new German states. In particular, it upheld the traditional laws concerning intermarriage among members of the nobility, taxation privileges, freedom of movement within the territories of the member states of the German League, exemption from military service, privileged status before the court, and the right to administer justice in accord with state law in their own territories. Cf. Gerner, ibid., pp. 253 f.

[194] *Proceedings*, sect. IV, pp. 141 ff.

116   tone. (On June 6, Consul Griesinger read comments relating to a petition of the nobility which he had been asked to present to the Assembly.[195] Since, however, his comments represented substantial content, the Assembly naturally neglected to discuss them, much less to make any decision regarding them.) On June 26 the rest of the kingdom's nobility followed suit.[196] On that same day further mediatized princes, who until then had been awaiting the Vienna Congress's decision on their constitutional status und hence understandably had abstained from participating in the Assembly's proceedings, joined in them now that the Congress was over. As Prince von Oettingen-Wallerstein[197] declared, they thereby laid claim to their rights under the new Articles of Confederation as the highest nobles in the states within which their possessions lay, and to any other rights and privileges as may in the future be conferred upon them.[198]

A number of princes failed to appear this time as well, and a number of new members appeared in place of those who had laid down their mandates. It seems that neither the resignation nor the appointment of Assembly members was in any way regulated and that the ministry allowed it to occur freely without there being anything pertaining to it in the royal Constitutional Charter. Indeed, though it is an essential element in any political assembly, the Estates Assembly adhered to no protocol at all. On the occasion of the opening day of the new session, for instance, when so much princely grandeur joined their ranks, they paid their respects to the nobles with the same gesture they had previously used to signal their vote.[199] Though the status of the mediatized princes within the state and within the Assembly was still somewhat vague, for the Assembly (which was itself persistently vague as to its relation to the state) it was sufficient that they now saw themselves as mediatized princes *within the kingdom*. If, however, the Assembly had been able to enter into substantial discussion of constitutional issues, the insufficient determinacy of the nobility's status would soon have become apparent.

In his resolution of October 16, the king had asked the Estates to instruct their previously appointed negotiators in such a way that a settlement could be reached on all the relevant issues. The Estates' answer came in the form

---

[195] Ibid., sect. VI, p. 113.   [196] Ibid., sect. X, p. 24.

[197] Ludwig, Prince of Oettingen-Wallerstein (1791–1870) began his political career as a non-elected member (*Virilstimmführer*) in the Estates Assembly, where he was a member of the instruction committee entrusted with compiling a list of the articles of the old constitution to be included in the Estates' revision.

[198] *Proceedings*, sect. X, p. 26; cf. sect. I, p. 15.

[199] At the first Assembly meeting, the deputies had signaled their vote by rising from their seats: cf. Gerner, *Vorgeschichte und Entstehung*, pp. 75, 77.

of a twelve-page petition in small print which the Assembly owed to Mr.
Bolley.[200] It rehashes the same old views in the usual manner, and it would   **117**
be superfluous to quote from it, with the exception of one passage (p. 269),
where it is said that even a superficial acquaintance with Württemberg's
constitution is sufficient to be convinced that it forms a self-contained and
integral unity. In one sense that may be true, though barely so since even
a superficial acquaintance would actually entail more scrutiny than such a
conviction, or rather judgment, could bear. We also read that the Estates
cannot allow the people of Württemberg to be torn from their history and
for the articles of their former constitution to be made into antiques. They
would have done better, however, to ask whether a people which till now
has not been an independent state, but rather part of another people, can
be said to have a history at all, and whether a people can have a history
without having a state.[201]

We mentioned above that in this petition the Estates confessed themselves unable to list the rights of the subjects of Württemberg, since they did
not have access to the old Estates archive – as though a constitution were
a codification of criminal law, civil law, etc., and as though the royal Constitutional Charter had invalidated any such laws! The petition concludes
with the simple and monotonous request that the king solemnly recognize
the legitimacy and validity of the old constitution of Württemberg for the
whole kingdom, excepting only such modifications as prove necessary or
convenient by mutual agreement.

In the beginning, the Estates had admitted no modifications to the old
constitution except those pertaining to the incorporation of the nobility
and the common rights of protestants and catholics. Now they seemed to
want the results of the present deliberations to go into effect *in addition to*
the chaos of the former laws of the land that were listed above. But if the
regulations of those two issues were all that was to be passed, then it would
have been the same untenable business, or rather the completely empty
illusion it had been from the start – nothing but the old constitution of
the duchy applied, to the great detriment and repression of the rights of
the new territories, to what was now the kingdom of Württemberg. Yet
of course there was more at stake than just those two issues, and in due
course that would of itself have become evident. Indeed, the conclusion
of the Estates' petition is framed in far more general terms. The difference
between the king's will and the Estates' demands came down to this. Was

---

[200] *Proceedings*, sect. XI, pp. 263–286.
[201] Cf. *Encyclopedia*, §549; *PR*, sect. 341–353; see also *Vorlesungen über die Philosophie der Geschichte*
(*Werke*, vol. XII, p. 56): "World history only deals with peoples who have formed a state."

the object of negotiations to be the royal constitution and the modifications to be made to it, or was it to be the old constitution of Württemberg and the modifications to be made to it? When it happens in the course of diplomatic negotiations that the one side demands that their proposition be discussed with a view to modifying it, and the other side demands the same, well, then since the object is the same the wiser man will yield, as the saying goes.

In a royal edict of November 13, the Estates' main legal claims were discussed, especially those pertaining to the incorporation of the nobility, and their unfoundedness was demonstrated in a separate appendix. The edict also reiterated the central point at issue, namely that of creating a constitution that would unify both the old and the new territories under a single government. The king stressed that in view of the dissolution of the Holy Roman Empire and the consequent lack of any higher judge to clarify legal uncertainties, he was unable to grant general recognition to the old contracts between the Estates and the dukes without first going into the legal content of each and every one. Therefore a complete and thorough exposition of those contents would be indispensable, scattered as they were in a multitude of documents and more often than not of dubious legitimacy. Otherwise the articles of the constitution would remain the possession of a privileged few (i.e., the committee heads of olden days, especially the consuls), and not the common property of the people. The edict went on to say that in case no settlement was reached and the Estates persisted in their refusal to participate in negotiations, the king would have no recourse but to retain the current mode of representation in the territory of Old Württemberg while introducing a truly national representation in the new territories based on a new constitution that integrated the present and former laws of those regions. Furthermore, in a second appendix the king laid down the fundamental points which, as any unbiased observer (indeed!) would have agreed, formed a suitable basis for the negotiation of a good constitution.

The inherent rationality of the matter[202] came through at least to the extent that the Estates acceded to the (albeit merely formal) step of beginning negotiations. Prince von Oettingen-Wallerstein motioned that after a suitable interval the Assembly members should present their views on the royal edict and then submit them to examination by a committee.[203] This proposal deviated markedly from the usual course of handing over such

---

[202] The German phrase is *die Vernunft der Sache*.   [203] *Proceedings*, sect. XIII, p. 138.

matters directly to a committee whose decision the Assembly would auto-
matically and unanimously accept, for such committees seemed to have
attained a monopoly on the Assembly's agreement. It had recently become **119**
popular, however, to appoint four speakers instead of a committee, since
the individual members of the examining committees were in the habit
of presenting their separate written statements to the Assembly anyway.
Apparently it had come to the point that even a committee of just a few
members was incapable of coming to a consensus, producing a series of
monologues instead. In the meetings that followed, many statements were
read, of which several argued that even now it was too early to enter into
negotiations, appealing for example to the principle *de juribus singulorum*,
which could not be decided by a simple majority in the Assembly. This
principle had been much hallowed in the law of the Holy Roman Empire,
the fundamental flaw and injustice of which consisted precisely in the fact
that the rights of the state had become *jura singulorum*.[204]

Among the more reasonable voices, von Varnbüler[205] replied to Lang,[206]
who had admonished the Assembly to heed its conscience and cried out
"with pathos": "No negotiations!", that that proposal was the greater threat
to conscience, for if they followed his advice they might end up with no
constitution at all.[207]

It is not going to help the people for the old constitution to remain valid merely
on paper, and it will not help us any to quote from learned treatises when one day
the people cry out to us, "The stakes were high and you bet all on nothing. They
wanted to give us a say in legislation, the right to approve taxation, the restoration
of church property, administration of public expenditures, personal liberty, legal
accountability of civil servants, the right to emigrate, and the permanent representation of the Estates – and you threw it all away! Who is to blame that we have
lost everything?"

It is remarkable that it was the members of the nobility who often
distinguished themselves before the other deputies by their more moderate
and unbiased views.

---

[204] As indicated in the text, *jura singulorum* (literally *individuals' rights*) are rights such that a member
of a political body holding *jura singulorum* cannot be overridden by a majority vote.
[205] Karl Eberhard Friedrich von Varnbüler (1776–1832), a non-elected member of the Assembly (*Viril-
stimmberechtigter*), was also one of the Estates' negotiating commissioners. He is notable in German
cultural and economic history for having pioneered new agricultural methods, which he propogated
in his periodical, the *Annalen der Württembergischen Landwirtschaft*.
[206] Friedrich Ludwig Lang represented Maulbronn at the Estates Assembly. He was a member of the
committee for preparing negotiations with the royal commissioners and on the committee on the
notary abuses. He voted against accepting the royal constitution on June 2, 1817.
[207] *Proceedings*, sect. XV, p. 59.

Mr. Bolley found it necessary to defend himself against the murmurs of disapproval that had not escaped his notice during his speech.[208] He felt that the reproach of bitterness and contempt was misdirected and attributed **120** the offence he had caused to the fact that he had held forth in such a loud voice.[g] It seems that the Assembly had tired of the previous petitions' style and digressiveness, and on November 23, in a vote of fifty-seven to forty-nine, the Assembly approved an unassumingly formulated draft by Weishaar free of bitterness, self-righteousness, and disparagement of the king's intentions. In that address the Assembly expressed its gratitude and relief that all obstacles to successful negotiations had now been removed and announced the imminent appointment of the Estates' negotiators. In the meeting after this motion had already passed, and while the votes for the negotiators were already being counted, Mr. Bolley tried once more to persuade the Assembly to insert reservations and qualifications into the petition, arguing that its excessive diplomatic openness was untrue to the character of the Estates thus far. And indeed, the plain, open, and simple style of the petition contrasted strongly with that of the preceding petitions. Still, the Assembly did not waver in its decision.

It was proposed that the Estates' negotiating commissioners should be instructed to press only for an accessory agreement.[209] Although this proposal was rejected, Mr. Bolley managed to persuade the Assembly to include a clever amendment stipulating that the commissioners declare at the earliest opportunity that the Estates desired an agreement in keeping with their previous applications and petitions to the king – the applications and petitions, that is, which had limited negotiations to an accessory agreement.[210] The object of the negotiations, however, was the whole gamut of constitutional issues. The commissioners from both sides

---

[g] [Footnote in the original:] Prince von Waldburg-Zeil remarks in sect. XVI, p. 161, that "most of the written statements were read so fast and so loudly" (Mr. Bolley alone had been entrusted by the responsible committee with reading a number of statements pertaining to the draft of a petition, after having read that draft himself in the previous meeting), "that if one had not been given precise instructions in advance" (as the committee had) "one could not grasp all of the content." The circumstances mentioned above combine easily with the reading of written statements, but they are not conducive to an Assembly's achieving any insight into the matter at hand, for it inclines them rather to depend entirely on their committees and grant unanimous approval to their recommendations.

[208] Ibid., p. 6.

[209] An accessory agreement (*accessorischer Receß*) in the legal parlance of the time is an agreement whose fulfillment depends upon some further conditions' being met. Bolley was of the opinion that such a tactic would ensure that the old constitution remain the basis of negotiations; cf. Gerner, *Vorgeschichte und Entstehung*, p. 301.

[210] *Proceedings*, sect. XVI, p. 47.

held their first conference on December 4, 1815. At a later date (January 17, 1816) the Estates' commissioners were joined by seven more deputies to form an instruction committee with twelve members (later – February 29 – increased to twenty-five). These members' work consisted mostly in compiling material on chapters of the old constitution according to a certain plan and then editing it into an ordered series of propositions, the content and formulation of which the committee had to agree upon before passing them on to the negotiators. The Estates had already demonstrated their unwillingness or inability to turn their attention to universal principles or to take them as their starting-point, and the "fundamental articles" included in the royal edict of November 13 were no exception, for the Assembly completely ignored them.[211] Since all their proceedings were based on the compilations of details, it was natural that the need arose to reduce all that material to general propositions, and Prince von Oettingen-Wallerstein motioned that they do so.[212] Such an ascent to the universal is integral to the formal side of the political education of a new Estates Assembly.

The fruits of their labors appeared in print in 1816 under the title *Draft of the Renewed Constitutional Charter of Württemberg, Based on the Resolutions of the Estates' Instruction Committee*.[213] This work not only differs in appearance from any mere collection of resolutions by the *Landtag*, legal miscellanies, etc., for its content also deviates in essential points from that of the old constitution. The very existence of such an ordered body of determinate propositions reduces the old constitutional laws to mere "antiques." The so-called "General Clause" appended to the work stipulates that all the common and house laws[214] of the former duchy remain in effect, to the extent that they are not explicitly modified or superseded by the new constitution, a demand that had been dear to the Estates from the beginning. Such a clause is due in part simply to an innocent need to ease the formal conscience, in part, however, also to the fact that, although a constitution is something solid, it is not utterly fixed and unmoving, and the sessions of an Estates Assembly represent the constant and uninterrupted development of the constitution. That is the true general clause that the world spirit appends to every constitution.

---

[211] Appendix B of the royal edict of November 13, 1815, presented fourteen so-called fundamental points worked out by Wangenheim as a new framework for negotiations. Cf. Gerner, *Vorgeschichte und Entstehung*, pp. 279–284.

[212] *Proceedings*, sect. XVII, pp. 58 and 145.

[213] In the original: *Entwurf des zu erneuernden Württembergischen Verfassungsvertrags, nach Beschlüssen des ständischen Instructions-Comité* (1816), p. 238.

[214] The house laws (*Hausgesetze*) were norms established by individual families of the high nobility which governed the line of succession, marriage, and inheritance practices, and similar matters.

The Estates Assembly's activity, as soon as it was directed toward a determinate content (for otherwise it would not have really been *work*), even in the present form of a mere revision of a draft of the constitutional charter, immediately caused them to forget the contentless formal principle of right that hitherto had been their highest aim. A concentrated effort to frame a whole constitution and its determinate articles is in itself incompatible with blind adherence to the positive determinations contained in a confused and scattered manifold of countless documents and edicts, for it requires the use of one's own understanding and reason, as in the case of the so-called natural law of states. The most important results always consist in the effects which the very nature of things[215] brings about unconsciously in people's heads against their own most stubbornly held and ardently professed convictions, and hence a far-sighted ministry like that in Württemberg will overlook the temporary manifestations of passion, prejudice, and perverted notions that precede those more lasting effects.

The proceedings of the Assembly from December 1815 to December 1816 dealt only in part with these questions, being also concerned with other constitutional issues, among them the extension of the rights of the mediatized princes. As touched on above, it remains to this very moment unclear how a German Estates Assembly is to be instituted as long as the status of the nobility has not been settled. At first it seemed as though the Assembly might become an instrument for achieving the goals of the nobility; had that been the case, then the Estates would have revealed that they were not yet organized. Some of the issues with which the Assembly were concerned have already been discussed, while others of them are relatively insignificant and can be passed over here. (We have for instance already spoken of the notaries' abuses.)

Among the more notable issues was the king's announcement of the annual taxes and their collection. Since October 20, 1815, the king had also begun sending the Estates his ministers' commentary and evaluation of the Assembly's list of complaints, as well as a number of constitutional modifications it had occasioned. The ministers' commentary exposes the shallowness of some of the views expressed in the complaints. The Assembly appointed a committee to consult on these issues, but like most of the similar committees formed by the Assembly, it was later disbanded without ever having produced results. On February 29, all of the Assembly's members who did not belong to the negotiating committee were united in

---

[215] In the German original the phrase is *die Natur der Sache*.

a grand committee with several sub-divisions which were to divide up the complaints and other material among themselves to be prepared for negotiations. Yet neither did any of these various sub-committees ever produce any results. Had their work contributed to successful negotiations with the ministry, then what they had adamantly refused before would have come to pass, namely a serious consideration of the various complaints. Though pressing current affairs such as the decree and collection of the annual taxes occasionally drove the Assembly to try to undertake practical measures, such attempts immediately collided with their lack of any determinate status. They could exercise participatory rights neither as the Estates Assembly of Old Württemberg, for that Assembly no longer existed; nor could they claim the rights granted them in the royal charter, for these they refused to accept; nor finally could they appeal to the new settlement, for this had not as yet been reached. This quandary was to remain an issue in a later discussion, too, that took place in June 1816: the Assembly was at a loss to determine the extent of the Assembly's competence or even the extent to which it had been constituted.[216] This lack of any determinate status was grounds for the royal ministry to reject the Assembly's attempts to claim rights as a legally constituted body.

[THE DIVISION OF THE ASSEMBLY INTO A NEGOTIATING COMMITTEE AND AUXILIARY SUB-COMMITTEES]

The Assembly had transferred responsibility for proceedings relating to the constitutional comparison to its commissioners and committees. At first (beginning December 1, 1815) the meetings were kept closed and their minutes separate from those of the Assembly, but it opened its proceedings once the committee had been given responsibility for preparing negotiations on January 25, 1816. As early as January 15, 1816, the commissioners had motioned not to present the individual phases of their work on the constitution to the Assembly, but rather to wait until they had completed their work and then to present the whole.[217] On February 13, 1816, Mr. Knapp[218] warned the committee that on this proposal, apart from the fact that "diplomatic" proceedings were not in keeping with the true relations

---

[216] *Proceedings*, sect. XXV.   [217] Ibid., sect. XVII, p. 144.

[218] Gottfried Gabriel Knapp (1764–1828) represented Gaildorf in the Estates Assembly from 1815 to 1817. Knapp was an opponent of the royal constitution and voted against accepting it on June 2, 1817.

between the king and the Estates, only five of the twelve committee members would be actively engaged in work on a regular basis, and the other seven only occasionally, while all the others would for the most part be occupied with issues of little or no significance.[219] As to how the Assembly was to pursue its calling in regard to the constitution while the committee was busy negotiating, it was resolved on February 29, 1816, that the whole draft of the constitution was to be presented to the Assembly at some future date for deliberation and not one section at a time, and that in the meantime the committee would at intervals report to the Assembly on the general progress of the negotiations.[220] It was after this resolution that the previously mentioned grand committee comprehending all the remaining members of the Assembly was established.

Thus the Assembly ultimately found themselves in precisely the form that the king had proposed at the time of the Assembly's adjournment at the end of July, 1815,[221] and which had elicited so violent a passion in them that they believed themselves to have nothing left to lose. Neither the fact that the Assembly had no important say in regard to the constitution for a full year, nor consideration of the high costs of maintaining the Assembly members had prevented them from meeting regularly. Mr. Knapp said in a statement from February 9, 1816, that the question was frequently and justly being raised, "What is the use of an Assembly of more than one hundred men that costs more than one hundred ducats a day, when only a handful are responsible for the business of the Assembly and are sufficient to attend to it?"[222] To this the Assembly had no answer.

In the course of the ensuing year, the committee was occasionally called on to read individual sections of the constitutional draft or other statements and papers relating to it to the Assembly. In effect, though, the newspapers and journalists played a greater role in the proceedings and discussions of the Assembly. Its members were so estranged by the right to free speech and the opinions whose expression it inspired, which differed markedly from the former hymns of praise they had been accustomed to hearing, that they deliberated as intensely on newspaper articles and pamphlets as they did on royal edicts, appointing committees and writing articles in book length intended to justify the Estates and to "refute" what they

---

[219] *Proceedings*, sect. XIX, p. 75.   [220] Ibid., sect. XX, p. 28.
[221] The royal edict of July 21, 1815, had called for an adjournment of the Assembly and the continuation of negotiations by four commissioners. The negotiating commissioners in February, 1816, numbered five.
[222] *Proceedings*, sect. XIX, p. 23.

referred to as "cooked-up libel." These lengthy and often laughable tracts were read before the Assembly.

In the meeting on September 17, 1816, it was announced that the instruction committee had ended its work on the constitution, the results of which were now to be gradually presented to the Assembly.[223] Some of them were actually read to the Assembly. Even so, in this last quarter of the year the Assembly still did not manage to initiate serious deliberation on the constitution, much less come to any decision concerning it. On October 24, 1816, shortly before Friedrich I's death during the night of October 29, indignation over the notary abuses was again aired before the Assembly.[224] The report of an unusually scandalous case had torn the Assembly from its habitual lethargy. The committee charged with investigating the notary abuses was augmented. Since an excess of responsibilities in connection with the constitutional draft prevented Mr. Knapp from finishing his report,[225] and seeing as how the Assembly itself had come to no decision, a new petition was submitted to the new king on November 21,[226] requesting that he institute a bilateral commission composed of members from both the royal government and the Estates to finish the task with which the Estates had been entrusted. The petition argues in favor of including royal deputies in the commission, saying that they would bring to the commission long experience of a kind that only high-ranking officials can have – an admission that the Assembly perhaps should have considered when they started compiling their list of complaints, organizing the Estates, and in other such matters. Now, however, since "every month that we delay inflicts severe damage on the land and its people" (why then had the Assembly hesitated with its work for so many months? – the first committee had been formed on May 13, 1815, eighteen months previously), the committee submitted an appraisal suggesting provisional measures. It is noteworthy that the Assembly itself did not accept credit or responsibility for this paper and thus even now had failed to make any recommendations of its own on how to improve the situation.

On December 6 the king informed the Estates that the privy council would now begin examining both the draft for a constitutional charter

125

---

[223] Ibid., sect. XXX, part 1, p. 32.   [224] Ibid., sect. XXXII, p. 48.

[225] Knapp's report did not appear until 1817, when it was published separately under the title *On Württemberg's Notary System: A Report Originally Intended for the Estates Assembly* [German: *Ueber das Württembergische Schreibereiwesen. Eine für die Stände-Versammlung bestimmt gewesene Relation*].

[226] *Proceedings*, sect. XXXIII, pp. 99 f.

and the alternative draft that the Estates had worked out on its basis, and that the Assembly would therefore be adjourned until January 15, 1817. Hereupon the Assembly ended its session.[227]

[CONCLUSION]

The aim of this extensive report would be sorely misconstrued if it were taken as a defense of anything other than the concept of land estates and the supreme interest attaching to it against an actuality that was so highly inappropriate to it and at the same time so presumptuous. By publishing the minutes of its proceedings, the actual Assembly has presented itself for public scrutiny and judgment. In conclusion, it remains only to mention the curious end result and fate of this assembly: never in the long and expensive course of its proceedings did it ever reach either an agreement with the king or even a decision among its own members regarding any substantial constitutional issue.

[227] Ibid., p. 150.

Excerpts from letters by Hegel, Jacobi, and Jean Paul concerning Hegel's review of Jacobi's works

Hegel's letter to Immanuel Niethammer, dated April 19, 1817, indicates that he consciously intended his lengthy and for the most part positive review to help effect a reconciliation with Jacobi, whom his scathing remarks in *Faith and Knowledge* (1802) had deeply estranged. Hegel writes,

[A]s I see, the main letter I wrote to Munich reached its addressee, and I am very pleased at your news that I succeeded in expressing and fulfilling my intention in the review. I thank Jacobi warmly for the friendly welcome he gave to this essay. An Encyclopedia is supposed to be ready by Easter. 6 sheets of it are printed. Copies for you and Jacobi have been ordered. I do not begrudge God that he makes things so miserable for us, but rather that in the end he does not allow our achievements to reach the degree of perfection we wanted and of which we could have been capable.[1]

Just a few months later, Hegel was instrumental in persuading the University of Heidelberg to grant Jacobi's close friend Jean Paul, the novelist, an honorary doctorate, and no doubt this new friendship between Hegel and Jean Paul also helped facilitate the rapprochement between Hegel and Jacobi.[2] In any case, in a letter dated September 3, 1817, Jean Paul confirms

---

[1] Johannes Hoffmeister, ed., *Briefe von und an Hegel* (Hamburg: Felix Meiner Verlag, 3rd ed., 1969), vol. II, Letter 316, p. 152. Hegel is referring to the first edition of his *Encyclopedia of the Philosophical Sciences*, which came out not, as planned, at Easter, but in June of 1817. Friedrich Immanuel Niethammer (1766–1848) was a close friend of Hegel's at least since Hegel's arrival in Jena in 1801. Also trained at the protestant seminary in Tübingen, where Hegel, Schelling, and Hölderlin had received their education, Niethammer (who was four years older than Hegel) had come to Jena in 1790, soon becoming a member of Reinhold's philosophical circle. In the mid-1790s, Niethammer was co-editor (with Fichte) of the *Journal einer Gesellschaft Teutscher Gelehrten* (*Journal of a Society of German Scholars*). He participated in Hegel's habilitation examination in 1801. From 1807 onward, Niethammer played a significant role in Hegel's gradual reconciliation with Jacobi. See Walter Jaeschke, *Hegel Handbuch. Leben-Werk-Wirkung* (Stuttgart/Weimar: J. B. Metzler, 2003), pp. 32–34.

[2] During Jean Paul Friedrich Richter's (1763–1825) first visit to Heidelberg in the summer of 1817, Hegel suggested that he be awarded an honorary doctorate. There was some initial resistance stemming from questions as to Jean Paul's Christian faith and his love of drink, but Hegel overcame it. Together with Friedrich Creuzer, the scholar of comparative mythology, Hegel handed over the honorary diploma to Jean Paul personally on July 17, 1817. Cf. Jaeschke, *Hegel Handbuch*, pp. 40 f. See also the colorful

Jacobi's impression of a convergence, writing, "Hegel has come much closer to you, except for just one point concerning the will."[3]

Two passages from Jacobi's correspondence are especially relevant, for in them he relates his perception of Hegel's review and of the points of similarity and difference between his own philosophical outlook and that of his younger philosophical contemporary:

You will have seen Hegel's review of my third volume in the *Heidelberger Jahrbücher*. Although he does me bitter injustice on at least three points, on the whole his work made me very happy, and I only wish I could understand everything he says. But I am not able to see anything through to the end because my eyes and memory are failing.[4]

A short time later, Jacobi goes into greater detail:

As it seems to me, you do not understand my *salto mortale* (which you refer to in your letter from January as a *salto fatale*) as I understand it and as anyone must understand it who has ever seen a daring acrobat perform the reversal in mid-air referred to by that name. What I have in mind is not at all plunging from a cliff headlong into the abyss, but rather a broad leap across both cliff and abyss in order to land firmly and in one piece on the other side.

In his review of my third volume, Hegel praises my leap, saying: "In his innermost, Jacobi had made just this transition from absolute substance to absolute Spirit and

---

account in Terry Pinkard, *Hegel: A Biography* (Cambridge: Cambridge University Press, 2000), pp. 377–381.

3 Günther Nicolin, ed., *Hegel in Berichten seiner Zeitgenossen* (Hamburg: Meiner, 1970), p. 156.

4 Excerpt from Letter 359 from Friedrich Heinrich Jacobi to Jean Paul (Munich, May 11, 1817). This and the following excerpt, from Jacobi's letter to Johann Neeb (Munich, May 30, 1817), are taken from *Friedrich Heinrich Jacobis Auserlesener Briefwechsel*, ed. Friedrich Roth (Leipzig: Gerhard Fleischer, 1827), vol. II, p. 464 and pp. 466 f., respectively. – Neeb (1767–1843) pursued a number of vocations in the course of his life. Throughout the 1790s he was a catholic priest, though he left the church in 1803, apparently in order to marry; during the same period and into the first decade of the nineteenth century he was professor of philosophy in Bonn and Mainz but relinquished his chair during the French occupation. In the late 1790s he made the acquaintance of Friedrich Hölderlin, who invited him to contribute to a journal which was then in the planning (*Iduna*) but which failed to materialize. Neeb also served as mayor of Niedersaulheim (near Mainz) and seems to have met with success as a farmer. Neeb's philosophical career began under Kantian auspices (*Über Kants Verdienste um die Interessen der philosophischen Vernunft*, Bonn, 1793). Mid-decade, he shifted somewhat to a Reinholdian position (*System der kritischen Philosophie, auf den Satz des Bewußtseins gegründet* [Frankfurt am Main: Andräische Buchhandlung, 1795/6], 2 vols. Although Neeb had already articulated views explicitly informed by Jacobi's arguments in the *Spinoza Letters* (see Neeb's *Vernunft gegen Vernunft oder Rechtfertigung des Glaubens* [Frankfurt am Main: Andräische Buchhandlung, 1797]), the two men's friendship dates from a later period: Neeb intervened in the debate between Schelling and Jacobi "on divine things" with an open letter adressed to the latter (*Über den Begriff von Gott und göttliche Dinge nach der neuesten Philosophie*), which also marks the beginning of their private correspondence. Neeb includes the letter in his *Vermischte Schriften* (Frankfurt am Main: Hermannsche Buchhandlung, 1817), pp. 61–71. All the titles mentioned are available as reprints in the series *Aetas Kantiana* (Brussels: Culture et Civilisation), pp. 1968 ff.

had proclaimed with an irresistible *feeling of certainty*, '*God is Spirit, the Absolute is free and has the nature of a person.*'[5] He adds: "It was of the utmost significance that Jacobi brought out the moment of immediacy in our knowledge of God so distinctly and emphatically."[6] Hegel's only criticism is that for me "the transition from mediation to immediacy has more the character of an external rejection and dismissal of mediation, for that immediacy is a living, spiritual immediacy that only arises within a self-sublating process of mediation."[7]

The difference between Hegel and myself consists in this. Although he, too, holds Spinozism to be the final, true result of thinking to which every consistent philosophy must lead ("that substantial absolute, in which everything goes under and all individual things are negated and extinguished"),[8] he seeks to pass through it into a system of freedom *without a leap* by traversing a still higher pathway of thought, which however is the same as (and thus not really higher than) the usual pathway; whereas I only get there by way of a premature leap from the springboard of a merely substantial knowledge which he, too, accepts and presupposes, but which he thinks we need to treat differently than I do. He thinks my method is like the one we follow as living beings when we transform food into juices and blood by way of unconscious digestion, unaided by the science of physiology. He may well be right, and I would gladly join him in testing every means available to unaided reason, if only my old man's head were not too weak for it. Now I take consolation by applying one of Kästner's canny thoughts to myself, who once said in one of his excellent observations on the way in which universal concepts are present in the mind of God, "I would rather learn about the lynx from a hunter than listen to an adherent of method tell me that it is a cat with a shortened tail and ears that are bushy at the tips."[9]

---

[5] See above, p. 9.   [6] See above, p. 9.

[7] Jacobi's quotation draws two separate passages from Hegel's text together without indicating the ellipsis. See above, p. 10.

[8] Here again, Jacobi tacitly elides two separate passages from Hegel's text. Cf. above, p. 8.

[9] Abraham Gotthelf Kästner (1719–1800) was a prominent mathematician in his own right and the teacher of both Lichtenberg and Gauss. He remains perhaps best-known for his aphorisms and epigrams, collected in his *Vermischte Schriften* (Altenburg, 1783), 2 vols.

Further reading

Recommended primary and secondary sources on the constitutional debate in Württemberg 1815–1819 and on Hegel's relation to it:

1 HEGEL IN HEIDELBERG

Hans-Georg Gadamer, "Hegel und die Heidelberger Romantik," in Gadamer, *Hegels Dialektik. Sechs hermeneutische Studien* (Tübingen: J. C. B. Mohr, 1980), pp. 87–97.

2 HEGEL AND THE CONSTITUTIONAL DEBATE IN WÜRTTEMBERG

P. Gehring, "Um Hegels Landständeschrift. Friedrich List im Spiel?" *Zeitschrift für philos. Forschung* (1969): 110–129.

Rudolph Haym, *Hegel und seine Zeit* (Berlin: Rudolph Gaertner, 1857), pp. 347–356.

Rolf K. Hocevar, *Stände und Repräsentation beim jungen Hegel. Ein Beitrag zu seiner Staats- und Gesellschaftslehre sowie zur Theorie der Repräsentation* (Munich: C. H. Beck, 1968), pp. 183–208.

Christoph Jamme, "Die Erziehung der Stände durch sich selbst. Hegels Konzeption der neuständisch-bürgerlichen Repräsentation in Heidelberg 1817/18," in *Hegels Rechtsphilosophie im Zusammenhang der europäischen Verfassungsgeschichte*, ed. Hans-Christian Lucas and Otto Pöggeler (Stuttgart-Bad Cannstatt: Frommann-Holzboog, 1986), pp. 149–173.

Otto Pöggeler, "Die Heidelberger Jahrbücher im wissenschaftlichen Streitgespräch," in *Heidelberg im säkularen Umbruch. Traditionsbewusstsein und Kulturpolitik um 1800*, ed. Friedrich Strack (Stuttgart: Klett-Cotta, 1987), pp. 154–181.

"Hegel und der Stuttgarter Landtag," in *Kant oder Hegel? Stuttgarter Hegel-Kongreß 1981*, ed. Dieter Henrich (Stuttgart: Klett-Cotta, 1983), pp. 59–79.

Franz Rosenzweig, *Hegel und der Staat* (Munich and Berlin: Oldenbourg, 1920), vol. II, pp. 30–62.

3 LITERATURE ON THE HISTORY OF WÜRTTEMBERG AND THE PROCEEDINGS OF THE ESTATES ASSEMBLY 1815–1819 AND HELPFUL LITERATURE ON GERMAN CONSTITUTIONAL HISTORY

Hartwig Brandt, *Parlamentarismus in Württemberg 1819–1870. Anatomie eines deutschen Landtags* (Düsseldorf: Droste, 1987).

Brandt's important study focuses on the period after the constitution was ratified in 1819, but the introductory chapter offers a servicable overview of the history of Württemberg's Estates and an analysis of the events leading up to and the interests involved in the constitutional debate from 1815 to 1819. Brandt also helpfully places the debate in the context of German constitutional history.

Joachim Gerner, *Vorgeschichte und Entstehung der württembergischen Verfassung im Spiegel der Quellen (1815–1819)* (Stuttgart: W. Kohlhammer, 1989).

Gerner offers a comprehensive study of the constitutional debate in Württemberg from King Friedrich's early initiative in January of 1815 until the ratification of a new constitution in Sepetember of 1819. For those with some knowledge of German, Gerner's study is a useful complement to Hegel's portrayal and analysis of events, since Gerner is able to make use of many sources to which Hegel would not have had access, including the private correspondence of the participants in the debate and records of discussions that took place within the royal cabinet. In addition to helpful information on the mode of the election and appointment of Assembly members, Gerner also offers a sociological profile of the Estates Assembly, shedding light on professional backgrounds and social allegiances.

Rolf Grawert, "Der württembergische Verfassungsstreit 1815–1819," in *"O Fürstin, der Heimath! Glükliches Stutgard." Politik, Kultur und Gesellschaft im deutschen Südwesten um 1800*, ed. Otto Pöggeler and Christoph Jamme (Stuttgart: Klett-Cotta, 1988), pp. 126–158.

Walter Grube, *Der Stuttgarter Landtag 1457–1957* (Stuttgart: E. Klett, 1957).

E. Hölzle, *Württemberg im Zeitalter Napoleons und der Deutschen Erhebung* (Stuttgart, Berlin: W. Kohlhammer, 1937).

Michael Stolleis, *Geschichte des öffentlichen Rechts in Deutschland 1800–1914* (Munich: Beck, 1992), pp. 121–186.

Dieter Wyduckel, "Die Idee des Dritten Deutschlands im Vormärz. Ein Beitrag zur trialistischen Verfassungskonzeption des Freiherrn von Wangenheim," in *"O Fürstin, der Heimath! Glükliches Stutgard." Politik, Kultur und Gesellschaft im deutschen Südwesten um 1800*, ed. Otto Pöggeler and Christoph Jamme (Stuttgart: Klett-Cotta, 1988), pp. 159–183.

4 SOURCES

August Ludwig Reyscher, *Historisch und kritisch bearbeitete Sammlung der Württembergischen Gesetze*. Vols. I–III, part 3: *Die Staats- und Grundgesetze vom Jahre 1806 bis Ende des Jahres 1828* (Stuttgart and Tübingen: Cotta, 1828).

Die Verhandlungen in der Versammlung der Landstände des Königreichs Württemberg 1815–1819. Vols 45 (Stuttgart 1817 ff.). Abt. 1815–1819.

5 LEXIKA

Eugen Haberkern/Joseph Wallach, *Hilfswörterbuch für Historiker. Mittelalter und Neuzeit*, 2 vols. (München: Francke, 1995).

Deutsches Rechtswörterbuch. Wörterbuch der älteren deutschen Rechtssprache (Weimar: H. Böhlaus Nachfolger, 1914 ff.).

Glossary of translated terms: German to English

Abgaben	levies
Adel	nobility; *hoher/niederer Adel* high/low nobility
Adresse	petition
Advokat	advocate
Agnaten	male heirs
Ahnung	intimation
Allerhandordnungen	legal miscellanies
allgemein	universal; *Allgemeinheit*, universality; *allgemeine Landstände* general estates
Amt	office; district
Amtschreiber	district notary
anderes	(an or the) other
Anschauung	intuition; *erkennende Anschauung* cognitive intuition; *intellektuelle Anschauung* intellectual intuition; *Vernunft-Anschauung* intuition of reason
an und für sich	in and for itself
Armenfonds	charity
Armenkasse	charity
Artikel	article
aufheben	sublate; cancel; (rarely) negate; *Aufhebung*, *Aufgehobensein* sublation
Aufklärung	Enlightenment
Ausschuß	committee; *bleibender Ausschuß* permanent committee; *innerer Ausschuß* inner committee
Ausschußwesen	committee system
bedingt	conditioned
Begierde	desire
Begriff	concept
begründet	grounded
Beilage	supplement

143

Beruf	calling
Beschwerde	grievance
Besoldung	salary
Besonderung	particularization
bestimmt	determinate; *Bestimmtheit* determinateness
Bestimmung	determination; *Erkenntnis-Bestimmung* determination of knowledge; *Reflexionsbestimmung* determination of reflection; *Verstandesbestimmung* determination of the understanding
Bevollmächtigter	authorized representative
Bewegung	movement
Beweis	proof; *werktätiger Beweis* proof by deeds
Bewußtsein	consciousness; *sinnliches Bewußtsein* sensuous consciousness; *reflektierendes Bewußtsein* reflective consciousness; *natürliches Bewußtsein* natural consciousness
Beziehung	relation
Bild	image
Bildung	culture, cultivation, education; *formelle Bildung* education of the understanding
Bürger	burgher
bürgerlich	burgher, bourgeois
Bürgermeister	chief accountant
Bürgerrecht(e)	civil right(s)
Casse	see *Kasse*
Charte constitutionelle	Constitutional Charter
Civilliste	civil list
Comité	committee
Comitéherr	member of the committee
Commissar	see *Kommissar*
Communordnung	see *Kommunordnung*
Concussion	extortion
Constituiring	structuring
Consul	see *Konsul*
Darstellung	account, exposition, manifestation
Dasein	existence
delikat	tactful
Denken	thought, thinking
Denkmöglichkeit	logical possibility

Deputation	deputation; *gemeinschaftliche herr- und landschaftliche Deputation* bilateral deputation (consisting of representatives of both the government and the land estates)
Deputierter	deputy
Deutschheit	Germanness
Dialektik	dialectic; *dialektisch* dialectical
Diäten	allowances
Ding-an-sich	thing-in-itself
Domanialeigentum	domanial possession, domanial property (of the king)
Dorf	village
Einbildungskraft	imagination
Eingabe	petition
Eingebung	sudden inspiration
Einheit	unity
Einkünfte	revenue
Einmütigkeit	unanimity
Einsicht	insight, oversight
Empfindung	sentiment
endlich	finite; *Endlichkeit* finitude
Entfremdung	alienation
entgegensetzen	oppose
Entschließung	resolution, decision
Erblande	Württemberg's original territories
Erbschaftsteilung	division of an inheritance
Erlaß	decree
Erkennen (das)	cognition, recognition
erkennend	cognitive
Erkenntnis	cognition; knowledge; *Erkenntnis seiner selbst* self-knowledge
erklären	claim, declare, explain
Erklärung	claim, declaration, explanation
Erschaffen aus Nichts	creation ex nihilo
Erscheinung	appearance; *Erscheinungswelt* world of appearance
Erziehung	education
evangelisch	protestant
Fleck	township
Forstamt	forestry department; *Forstordnung* forestry regulations; *Forstwirtschaft* forestry
Freiheit	freedom

Freiheitsrechte	civil liberties
Freizügigkeit	liberality
Fürst	prince, monarch; *fürstliche Diener/fürstliche Bediente* those in service of the prince/prince's servants
Garanten	guarantors
Gedanke	thought
Gedankendinge	entia rationis
Gediegenheit	solidity
Gefühl	emotion, feeling
Gegensatz	opposition
Gegenstand	object
Gegenstoß gegen sich	repelling that is in itself its own self-repelling
Geheimer Rat	privy council; *Geheimrat* privy councillor
Geist	mind, spirit
Geistestätigkeiten	mental activities
geistreich	with ésprit
Gelder	funds; *Landesgelder* funds belonging to the Estates; *öffentliche Gelder* public funds; *private Gelder* private funds; *verwilligte Gelder* allocated funds
Geltung	validity
Gemeinde-Vermögen	assets of local government
Gemeindekasse	municipal treasury
General-Klausel	General Clause
Gerichtsbarkeit	jurisdiction; *nicht-streitige Gerichtsbarkeit* non-contentious jurisdiction
Gerichtsschreiber	court notary
Gesetz	law; *sittliches Gesetz* moral law
Gesetzbücher	statute books
Gesetzgebung	legislation
Gesinnung (politische)	(political) attitude
Gestalt	form; *unter der Gestalt des Ewigen* sub specie aeternitatis
Gestaltung	form
Gewißheit	certainty; *Gewißheit seiner selbst* certainty of self
Gewohnheit	habit, custom, mores
Glauben	belief, verb: believe
Gleichgültigkeit	indifference
Grund	ground, reason
Grundgesetz	fundamental law
Grundlage	foundation

Grundsatz	principle; *Grundsatz der Reziprozität* principle of reciprocity
Grundvertrag	fundamental contract
Gültigkeit	validity
Gutachten	appraisal, assessment
Haus-Grundgesetze	house laws
Heiratspakte	marriage agreements
Herzog	duke
Hexenräuche	sorcerer's smoke
Hofrat	court councillor
Hoheitsrechte	sovereign rights
Ich (das)	the I, the ego
Idee	idea
Instruktions-Comité	instruction committee
Intelligenz	intellectuals
Jahressteuer	annual tax
jenseits	beyond
Jura	law (as a subject of study)
Justizamt	department of justice
Kameralistik	economy; *Kameralverwaltung* economic administration
Kammereinkünfte	(royal) chamber income
Kasse	cash, fund, treasury
Kaste	caste
Kastenordnung	church regulations
Kirchenfond	ecclesiastic assets; *Kirchengut* church property; *Kirchenordnung* church regulations
Komitee	committee; *Komitee aus mehreren Sektionen* grand committee
Kommissar	commissioner; *ständischer Kommissar* estates commissioner
Kommune	municipality; *Kommunalbeamter* local offical; *Kommunordnung* local adminstrative regulations
königlich	royal
Konsul	consul
Kopula	copula
Kriegsbedürfnisse	war funds
Landes-Grundgesetz	common law
Landesherr	prince, ruler
Landeskasse	estates treasury
Landesordnung	administrative regulations

Landplage	plague upon the land
Landrechte	code of law
Landschaft	estates (considered collectively and in actual assembly, rather than severally and as distinct social classes)
Landschaftsarchiv	estates archive
Landstand	estate; *allgemeine Landstände* general estates
Landtag	estates assembly, parliament
Landvogt	provincial governor
Maßstab	standard
Mechanismus	mechanism
Metaphysik	metaphysics; *vormalige Metaphysik* metaphysics of the old school
Ministerium	ministry
Mitte	middle term (of a syllogism, in contradistinction to the extreme terms)
Mittelstand	middle class, intermediate class
Möglichkeit	possibility
moralisch	moral
Nachsteuer	supplementary tax
National-Repräsentation	national representation
negativ	negative
Negativität	negativity
Neuwirtemberg	New Württemberg
Nicht-Ich	non-I
nichtig	illusory; *Nichtigkeit,* Nullität nullity
Nichtigkeit	vacuity
Nichts	nothingness
Notwendigkeit	necessity
Nützlichkeit	utility
Oberamt	superior district
Objekt	object
Objektivität	objectivity
öffentlich	public
Parlament	parliament
Patrimonial-Eigentum	private property (of the king)
Pension	regular payments
Persönlichkeit	personality
Pflicht	duty
Plenarversammlung	plenary assembly
Polizeiamt	department of the police

Positive (das)	positivity
positives Recht	positive law
Präliminarartikel	preliminary articles
Prästationen	proceeds from vassals
Prinzip	principle; *Prinzip der Abscheidung in sich selbst* internal principle of separation
Privatrecht	private right
prozessualisch	legalistic
Protestant	protestant
Prüfung	examination; oversight
Publikum	public, readers
Realisation	realization
Realität	reality
Rechner	accountant
Rechnung	account
Recht	right; *Recht des freimütigen Urteils* right to free speech; *Petitionsrecht* right to petition
Referent	speaker
Regierungszeit	regency
Reglement	protocol
Reich(e)	empire, realm(s)
(Reichs)matrikel	quota list
Reichstag	Imperial Diet
Reichsterritorium	territory of the empire
Repräsentant	representative
Reskripte	edicts
Rezeß	resolution; *azzessorischer Rezeß* accessory agreement
Romantik	romanticism
Satz	article
Schein	appearance, illusion
Schluß	syllogism
Schranke	limitation
Schreiber	notary; *Schreiberei-Institut* notary institute; *Schreiberei-Unfug* notary abuses; *Schreiber-Stand* caste of notaries; *Schreib-Monopolist* notary-monopolist
Schuldentilgungskasse	fund for the amortization of debts; *Schulden-Zahlungs-Behörde* office for the payment of debts
Sein-Sollen	ought

Sektion	sub-committee
Selbstbestimmung	self-determination
Selbstbewußtsein	self-consciousness
Selbstgefühl	sense of self
Selbsttaxation	self-taxation
Sinn des Staates	sense of the state
Sitte	custom, mores
sittlich	ethical
Sittlichkeit	ethical life
Sitzung	meeting, session
sollen	ought
Staat	state; *monarchischer Staat* monarchic state
Staatsanlehen	state bond
Staatsausgaben	state expenditure
Staatsbeamte	state officials
Staatsbedürfnisse	state financial needs
Staatsbürger	citizen
Staatsdiener	civil servants; *Verantwortlichkeit der Staatsdiener* legal accountability of civil servants
Staatseinnahmen	state revenue
Staatseinrichtungen	state institutions
Staatsminister	minister of state
Staatsministerium	ministry of state
Staatsrat	council of state
Staatsrecht	law of states; *natürliches Staatsrecht* natural law of states
Staatsregierung	state government
Stadt	town
Stadtschreiber	town notary
Standesherr	mediatized prince
Standpunkt	standpoint
Steuer	taxes
Steuerempfangbücher	tax receipts
Steuerrepartition	distribution of taxes
Steuerzettel	tax forms
Substantielle, das eine	the one substantial being
Tätigkeit	activity
Testament	will
Totenkopf	caput mortuum
Trieb	passion, striving
Trockenheit	inanity

Truhe, geheime	secret fund
Tugend	virtue
unbestimmt	indeterminate; *das Unbestimmte* indeterminacy; *das absolut Unbestimmte* absolute indeterminacy
undeutsch	un-German
unendlich	infinite
unerweislich	indemonstrable
Unrecht	injustice
Unterhandlung	negotiation; *Unterhandlungs-Comité* negotiating committee; *Unterhandlungskommissar* negotiating commissioner
Unterschied	difference; *sich in sich bewegendes Unterscheiden* internal movement of self-differentiation
unvernünftig	non-rational
Ursache	cause
ursprünglich	original, originary
Urteil	judgment; *synthetisches Urteil a priori* synthetic judgment a priori
Vereinzelung	particularization
Verfassung	constitution; *ehemalige ständische Verfassung* old Estates constitution; *positive Verfassung* positive constitution; *Verfassungsentwurf* constitutional draft; *Verfassungsrechte* constitutional rights; *Verfassungsurkunde* constitutional charter; *Verfassungsvergleich* constitutional comparison
Verhältnis	relation
Verhandlung	negotiation
Verknüpfung	connection
Verlassenschafts-Gant-Inventare	estate auction inventories
Vermittlung	mediation
Vermögen	assets; *Bestimmung des steuerbaren Vermögen* calculation of taxable assets
Vernunft	reason
vernünftig	rational
Verordnung	decree
Verschiedenheit	difference, diversity
versenken	immerse
Verstand	understanding
Verstandesbestimmung	determination of the understanding
vertagen	adjourn

Vertrag	compact, contract, treaty; *Vertragsverhältnis* contractual relation
Verwalter	administrator; *Stiftungs-Verwalter* trustee
Virilstimmführer	non-elected member
Volk	people; *Volksadresse* popular petition; *Volksgeist* spirit of the people
Vollversammlung	plenary assembly
Voraussetzung	presupposition
Vorstellung	idea, (mere) representation, imagination
wahr	true; *das Wahre* the true
Wahrheit	truth
Wahrnehmung	perception
Weltgeist	world spirit
Wesen	entity; essence
Wesenheit	essentiality, essential constituent
Widerspruch	contradiction
Wille	will
Wirken	(effective) activity
Wirklichkeit	actuality
Wissen	knowledge
Wissenschaft	science; *wissenschaftlich* scientific
Zauberformel	magic formula
Zeitgeist	spirit of the times
Zergliederung	analysis
Zusammenrufen	convene
Zusatzartikel	amendment
zurücknehmen	revoke

Glossary of translated terms: English to German

accessory agreement	*azzessorischer Rezeß*
account	*Darstellung, Rechnung*
accountability of state servants	*Verantwortlichkeit der Staatsdiener*
accountant	*Rechner*
activity	*Tätigkeit, Wirken*
actuality	*Wirklichkeit*
administrative regulations	*Landesordnung*
administrator	*Verwalter*
advocate	*Advokat*
alienation	*Entfremdung*
allowances	*Diäten*
amendment	*Zusatzartikel*
appearance	*Erscheinung, Schein*
appraisal	*Gutachten*
article	*Artikel, Satz*; preliminary article *Präliminarartikel*
Assembly	*Versammlung*; plenary assembly *Plenarversammlung, Vollversammlung*; assets *Vermögen*; assets of local government *Gemeinde Vermögen*; ecclesiastic assets *Kirchenfond*
belief	*Glauben*
beyond	*jenseits*
burgher	*Bürger, bürgerlich*
calculation of taxable assets	*Bestimmung des steuerbaren Vermögens*
calling	*Beruf*
caput mortuum	*Totenkopf*
cash	*Kasse*
caste	*Kaste*; caste of notaries *Schreiber-Stand*
cause	*Ursache*
certainty of self	*Gewißheit seiner selbst*

chamber income	*Kammereinkünfte*
charity	*Armenkasse, Armenfonds*
chief accountant	*Bürgermeister*
church property	*Kirchengut*
church regulations	*Kirchenordnung, Kastenordnung*
citizen	*Staatsbürger*
civil liberties	*Freiheitsrechte*
civil list	*Civilliste*
civil right(s)	*Bürgerrecht(e)*
civil servant	*Staatsdiener*
code of law	*Landrechte*
cognition	*Erkennen*
cognitive	*erkennend, wissend*; cognitive movement in itself *wissende Bewegung in sich selbst*
commissioner	*Kommissar*
committee	*Ausschuß, Comité*; committee report *Relation des Comités*; committee system *Ausschußwesen*; inner committee *innerer Ausschuß*
common laws	*Landes Grundgesetze*
common sense	*gesunder Menschenverstand*
concept	*Begriff*
conditioned	*bedingt*
consciousness	*Bewußtsein*; natural consciousness *natürliche Bewußtsein*; consciousness of reason *Bewußtsein der Vernunft*; reflective consciousness *reflektierendes Bewußtsein*
constitution	*Verfassung, Recht*; old estates constitution *ehemalige ständische Verfassung*; positive constitution *positive Verfassung*; royal constitution *königliche Verfassung*
constitutional charter	*Verfassungsurkunde, charte constitutionelle*; constitutional comparison *Verfassungsvergleich*; constitutional draft *Verfassungsentwurf*; constitutional rights *Verfassungsrechte*
consul	*Konsul*
contract	*Vertrag*
contradiction	*Widerspruch*
convene	*zusammenrufen*
copula	*Kopula*

council of state	*Staatsrat*
court councillor	*Hofrat*
court notaries	*Gerichtsschreiber*
creation ex nihilo	*Erschaffen aus Nichts*
cultivation	*Bildung*
culture	*Bildung*
custom	*Sitte*
decree	*Verordnung*; royal decree *königlicher Erlaß*
deputation	*Deputation*; bilateral deputation (consisting of representatives of both the government and the land estates) *gemeinschaftliche herr und landschaftliche Deputation*
deputy	*Deputierter*
determinate	*bestimmt*; determinateness *Bestimmtheit*,
determination	*Bestimmung*; determination of the understanding *Verstandesbestimmung*; determinations of knowledge *Erkenntnis-Bestimmungen*; determinations of reflection *Reflexionsbestimmungen*
dialectic	*Dialektik*; dialectical *dialektisch*
difference	*Unterschied*, *Verschiedenheit*
distribution of local expenditures	*Repartition der Communial Ausgaben*; distribution of taxes *Steuerrepartition*
district	*Amt*; superior district *Oberamt*
district notary	*Amtschreiber*; town notary *Stadtschreiber*
division of an inheritance	*Erbschaftsteilung*
domanial possession, domanial property	*Domanialeigentum*
duke	*Herzog*
duty	*Pflicht*
economic administration	*Kameralverwaltung*
economy	*Kameralistik*
edict	*Reskript*
education	*Bildung*; education of the understanding *formelle Bildung*; political education *politische Erziehung*
ego	*das Ich*
emotion	*Gefühl*
empire	*Reich*
entia rationis	*Gedankendinge*

entity	*Wesen*
essence	*Wesen*; essential constituents *die Wesenheiten*; essentiality *Wesenheit*
Estate	*Landstand*; Estates (considered collectively and in actual assembly, rather than severally as distinct social classes) *Landschaft*
Estate auction inventories	*Verlassenschafts-Gant-Inventare*
Estates archive	*Landschaftsarchiv*; Estates Assembly *Landtag, Landständeversammlung, Ständeversammlung*; Estates commissioner *ständischer Kommissar*; estates treasury *Landeskasse*; general Estates *allgemeine Landstände*
ethical life	*Sittlichkeit*; ethical sphere *sittliche Sphäre*
existence	*Dasein*
exposition	*Darstellung*
extortion	*Concussion*
feeling	*Gefühl*
finite	*endlich*; finitude *Endlichkeit*
forestry	*Forstwirtschaft*; forestry department *Forstamt*; forestry regulations *Forstordnung*
form	*Form, Gestaltung*; form of knowledge *Form der Erkenntnis*; scientific form *wissenschaftliche Form*
foundation	*Grundlage*
freedom	*Freiheit*
fund	*Kasse*; secret fund *geheime Truhe*
fundamental contract	*Grundvertrag*
fundamental law	*Grundgesetz*
funds	*Gelder*; allocated funds *verwilligte Gelder*; emergency war funds *außerordentliche Kriegsbedürfnisse*; funds belonging to the estates *Landesgelder*; fund for the amortization of debts *gemeinschaftliche Schuldentilgungskasse*; public funds *öffentliche Gelder*; private funds *private Gelder*; general estates *allgemeine Landstände*
Germanness	*Deutschheit*
God	*Gott*
governor	*Regierungspräsident*
grand committee	*Komitee aus mehreren Sektionen*

grievance	*Beschwerde*
ground	*Grund*; grounded *begründet*
habit	*Gewohnheit*
house laws	*Haus Grundgesetze*
I (the)	*das Ich*
idea	*Idee*
illusion	*Schein*; illusory *nichtig*
image	*Bild*
imagination	*Einbildungskraft, Vorstellung*
imperial court councillor	*Reichshofrat*
Imperial Diet	*Reichstag*
in and for itself	*an und für sich sein*
inanity	*Trockenheit*
income	*Einkünfte*
indemonstrable	*unerweislich*
indeterminacy	*Unbestimmtheit*; absolute indeterminacy *das absolut Unbestimmte*
indifference	*Gleichgültigkeit*
injustice	*Unrecht*
inquiry	*Untersuchung*
instruction committee	*Instruktions-Comité*
intellectuals	*Intelligenz*
intermediate class	*Mittelstand*
intimation	*Ahnung*
intuition	*Anschauung*; infinite intuition *unendliche Anschauung*; intellectual intuition *intellektuelle Anschauung*; intuition of reason, rational intuition *Vernunft-Anschauung*
judgment	*Urteil*; synthetic judgment a priori *synthetisches Urteil* a priori
jurisdiction	*Gerichtsbarkeit*; non-contentious jurisdiction *nicht-streitige Gerichtsbarkeit*
knowledge	*Erkenntnis*; knowledge of God *Wissen von Gott*; scientific knowledge *wissenschaftliche Erkenntnis*
law	*Recht*; law as a subject of study *Jura*; private right *Privatrecht*; good old law/good old constitution *gutes altes Recht*; positive law *positives Recht*
legal formalism	*formelles Recht*
legal miscellanies	*Allerhandordnungen*

legal system	*Recht*
legislation	*Gesetzgebung*
levies	*Abgaben*
liberality	*Freizügigkeit*
limitation	*Schranke*
local adminstrative regulations	*Communordnung*
local officials	*Kommunalbeamte*
magic formula	*Zauberformel*
male heirs	*Agnaten*
manifestation	*Darstellung*
marriage agreements	*Heiratspakte*
means	*Mittel*
mediation	*Vermittlung*
meeting	*Sitzung*
member	*Mitglied*; member of the committee *Comitéherr*; non-elected member *Virilstimmführer*
mental activities	*Geistestätigkeiten*
metaphysics	*Metaphysik*; metaphysics of the old school *vormalige Metaphysik*
middle class	*Mittelstand*
middle term (of a syllogism)	*Mitte*
mind	*Geist*
minister of state	*Staatsminister*
ministry	*Ministerium*; ministry of state *(königliches) Staatsministerium*
monarch	*Fürst*; monarchic state *monarchischer Staat*
moral law	*sittliches Gesetz*
moral sphere	*moralische Sphäre*
mores	*Sitten*
movement	*Bewegung*; internal movement of self-differentiation *sich in sich bewegendes Unterscheiden*
municipality	*Kommune*
municipal treasury	*Gemeindekasse*
national representation	*National Repräsentation*
natural law of states	*natürliches Staatsrecht*
necessity	*Notwendigkeit*
negate	*negieren*, (rarely:) *aufheben*
negative	*negativ*; negativity *Negativität*

negotiation	*Unterhandlung*; negotiating commissioner *Unterhandlungskommissar*; negotiating committee *Unterhandlungs Comité*
New Württemberg	*Neuwirtemberg*
nobility	*Adel*; high/low nobility *hoher/niederer Adel*
non-I	*Nicht-Ich*
non-rational	*unvernünftig*
notary	*Schreiber*; notary abuses *Schreiberei-Unfug*; notary institute *Schreiberei-Institut*; notary-monopolist *Schreib-Monopolist*
note	*Note*
nothingness	*Nichts*
nullity	*Nichtigkeit*; political nullity *politische Nullität*
object	*Gegenstand, Objekt*; objectivity *Objektivität*
office for the payment of debts	*Schulden-Zahlungs-Behörde*
Old Württemberg	*Altwirtemberg*
one absolute substance	*das Absolut-Eine*
one substantial being	*das eine Substantielle*
original	*ursprünglich*
originary	*ursprünglich*
other (an or the)	*Anderes*
ought	*sollen, sein sollen*
parliament	*Parlament*
particularization	*Vereinzelung, Besonderung*
passion	*Trieb*
people	*Volk*
perception	*Wahrnehmung*
personality	*Persönlichkeit*
petition	*Adresse, Eingabe*; popular petition *Volksadresse*
(political) attitude	*(politische) Gesinnung*
positivity	*das Positive*
possibility	*Möglichkeit*; logical possibility *Denkmöglichkeit*
prelate	*Prelat*
prince	*Landesherr*; mediatized prince *Standesherr*
principle	*Prinzip*; internal principle of separation *Prinzip der Abscheidung in sich selbst*; principle of reciprocity *Grundsatz der Reziprozität*
privy council	*Geheimer Rat*
proceeds from vassals	*Prästationen*
proof	*Beweis*; proof by deeds *werktätiger Beweis*

property	*Eigentum*; private property of the king *königliches Patrimonial Eigentum*
protestant	*evangelisch, protestant*
protocol	*Reglement*
provincial governors	*Landvogten*
public	*öffentlich*
quota list	*(Reichs)matrikel*
rational	*vernünftig*
reality	*Realität*
realm(s)	*Reich(e)*
reason	*Vernunft, Grund*
recognition	*Erkennen*
reflect	*reflektieren*; reflection *Reflexion*
regency	*Regierungszeit*
relation	*Beziehung, Verhältnis*
repelling that is in itself its own self-repelling	*Gegenstoß gegen sich*
representation	*Vorstellung*
representative	*Repräsentant*; authorized representative *Bevollmächtigter*; people's representatives *Repräsentanten des Volks*
resolution	*Rezeß*, Resolution, *Entschließung*
revenue	*Einkünfte*
right	*Recht*; right to free speech *Recht des freimütigen Urteils*; right to petition *Petitionsrecht*; sovereign right *Hoheitsrecht*
romanticism	*Romantik*
ruler	*Landesherr*
salary	*Besoldung*
science	*Wissenschaft*
self-consciousness	*Selbstbewußtsein*
self-determination	*Selbstbestimmung*
self-knowledge	*Erkenntnis seiner selbst*
self-taxation	*Selbsttaxation*
sense of self	*Selbstgefühl*
sense of the state	*Sinn des Staates*
sentiment	*Empfindung*
session	*Sitzung*
sorcerer's smoke	*Hexenräuche*

speaker	*Referent*
spirit	*Geist*; spirit of the people *Volksgeist*; spirit of the times *Zeitgeist*
state bond	*Staatsanlehen*
state expenditure	*Staatsausgaben*
state financial needs	*Staatsbedürfnisse*
state government	*Staatsregierung*
state institutions	*Staatseinrichtungen*
state officials	*Staatsbeamte*
state revenue	*Staatseinnahmen*
statute Statut; statute books	*Gesetzbücher*
structuring	*Constituirung*
sub specie aeternitatis	*unter der Gestalt des Ewigen*
sublate	*aufheben*; sublation *Aufhebung, Aufgehobensein*
substance	*Substance*
supernatural	*übernatürlich*
supplement	*Beilage*
tactful	*delikat*
tax	*Steuer*; annual tax *Jahressteuer*; supplementary tax *Nachsteuer*; tax form *Steuerzettel*; tax receipt *Steuerempfangbücher*
territory of the empire	*Reichsterritorium*
thing-in-itself	*Ding-an-sich*
thought	*Gedanke, das Denken*
town	*Stadt*
township	*Fleck*
treasury	*Kasse*
treaty	*Vertrag*
trustee	*Stiftungs-Verwalter*
unanimity	*Einmütigkeit*
understanding	*Verstand*; finite understanding *endlicher Verstand*
un-German	*undeutsch*
unity	*Einheit*; substantial unity *seiende Einheit*
universal	*allgemein*; abstract universal *abstrakte Allgemeinheit*
universality	*Allgemeinheit*
utility	*Nützlichkeit*
vacuity	*Nichtigkeit*
validity	*Geltung, Gültigkeit*

village	*Dorf*
will	*Wille, Testament*
world	*Welt*; world of appearance *Erscheinungswelt*; world spirit *Weltgeist*
Württemberg's original territories	*Erblande*

Index

Made in the USA
Middletown, DE
10 February 2019